The Jews and the Mosaic Law

Isaac Leeser

1806 - 1868

APPLEWOOD BOOKS

Bedford, Massachusetts

The Jews and the Mosaic Law
was originally published in
1833

ISBN: 978-1-4290-1912-5

APPLEWOOD'S
American
Philosophy AND *Religion*
SERIES

For a free copy of our current print catalog featuring our bestselling books, write to:

APPLEWOOD BOOKS
P.O. Box 365
Bedford, MA 01730

For more complete listings, visit us on the web at:
awb.com

Prepared for publishing by HP

THE

JEWS AND THE MOSAIC LAW.

PART THE FIRST:

CONTAINING

A DEFENCE OF THE REVELATION OF THE PENTATEUCH, AND
OF THE JEWS FOR THEIR ADHERENCE TO THE SAME.

BY ISAAC LEESER,

READER OF THE PORTUGUESE JEWISH CONGREGATION IN PHILADELPHIA.

אמרתי להוללים אל תהלו
ולרשעים אל תרימו קרן :

" I said to those who derided, deride ye not;
And to the wicked, raise ye not the horn."
PSALM lxxv. v. 5.

PHILADELPHIA:
PRINTED FOR THE AUTHOR.
AND SOLD BY
E. L. CAREY & A. HART, PHILADELPHIA; CAREY, HART & CO. BALTIMORE;
D. W. HARRISON, CHARLESTON, S. C.; E. BLOCK, CINCINNATI, OHIO;
AND MOSES SARFATY, KINGSTON, JAMAICA.
5594.

A. WALDIE, PRINTER.

Dedication.

TO RABBI B. S. COHEN,

PRINCIPAL OF THE JEWISH INSTITUTE AT MÜNSTER IN WESTPHALIA.

Respected Friend,

No apology will be necessary for inscribing this volume to you. The friendship with which you were kind enough to regard me when yet a child, is sufficient warrant for me to hope, that a work of maturer years will not be received with indifference by one, who, though from his varied learning well capable of judging, will yet be indulgent to errors, and perhaps misapprehensions, almost inseparable from youthful productions.—It had been my intention to have dedicated this first production of mine, to my late venerated teacher, Rabbi Benjamin Jacob Cohen, your friend and my benefactor; but since it was the will of our Father in heaven, to deprive me of this excellent guide of my infancy, and the world of an active friend, and religion of a zealous defender: I know no one, to whom I could with more propriety dedicate it, than to you. Perhaps you may find, that the sentiments, imbibed in part under your excellent instruction, and which were dear to me when I had the pleasure of daily enjoying a friendly intercourse with you, are yet remembered and cherished by me, at this distance of time and place. If so, you will doubtlessly be pleased at the discovery; and you may be assured, that to receive your approbation will be one of the most pleasing fruits, which I can hope to reap from my labours.—Farewell, dear friend, and believe me, that I find a great degree of consolation in the idea, that the Almighty has preserved you, whilst He has deprived me of my first teacher and friend; and that it shall ever be cause of joy to be informed of your welfare and prosperity to

Your obliged servant,

ISAAC LEESER.

TO THE READER.

This book, now for the first time published, was composed more than four years ago, whilst I was engaged in pursuits quite uncongenial to literature. Many a time, after a day of active application to business, have I spent the hours of night in writing. Books for reference I had but few; and the reader will therefore excuse the brevity with which many points are treated, which no doubt would have received more attention, could I have had authorities to refer to. In some respects this may have been an advantage, as it prevented me from being too much trammeled by the opinions of others. The reader may be assured, however, that since my residence in Philadelphia I have omitted no opportunity of correcting and altering many passages which I thought required it; and even while the work was going through the press I have made a great number of additions and alterations, at times amounting to nearly an entire page. With all this care I do not flatter myself that the book is free from fault, nor can I even say that it meets my own approbation in every instance; for many a sentence had to pass as it stood, because I did not discover its defectiveness till it was too late. One thing, however, I hope, that no error in point of fact, and no great want of connection in reasoning, will be discovered; at least I have done all I could to avoid it. It becomes me not, however, to be too solicitous of engaging the favourable opinion of the reader: the book itself is before him; and let him condemn or approve, as he may think proper after mature reflection. In conclusion, I must remark, that vanity had but a small share in inducing me to make public a book laying so long dormant; the reasons assigned in the preface, written at Richmond on the day it is dated, are yet operative, as no book of the kind required has made its appearance since then. But my own opinion of the humble value of my labours has not been changed; and I therefore insert the preface, though in some respects it is not quite as applicable as it was four years ago. To say that I should not be highly delighted if I meet with approbation and success, would be the excess of ill disguised affectation; but I may freely say, with justice to myself, that a fair criticism, even if it should strip my work of all value, will not be at all unwelcome to me, although mortifying to my self-love; the object of my enquiry and of this publication is the search for and maintenance of truth, but not the acquisition of fame; and as the humble inquirer for truth, I dare not be offended if I have been found wanting either in talent in my search for her, or in capacity whilst engaged in her service.

Philadelphia, Tishry, 5594.

PREFACE.

In presenting the following pages to the consideration of the public, I deem it unnecessary to inform them who and what I am; but, at the same time, I think it incumbent upon me to disclose the motives which induced me to add another theological work to the many already in existence; that it may not be supposed I undertook this difficult task from the mere love of writing, and of becoming an author.

Some time last fall (1828) a gentleman of this city showed me an article in the London Quarterly Review, in which our nation (the Jews) were very much abused, and their moral and religious character shamefully vilified. Though I felt very indignant at the time, I deferred noticing it publicly, until the article in question was republished in a New York paper, on the 26th of December last. I then thought it was high time to notice it, as I verily believed that its circulating without a reply would be extremely injurious to the interest of my brethren in this country. I therefore undertook, without being solicited by any one, the task of refuting the accusations it contained. I was at first very doubtful of success; but I had soon the satisfaction of discovering that my feeble efforts had met with favourable notice. A few weeks after the publication of the first essay, I was gratified with the mild and temperate piece which appeared under the signature of " A Professor of Christianity." After replying to him, I understood that several persons at a distance had read and approved of my labours. I must confess that I felt pleased at this mark of approbation from strangers, which I in the first instance hardly expected to receive from friends; but since it was so, I came to a determination to republish my two essays, to rescue them from the perishable state in which they had appeared. It being hinted to me by a friend*

* Mr. B. H. Judah, late librarian of the Richmond Library Company, who has died since this book was written; and I have to express here the obligation I am under to him, Mr. Jacob Mordecai, and Mr. Abraham H. Cohen, late Reader of the Richmond congregation, for many valuable suggestions.

that in that case I ought to add some proofs in favour of our observing the proper day of the week as the Sabbath, I followed his suggestion, and began immediately to embody my thoughts relative to the truth of the mission of Moses; and though I intended to say but little, the subject grew by degrees under my hands, till it assumed the shape in which it is presented to the *indulgent* reader. I had scarcely commenced, when I saw the reply of the "Professor of Christianity" to my second essay, but was prevented from answering him then, on account of the editors of the Richmond Whig (in which paper these four essays first appeared) having closed their columns against the further continuation of the controversy.*

Whatever opinion may be formed as to the merits of this my first work, I would beg my readers not to pronounce me guilty of presumption, in attempting to write on so grave and difficult a subject, as theology. My motives are simply these. I have beheld with grief and *shame* the efforts made of late by many, who dishonour the name of Israel, to lessen the respect our nation has ever felt for the law of Moses and the traditions of our ancestors. I waited, but found no one in this country, older than myself, attempting to enlighten the minds of my brethren; I could therefore no longer remain silent—I felt called upon to act, and I obeyed the inward call, not unmindful of what Hillel the ancient said: "And in a place, where there is no man, try even thyself to be a man." (Abothe II.) The infidel, indeed, clothed in his panoply of unbelief, thinks himself invulnerable, he defies the word of God, and exultingly asks for proof of the truths of revelation. But in times of old the Philistian Goliath was conquered by David, who, armed with a sling only, but coming in the name of the God of Israel, threw the stone, which entered the head of his *powerful* and armed antagonist, who sunk before the future king of Israel. Even so have I attempted to approach the armed infidel; who knows, but God may effect some good work through me, for He is ever powerful to assist them, who rely upon Him in truth and sincerity.—I dare not even flatter myself with the hope of success; but if I fail, I may con-

---

* I must once for all acknowledge the liberality of Mr. John H. Pleasants, the senior editor of the Whig, who so kindly offered to publish my essays; and I seize with unfeigned pleasure the present opportunity (the first that has offered) of returning him thus publicly my heart-felt thanks for the handsome manner in which he drew public attention to my first essay. I also think it an act of justice to mention, that I believe him to have been actuated by the best motives in discontinuing the controversy.

sole myself with the idea, that I have been defeated in a good cause; this disappointment even may stimulate me to make a second attempt, when I shall endeavour to avoid those faults which caused my failure in this first undertaking.

The liberal Christians (and to those alone I address myself) will easily discover, that the little I have said in relation to Christianity, was indispensably necessary to my plan. They moreover cannot be offended, at a liberal and candid view being taken of their belief by a Jew; for if he *is* wrong, they can easily reply to him; and I will just remark, that any strictures or hints, in relation to this book, shall be thankfully received by me, provided they be made in the spirit of candour and conciliation.

The body of the arguments, as far as the plan of arranging them is concerned, is altogether mine, as are also many of the arguments themselves. I will not assert, that the same have not been used before; but I may say with truth, that I have not intentionally borrowed from others. I consulted no books, besides those mentioned in the text, and even those I had not always before me; but quoted perhaps as often from memory, as from actual inspection. Be that as it may, I can assure the public that I have advanced neither argument nor assertion, which I did not subject to frequent examinations, and have asserted nothing which I in conscience did not believe founded in fact to the best of my knowledge. It would be the height of presumption in me to say, that I have made no *mistake*, for that only can be the case with inspired writers; and if I err not altogether, I do not remember to have read any book from a profane writer, where some error or other had not been committed. Should I have the good fortune, however, to see a second edition of this work called for, I will make those corrections and alterations, which may have been discovered to be necessary.

In some places I have followed the English version of the Bible, in others again I have attempted to translate the original myself; either because I did not consult the English at all, or because the common translation seemed to me incorrect.

No man can be more aware of the difficulty of doing justice to the subject under discussion, than myself; yet this did not deter me from the attempt, it rather stimulated me the more; first because I never saw a book in the English language written by a Jew, that treated of the evidences of his religion, if perhaps we except David Levy's answer to Thomas Paine, and Rabbi de Cordova's little book, Reason and Faith: and therefore I resolved to write, with the hope that some person more capable than myself, might undertake to discuss the subject, as its importance deserves, and follow up with more success, my humble beginning.—And secondly, having been taught by men distinguished for learning and piety, I thought that perhaps the instruction I had received from them might be made as beneficial to others as it had been to me.

These are the reasons and motives, which governed me in writing; but neither fame nor emolument was my object; for how can any man gain either by appearing as the champion of the hated and persecuted Jews? I was not however deterred from doing, what I conceived to be my duty, by the fear of ridicule or hatred; and I believe it to be obligatory upon every Jew, to defend his principles and religion from the obloquy generally cast upon them, at whatever hazard to himself. I must therefore entreat every liberal Christian, deist or Jew, to read what I have written in favour of our laws and ceremonies, and not condemn them before he knows some of the reasons which can be urged in their favour even by so obscure an individual as myself.

If I have succeeded in establishing the truth of our faith, let not the honour be ascribed to me; but to the excellence of that law, which can be defended so easily and with so little information, as I possess; but if I have failed, let not our law be rejected on that account, for though I could not do it justice, there are many amongst the descendants of the patriarchs, who are every way much better qualified to do so than

THE AUTHOR.

Richmond, Va. Sivan 9th, (June 10th,) 5589.

CONTENTS.

PART I.

ADVERTISEMENT.

Those persons desirous of possessing the "Instruction in the Mosaic Religion," translated from the German of Johlson, of Frankford on Maine, by the author of this book, will please to make early application to any of the agents for selling this book, or to the author himself, as but a small number of copies are yet unsold.

The author has been advised by several friends to print the discourses delivered by him on various occasions, either in book or pamphlet form, which latter mode, it is asserted, would give them a greater circulation. He has no objection whatever to make any of his writings public, if they are deemed of any service; but the encouragement hitherto extended to him, both in the sale of the first and subscriptions to the present work, does not authorise him to undertake a new book, especially in parts, as the trouble and expense attending a distribution in this way would evidently be very great. He therefore takes this method to announce to the friends of our religion, that, if they think his discourses of sufficient value to wish them published, they will be kind enough to communicate their willingness to *encourage* the undertaking, to Messrs. Carey & Hart, J. L. Hackenburg, or the author, Philadelphia; the Rev. Isaac B. Seixas, New York; Mr. Zalma Rehine, Baltimore; Mr. Jacob Mordecai, Richmond; Dr. Jacob de la Motta, and Mr. Nathan Hart, Charleston; Mr. Jacob de la Motta, Savannah; Mr. Eleazer Block, Cincinnati; and Mr. Moses Sarfaty, Kingston, Jamaica; or to any of the author's friends, who are requested to communicate to him, as soon as convenient, their success or failure. Those willing to subscribe will please to state how many copies they wish to take, and whether they wish the work in monthly parts, or in one or two volumes, according to the number of printed pages it may make. He cannot yet state the price which he will charge; but the public may rest assured that he will ask as moderately as possible; and he trusts that the two books which have been published already are sufficient evidence that he does not wish to make any undue profit by his writings. In conclusion, he must state, that he will not think himself bound to publish the aforesaid discourses, if the encouragement is not sufficient to secure him from loss; and that he will be determined about the *mode* of publication as circumstances may hereafter direct.

JEWS AND THE MOSAIC LAW.

PART I.

O LORD of the universe! who endurest for ever, we adore Thee; for Thou art the Creator of all nature, from Thee all, that is, derives its existence, and Thou hast the power to do with this, thy creation, as Thou pleasest. Thou changest the order of nature, as Thou desirest, without deranging its harmony; for Thou, nature's architect, knowest the secret springs of all existence. All is sustained solely by thy will; and if Thou but speakest, all must be annihilated.—O Fountain of eternal life! who didst choose our forefathers to be thy people, have mercy upon us their descendants, though fallen and degraded through our sins; let thy wisdom enlighten our minds, that we may understand the ways of thy law; that we may live according to thy commandments, and be worthy of thy love and protection! Hasten Thou also the time of our redemption through thy anointed, and show again, as thou hast promised, that thou art the God and Redeemer of Israel, when Thou displayest for a second time over us thy protecting arm, before the eyes of all nations. Amen.

1

CHAPTER I.

CONSCIENCE AND REVELATION.

In proving the truth of *Judaism*, or, to speak more correctly, the laws and ordinances contained in the Mosaic writings, and the books of the prophets who were the successors of Moses, it is necessary, first, to prove the truth of *Revelation* in general, and next, that what is commonly called the *Old Testament, can be true, without* at the same time admitting the authority of the *gospels* and *epistles* of that book, known as the New Testament.

Let us then enquire :—

" Is it rational to believe that the Almighty revealed himself to the children of Israel, as related by Moses; and is this assertion of the Jewish legislator borne out by historical facts ?"

The greater number of thinking men of our own days and of past times agree in asserting, that a revelation, so called, does really exist; but they differ very widely as to the *nature* of this revelation. The notion of the heathens, that the gods lived in familiar intercourse with men, and taught them the necessary mode of worship, has long since been given up by a great number of nations, who have adopted, in the place of heathen mythology, the tenets of the Koran or the Gospels; but immense bodies of men, and who are far more numerous than Christians or Mahomedans, yet believe in the just mentioned theory of revelation.—Another set of men, amongst whom the Jews stand pre-eminent, believe, that the Almighty, Eternal, and Only God made his will known to men, singularly pious and resigned to his will, and sent them as messengers to the rest of the world, to make known certain laws and regulations by which mankind should be governed; and to this idea the Christians and Mahomedans also adhere.—But there are some men who suppose that no *such* revelation was ever made; that is to say, that God never *spoke* to any man; but that He has revealed himself, that is, has made himself known, through his creation, and has at the same time implanted within the bosom of every individual of the human family a certain and infallible guide to righteousness, which, when attentively listened to, will invariably lead a man in the path of right and justice.—The notions of the' Pagans it is useless to examine here, as there are none amongst us who profess them; and then again, their nothingness must be admitted, if any one of the other two systems can be established as the correct one. And as those, who acknowledge only what they call the inward revelation, deny the *necessity* even of any other, it remains to be examined if there be actually such a thing as the infallible voice within, or, as it is commonly styled, *conscience.* If it should, therefore, be found, that *conscience,* properly so called, does not exist, or is inadequate to effect the purpose of a *general* revelation, that is, to teach every body under every circumstance the same: it must follow that conscience, or the inward monitor, cannot be the sole revelation; as, in that case, no universal standard, unvaried and infallible, of right, could be in existence; we should therefore be obliged to arrive at the conclusion, that there must be somewhere an *outward* revelation, or, in other words, a *promulgated law,* which must be the universal standard of right; and it would next be our business to seek, where this outward revelation, this promulgated law of God, could be found.—Since, however, it is very often asserted, that man can arrive at a knowledge of right of his own accord, we will briefly examine if this can be true, or if there be not some facts which clearly prove the contrary. Suppose that conscience were a proper teacher, and would always punish with inward remorse every aberration from the path of right: we might then place an implicit reliance upon it, and thus our own unassisted reason would be the only revelation necessary. But *is it true* that all men, when left to themselves, will think alike? Whence, then, the horrible modes of idolatry, which shock us so much in ancient, and even in modern, history? But grant even, that superstition may be made an engine in the hands of designing and interested men, to induce their fellow-men to disregard the voice of conscience, and follow the mad inventions of others; yet what can be urged in favour of inward revelation, when we find whole nations addicted to certain actions, which are condemned as unjust by others? It is well known that an ancient Greek legislator thought parricide such a monstrous crime, that he did not even specify the punishment, believing that no human being could ever be guilty of a crime so heinous and unnatural. But, for all that, we find that a certain American nation do not regard the killing of their aged parents in this light; for when a man is grown too old, according to their notions, that is, as soon as he has become unable to shift for himself, a grave is dug, into which he is compelled to descend, and is then strangled or tomahawked by the young men, who do this atrocious deed with the utmost unconcern, and even think they do him a service.—The free-thinkers also say, that incest is so contrary to the well-being of society, that it would not be permitted, although there were no prohibition against it to be found in the Bible. But even this is not true; for the Grecians, Persians, and Egyptians, the most *refined* nations of antiquity, married their sisters, or other near relations; and amongst the Lacedæmonians it often happened that the same woman was the wife of two men.* Amongst the Romans, also, incest was not very rare.— Most savage nations are addicted to stealing; and the Arabians of the present day will rob you, and entertain you very hospitably, after having emptied your pockets. They very often accost a traveller with—" Thy brother is hungry, thy sister is naked, and as

---

* Schiller,—the celebrated German poet and historian, and who was a liberal deist, that is to say, he believed in the truth of the Mosaic history, and applauded the beauty of the Mosaic code, without believing in a direct revelation from God to man,—thus speaks of the laws of Lycurgus, in his treatise entitled, " The Legislation of Lycurgus and Solon."

" From the married state itself all jealousy was banished. Every thing, even (female) modesty, the Legislator (Lycurgus) rendered subordinate to his chief design. He sacrificed female fidelity, to obtain healthy children for the state."

"As soon as the child was born, it belonged to the state. Father and mother had lost it. The elders (of the people) inspected it; if it was strong and well built, it was given over to a nurse; but if it appeared weak and badly shapen, it was thrown into a deep pit near Mount Taygetus." See *Schiller's Works*, Stutgard edition, vol. xvi. page 101.

I would hardly have dared to shock the finer feelings of my readers with the above extracts, which are almost too immodest for transcribing, were it not that some deniers of revelation had dared to place the Lycurgian laws in comparison with the Mosaic code, the spirit of uncleanliness and barbarity with the essence of chastity and benevolence. The subject deserves a much more extended notice than can be taken of it here; but it is likely, that at some future time I may recur to it, when a more fitting opportunity offers.

thou hast food and clothing to spare, it is but right, that thou shouldst give us, what we want." It is true, they return you enough to defray the expenses of travelling; but they are very careful to take first, whatever suits them.

The foregoing instances are undoubted facts, and they must go a great way to prove, that one set of men almost invariably thinks that right, which the other thinks wrong and criminal. Civilised nations of modern times detest theft, murder and incest, and believe them to be dangerous to the public welfare; whilst barbarous people commit these things without ever once *dreaming*, that they are doing wrong: nay even civilised nations of antiquity were not altogether exempt from *some* of these crimes at least. The unenlightened part of mankind of our own times have hardly any idea of what is, amongst Europeans and Americans, considered right and wrong: they frequently are generous, brave and hospitable; but we seldom or never find them possessed of those noble qualities of the soul, that nice sense of duty, which animate those who have drunk of the refreshing fountain of revelation.—But to return to our proposition: will it be said that the Hindoo believes himself impelled by *consience*, to sacrifice himself to his idol, the Juggernaut; or that he does think it wrong, uninformed as he is? Does the conscience of the European permit him to commit suicide, or not? Does the ignorant Arab think, that he commits any crime by robbing the wayfaring traveller? And did the Spartan woman suppose herself guilty of any sin by adultery?

The greater number of my readers, whatever their opinion relative to revelation may be, will agree with me in asserting, that it is the greatest sin to sacrifice ourselves or any other person to an idol; that suicide can hardly be defended by those even, who deny a future state; and I am sure, that there are not many honest men in civilised society, who would defend robbery with the same reasons the Beduin gives for his depredations.—We have thus seen, conscience allowing theft to the Arab, and self-destruction to the ignorant Hindoo and the desperate European, when he has lost his all, or ruined his neighbour; but that to the generality of mankind conscience forbids theft and the destruction of one's own life or that of another. It follows, therefore, that the *conscience of one man justifies what another's very justly condemns.* Can it then be said, that we may without fear give ourselves up to the guidance of our own reason (conscience), unassisted by the word, the *written* word of God, and do, what we of our own accord deem to be right? Will the philosophers allow *every* man to do what he likes? O no*—they will say: " *That* action will endanger your neighbour's safety, and *this* will be disagreeable to the majority of the people." This is all very well, but what can they say against incest, suicide and gambling, where one or more men injure *themselves alone*, without harming any one, except he be a party or accessary to their deeds by his own accord? If I have a large sum of money, and another man chooses to stake an equal sum against me, what right, it may be asked, have these philosophers to forbid his doing so? Does he, or does he not, injure society at large, if he loses? His conscience does not forbid it; he says, " My own reason tells me, it is perfectly right, that I, knowing what I am about, may lose all I possess, if it pleases my fancy." This, it must be obvious, is a fair defence of gaming with those, who acknowledge no other monitor, than that still voice within us, called conscience; but notwithstanding this, none is more loud in condemning this *really detestable* vice, than the philosopher, who denies all revelation. But does not any re-straint, laid upon a man in this respect, limit the observance of what the dictates of his conscience or reason allow him to do? So then we find, that not even freethinkers can allow us to be guided in all concerns of life by the dictates of our own reason alone. But we hear them say: " Since every man is not endowed with the same reasoning powers, and since all are not equally virtuous, not every man should be allowed to follow the bent of his own inclination, since this would be injurious to society ; but he is to submit to those rules and regulations, which wiser and better men, than himself, have prescribed to him."—But is this fair? From what source does the

* Even a Draco, who punished small and great crimes equally with death, because the smallest sin deserved death, and for greater ones he could find no severer punishment—even he made his laws, at least in letter " unchangeable laws."—*Schiller's Works*, vol. xvi. p. 122.

And the French revolutionary legislature solemnly decreed there was no God, and introduced an actress and worshipped her as the goddess of reason! and besides they tortured and butchered the catholic clergy for non-conformity to revolutionary laws.

philosopher derive the right to dictate laws to mankind from his study? How can he convince every one, that he is in possession of more wisdom and virtue than every other human being? How then dares he to appropriate to himself the privilege of thinking for so many of his fellow-mortals?—Now grant for argument's sake, that his superior wisdom and virtue, which are universally acknowledged, entitle him to this pre-eminence by the common consent of his contemporaries. But we ask, whence proceeds his wisdom? Has he obtained it by intuition? Is his knowledge derived from himself, or from some superior Being? Do his superior endowments make him more than man? do they render him immortal? do they make him infallible? Is he no longer liable to err because he is wise, because he is learned? Is his virtue of that kind, that it never yields to temptation? In short, can he cease to be man? No—he is still a mortal, prone to err, and he must at length descend to the grave, and there his body, as well as the remains of the most ignorant of men, will become a prey to worms.—Shall we then rely for our moral instruction upon a man—one destined to die—one, who cannot change even the smallest particle of nature—one, who, no less than the humblest of mortals, must look with astonishment at the great works of the great Creator? From this great Creator the wisdom of the philosopher is derived; it is He, who favoured him with more knowledge, than other men, and to Him his *spirit must return*, when his body is laid to moulder in the grave. Shall it now be said, that we are to listen to the instructions of the creature, but disregard those of the Creator? Or can it be supposed, that the almighty Author of all could not make as good laws for the government of mankind, as the man, to whom He has imparted but a small share of knowledge? Shall we shut out the light of the sun, because a taper also can give light?

But, ask our opponents: " Is it rational to suppose, that the Creator did promulgate his laws?" Yes, and we may be bold to say, that the contrary opinion must of necessity be absurd; as from the preceding remarks it will be apparent, that our own reason is not sufficient to show us the path of right; for that what is called conscience does not, cannot, *influence all alike*, and consequently cannot be the universal standard of right, since it leads different persons to different conclusions. This being admitted, (and the experience of every man will prove it so,) it must follow, that unless there be a revelation, that is to say, a declared and known law proceeding from God, the world is left without the knowledge of right and wrong; and thus the deniers of revelation must accuse the Deity of the greatest injustice, in creating so many beings, endowed with reason, and leaving them to proceed without a rule or guide, like a ship, tossed upon the billows of the tempestuous ocean, without rudder or compass!*—Let us then ask every thinking man, what is most reasonable to believe—that God made his will known to mankind, that

* Since, if you break down the moral influence of enacted laws in a community, mere brute force will never be able to maintain peace and order, as the history of all nations, where anarchy has reigned, clearly proves; and you would thus expose the whole world to mutual pillage and rapine, and subject the weaker to the insolent tyranny of the stronger; and we should see a spectacle exhibited, the most frightful ever yet experienced on earth. It is in fact the idea of a supreme legislative power being somewhere, which has been the foundation of civilised society in all ages, and where this has not been the case, disorder was ever the consequence. If we have now no declared will of the Deity, (which however the traditions of all nations clearly establish,) and as the enactments of man, even the cardinal points on which the structure of civil society rests, can be repealed by a succeeding generation, (witness the laws of Draco and Solon,) it will be evident that no moral system, even the emanation of the wisest men, can obtain sufficient moral force, to become a standard of right. This moral force, however, can only belong to a system derived from a Being not fallible himself, and whose wisdom cannot be gainsaid by a successor. It cannot be denied, that some persons have availed themselves of the actual existence of a revelation to promulge ideas of their own engrafted upon it, which were foreign to its nature; but this only proves the more clearly, the necessity of a knowledge of the pure source, even to the unbeliever, not to mention to any one founding his belief upon, and regulating his life by, revelation; since from it systems have sprung, which, although not possessing the whole strength and grandeur of the original itself, have nevertheless done so much towards civilising the world and exploding codes of laws disfigured by cruelty and immorality. What is more, this diversity of systems derived from the Pentateuch will upon reflection establish the truth of the latter; as its actual existence, and the knowledge they had of its being the work of inspiration, induced reformers to give to their own nations something resembling it, whilst they perhaps thought them not yet sufficiently enlightened to bestow the whole upon them. But there is no doubt, that a time will come, when the Mosaic code alone, under such modification (*to the nations*) as the Almighty may ordain, will be the law-book of all the earth. See Isaiah, chap. ii. and xi. Zachariah, chap. xiv. and many other passages in the prophets.

they might have a road to lead them on to happiness, or that He left them to grope about in darkness? Can it be believed, that He, who has provided for the smallest insect, which is invisible to the human eye, should leave his noblest work so unprovided, so destitute, so miserable? Did He give him an intelligent mind to make his station the more wretched, the more forlorn?

If philosophers would only reflect, to what ends their reckless denial of all revelation must lead them, I am confident, they would pause and shudder at the sight of the fathomless abyss, to which they so thoughtlessly hurry on themselves and others. They would not then so often think lightly of the word of Him, who is no less their God, than the God and Creator of the whole universe.

CHAPTER II.

WHO WROTE THE PENTATEUCH?

Before we adduce further proofs in favour of revelation, it will be necessary to enquire, if Moses actually wrote the books, which bear his name; and granted he did write them, if he be then entitled to belief, or in other words, if what Moses relates in his history did take place, at the time, place, and in the manner, he himself says it did happen.

First: " Did Moses write the *five books* (Pentateuch), which are designated by his name?" To this question we unhesitatingly answer, yes; for the following reason: If any man presents a book to the public, and alleges that he is the author of the same, he deserves, without doubt, to be believed, unless some other person should claim the authorship, and bring conclusive proof, that he, *and not the ostensible editor*, is the true author. Now we find, that Moses tells us, that he was commanded by God, whose messenger he purports to be, to write down all the transactions of his time, as they happened,

2

for we read in Exodus, chap. xxxiv. v. 27: "And the Eternal said unto Moses, Write thou these words; for according to these words I have made a covenant with thee and with Israel."

Here we find Moses announcing, that he had received an absolute injunction from the Deity, to write down the events of his time, and the laws which were communicated to him.

And in Deuteronomy (chap. xxxi. v. 24) we read that Moses relates his having completed the task thus imposed upon him by God; for there it is said:

"And when Moses had finished to write down the words of this law in a book, to their very conclusion;

25. Then Moses commanded the Levites, the carriers of the ark of the covenant of the Eternal, as follows:

26. Take this book of the law, and place it at the side of the ark of the covenant of the Eternal your God, and it shall be there as an evidence against thee (the whole nation of the Israelites)."

It is thus proved by the internal evidence of the books themselves, that they were written and compiled* by Moses; and even the account of the travels of the Israelites owes its origin to the same author, as he carefully noted down all the journeyings of the people under his charge, as he himself tells us in the 33d chapter of the book of Numbers.

How can it now be doubted, that Moses was the writer of the books in question?—Suppose a modern antiquarian were to attempt to demonstrate, that Cæsar was *not* the author of his Commentaries; or that Demosthenes did *not* deliver those splendid orations, which were for the last two thousand years supposed to be his: would not such an attempt be considered, by most men at least, as an evidence of insanity in the person who makes the attempt?—For how could he hope to convince the world of their error, except by prostrating at the same time all dependence upon history? The reason for this assertion is simply the following: if you deny, that a book, which

---

* I say compiled; for though there can be no doubt, that Moses was the *bona fide* author of the last four books of the Pentateuch, comprising the history of the Israelites during his life time; it is nevertheless more than probable, that the book of Genesis was in existence before Moses, and if even not in its present form, at least it may be presumed that he had ample materials in his possession, from which he *compiled* it, as will be more clearly shown in a subsequent chapter.

bears the name of any author, was written by the reputed author, you admit, that this book contains in this respect at least an untruth; and if it cannot be relied upon in so material a point, it ought not to carry any weight with it in other matters; for since the author has been convicted of not paying a strict regard to truth, how can you determine, (if you rely solely upon the internal evidence of the book itself,) what is true and what is *not* true? Not to come to this dilemma you must admit, that the *pretended* author was the *real* author; for to deny this, as has been said, would throw discredit upon the whole book.—The same is the case with every historical writing extant; and we are constrained to credit the authenticity of authorship, or else no monument of art, no building, no painting, in short nothing whatever, would be believed to be the work of the artist, to whom it is generally ascribed; and all history would be a mere romance, written perhaps like some fairy tale, to amuse children and frighten the ignorant. Nothing, of which we had not ocular proof, would then be believed by us, and nothing considered a reality, of which we had no perception with our senses. But where is the man to be found, who is willing to carry this principle to so great an extent? And yet I see no point, where to stop with any degree of safety. There are very few, who do not repose confidence in history, and believe things, though they never did come under their own observation. Many have never seen the emperor Napoleon, few have ever seen Sir Walter Scott; nevertheless they firmly believe that the former fought the many battles in Europe, Asia and Africa, in which he is *reported* to have been present; and that the latter wrote the life of Napoleon, and that moreover he is the author of that great number of books, of which he has avowed himself the author. It cannot indeed be well comprehended, how a single man, unaided, could possibly *write so much*, independently of the composition of so many works; but for all that, they believe, that Sir Walter did write all those books, the authorship of which he claims, chiefly because no other person has claimed the authorship and proved a superior title to the reputed author, although they themselves have never seen him write a single word.

But, some one may ask;

"If I am to believe the *identity* of books, which have been written so many centuries ago, what safeguard have I against being imposed upon by any book, which is given out as being the work of any author of antiquity?"

This, I confess, is a weighty objection, the more so, as *forged books* have very often been ascribed to writers, who perhaps had never even heard the names of those very works, said to be theirs. But let us examine the matter a little more closely, and see if the danger of being imposed upon be really so great as might perhaps appear at first sight. Let us for instance suppose; that a book should be published, purporting to have been written by *Julius Cæsar*, and giving an account of the *civil war*, which under Cæsar agitated the whole Roman empire; that further, this book should give an account of the events of the time, similar to that, which is contained in the book, commonly ascribed to Cæsar, on the same subject,—let us say, till his arrival in Greece; but in speaking of the battle of Pharsalus, in which Pompey was conquered, suppose it to state, that Cæsar's army was routed by that of Pompey, after which the latter held a triumphant entry into Rome, and that it was not till after a long war, that Cæsar conquered in a hard fought battle, in which Pompey was slain. What would every one's opinion be in finding such an account in a work said to be written by Cæsar? Surely, that Cæsar could *not* be the author, because the whole chain of events, which *preceded Cæsar's death*, belie the (fictitious) account just given, and the great dictator would not in all probability have committed any thing to writing, which he, as an eye-witness and the principal actor, must have known to be untrue.—Or if the book in question should say, that the German warriors in Cæsar's army were equipped after the fashion of Numidian horsemen—or if it were written in the monkish Latin of the middle age: in all these cases the book would no doubt be pronounced a forgery, without the slightest diversity of opinion; for circumstances, generally and upon the best possible evidence, admitted as facts, prove that Cæsar could not have written it, for he must have been intimately acquainted with the *history, manners* and *language* of his time.—But if, on the contrary, a book were found at present, written in the easy style of Cæsar, and giving such an account of events as would appear plausible, and not contradicted by well established histories of that period, and if there should be a clause in the work stating, that C. Julius Cæsar the Dictator had written it: could then any reasonable doubt be entertained of its authenticity? And I am free to assert, that most persons would regard the book as genuine, and they would require more proof, than the mere *dictum* of any man, to establish the contrary.*

The foregoing illustration it is hoped will have satisfactorily shown, that we may with a great degree of safety rely upon the identity of books of antiquity. I will now advance another position, which from its very nature is incontrovertible, namely: "*that what is once true must ever be so.*" If for instance it is true now, that Cæsar wrote the first seven books on the Gallican War, the same must be true two thousand years·hence, for what is once past, is *past*, and nothing can undo the past.

I must ask pardon of my readers for this long digression, which was considered necessary for the proof, or at least elucidation, of the assertion, " that Moses was the author of the books he professes to have written."—Almost every man admits the truth of profane history, at least so far as to believe, that the different books of all ages were written by those men, who claim to be the authors, unless perhaps it might be established, that there be some other claimants, who have superior titles to the reputed authors. The details of history are also admitted, unless their falsity can be proved.

Let us now ask all those, who deny the truth of our religion, why will you give credence to profane history, and not even believe, that our blessed legislator was the author of his own books; or rather that it was he who wrote them by the command of the Most High, if any one did? But you will say, " the books are of so great antiquity, that it may be fairly doubted, whether Moses wrote them, especially as we have no contemporary writer to prove the fact!" Is that your objection? well let us examine it a little more closely and ask : if Moses did not write them, who then was the author? Were the seventy elders, who made the translation, commonly called the *Septuagint*, for Ptolemy Lagos, the.authors?—No, for they were only the translators into Greek of this book—a book previously existing in Hebrew, and so much renowned for its wisdom, that a

---

* Although the above supposition may appear far-fetched, similar cases have nevertheless frequently occurred, both with works of ancient and modern authors; for example, the book of the Republic by Cicero, and Milton's book on Religion, which both have been discovered only very lately, as the learned reader will no doubt recollect.

Grecian king desired a transcript of it in his own language.*—But was it Ezra? No, for he could not be the compiler even, much less the author, as he speaks of the books as *already in existence*, nay as *existing even before his time*, and as being well known to the enlightened part of the people.—So *he* cannot be the man.—But was it Joshua, the immediate successor of Moses? Oh no, for to him it was commanded (Josh. i. 8.): " This book of the law shall not depart out of thy mouth, and thou shalt meditate therein day and night, that thou mayest observe to do all, which *is* written therein, for then wilt thou be prosperous and then wilt thou be wise." If the Pentateuch then was existing before Joshua, he cannot be the author of it; much less Ezra, who lived near a thousand years later. We must therefore come to the conclusion, that Moses—being the immediate predecessor of Joshua, and as the Jews had no legislator before him—must be the author† *de facto* of the books that bear his name. This he was in the time of Joshua, and *what was true then, is true now;* and, therefore, since Moses was the real author in those days, he must now also be considered as such, and this so long as the blue vault of heaven shall remain extended over this beautiful earth!

May God enlighten our minds and fortify us in his law, Amen!

---

* And it certainly can be no argument against the actual existence of the Pentateuch before this period, that the Greeks were not acquainted with it, as we find no mention made of it in their most ancient historian. For this may have been owing to their ignorance of what related to other nations, or to the contempt they uniformly expressed towards *barbarians* (all nations except the Greek), and they may have therefore concealed the knowledge they had of a book of wisdom and good laws belonging to another and distant people.—But the eagerness of Ptolemy to possess himself of this treasure clearly proves, not only that the Greeks were ignorant of its existence, but that its origin must have been referrible, even at that time, to very remote antiquity.

† See Appendix to Part I. for a refutation of some anachronisms, which it is pretended have been discovered in the Pentateuch.

CHAPTER III.

MOSES AN AUTHENTIC HISTORIAN.

Having in the preceding chapter endeavoured to establish, to the best of my limited abilities, that Moses was the author of the books, which are known by his name : we must now proceed to the *second* point of enquiry ;

" Is Moses entitled to credibility, as a historian ?"

Our conviction or knowledge may be referred as proceeding from three causes : *first*, we are convinced of any thing, that is, we know it to be true, because we were *eye-witnesses*, or have other *personal* knowledge of the fact; *secondly*, because we hear it related by persons, who profess to have seen or experienced it, and in whose veracity we place confidence ; and *lastly*, because we *read* events described in books, and though the author, or what is the same, the narrator, himself be not present, to tell us his narrative by word of mouth, we may nevertheless believe confidently, *first*, that the professed author was an eye-witness of the described event, or that his source of information was undoubted; and *lastly*, that his narrative is in conformity with truth, or, what is the same, that the events related actually occurred.

The *limited faculties* of man will not allow him, to be an eye-witness of many things ; and, since he cannot be at different places at the same moment of time, he must receive, whatever happens out of his presence, upon the good faith of others; for he would assuredly be, and ever remain, woefully uninformed of the affairs of life and the discoveries of science, should he reject every thing as untrue, which did not fall under his own personal observation.

Since our acquaintance with external facts can only commence from the time of our birth, we are thereby prevented from having *personal* knowledge of what occurred before our time ; we cannot resort to eye-witnesses for information, as every human being alive is comparatively of but recent date. If therefore we wish to be informed of what took place before our time, we must needs seek this information *from books ;* secondly, from those who have read them, in case we cannot read them ourselves, and lastly from monuments and popular tradition.

Of all the above sources of information, or conviction, *that* is undoubtedly the safest, which results from our own actual observation and the perception of our senses; the second best is that, which is derived from living witnesses, who impart to us what they know by experience; and the last is that, which is drawn from books, monuments and tradition.

Though, *generally* speaking, to see is to believe; we will yet frequently find, that we may be deceived, although we have the thing to be investigated actually before us. The reason of this is, that many things, presented to our view, are not sufficiently known or understood by us, to enable us to form a correct judgment; and even when this is not the case, we are frequently so much biassed by prejudice, as to suffer it to warp our judgment to such a degree, that we are led to judge altogether erroneously, though under other circumstances we would be able to form a strictly correct opinion, if our *feelings* were not enlisted, on the one side or the other.

When we derive our information from living witnesses, we are too apt to suffer *our* judgment to be swayed by the *feelings* of *our informants*, particularly, if our interest coincides, with theirs; so, on the contrary, we are often, from no other cause than private pique, predisposed to differ altogether with our informants, because we may prefer finding them, or their friends, in the wrong, or shut our ears against conviction, from a mere spirit of contradiction. But as we are here not so much personally engaged, as if we were the actors, or immediate spectators, we will frequently, upon reflection, be disposed to alter our opinions, and bring them down to a proper standard of reasoning, much oftener at least, than if our feelings were more immediately enlisted, by our personal observation or actual participation.

When at last books, monuments, or traditions, are our guides to knowledge, though we may *even here* be more inclined to one side, than the other, we will yet certainly, and almost invariably, be enabled to form a more *correct opinion*, than in the two first cases.

Thus we see, that each mode of acquiring information has its advantages and disadvantages; and indeed it often happens, that though we ourselves are unjust towards a third person, our neighbours will understand our dispute better, and, however favourably inclined towards us, will decide in his favour:—and again, posterity will esteem a man great and glorious, whom his contemporaries suffered to starve.

I am inclined to believe, that the foregoing will be sufficient to show, that we may derive *positive information* without ocular evidence, or else, that our mind must be a blank, and ignorant of the most important concerns of life, and of those things, which are the most conducive to our happiness. In fact, the world in general has ever thought so, since, from time immemorial, history has afforded instruction and amusement, and has been generally received as true; besides, the example of great deeds has roused many a noble mind into activity, which might otherwise have lain dormant, or exhausted its vigour in works, if not pernicious, at least useless to society.

But some one may ask : "How far is it reasonable to rely upon any thing I hear, or find related in books? what rule am I to observe, to guard myself against being imposed upon?" Here let us pause a moment, and reflect : how does it appear to our conviction, that any thing has *actually* occurred, and that our impression of any supposed fact is not a phantom of the imagination? First, from the effect the occurrence has produced; secondly, from preceding, accompanying, or subsequent circumstances; and lastly, from the impression it made at the same time upon others, if others there were, to witness the occurrence at the same time with us.—For instance, let us suppose, that a number of persons should be assembled in a well built house, and that this had the appearance of being a structure which could endure for ages. Now let us imagine, that a sudden concussion of the earth were to rend this building asunder, and bury the persons there assembled amidst the tumbling ruins; that only one should be dug out alive, and recover his recollection by degrees, after weeks of sickness and mental darkness, and then, finding himself surrounded by strangers, call for those who were with him when the earthquake took place; now even assume, that he receive at first an evasive reply, as for instance, that they would soon come; is it not highly probable, that his own returning reason will soon convince him of the reality of the case? his being where he is, will tell him, upon reflection, that something dreadful must have taken

3

place, and the sudden tumbling of the strong walls, the shock, which he himself experienced, will force upon him the melancholy conclusion, that he shall see his friends no more ; and no matter how faint his knowledge of the actual occurrence of the earthquake may be at first, the *effect* it had upon him will undoubtedly teach him that it actually did occur.—In the second case ; you are in a room, and hear a conversation, to which you pay no particular attention ; to be sure, you hear it, but yet do not think it of consequence enough to charge your memory with it. After some time suppose a friend comes to you, and asks : " Do you recollect what such a one said on that day ?" At first, you will barely recollect that a conversation took place at all ; but if he draws your attention to various circumstances, which accompanied this conversation, you will very probably recollect the whole or the essential part at least, which would have been absolutely impossible, but for the *accompanying circumstances.*—In the third place, let us suppose that a sudden meteor flashes before our eyes, but that its transit is so quick as to leave us in doubt if we are mistaken in our impression or not ; but if we hear others say that they too saw a meteor, we shall then be convinced of the truth of our *first* although *imperfect* impression.

In the same manner may historical correctness be tested ; first, by *effects* ; secondly, by *circumstances* which are known to have taken place ; and thirdly, by *general impression,* except when it is *contrary to previously well attested facts.*—Historical effect is every thing produced by events related in, or made known by, history ; thus is the independence of the United States an effect or consequence, in the first instance of the Declaration of Independence, and in the next, of the subsequent war.—In this class may also be reckoned what are called the remains of antiquity, as ruins, ancient buildings, monuments, and manuscripts.—To the second class belong conversations, said to have been held by persons, who are no more in being, which derive their claim to authenticity, merely from the known character of those persons ; further, such incidents as have been transmitted to us in historical records, which are rendered probable from the peculiar manner, lives, and character of persons or even nations. Of the former, I will only mention the few words said to have been spoken by Julius Cæsar, when he discovered Brutus amongst his assassins ; and of the latter, the conduct of Alexander of Macedon at the temple of Jupiter Ammon, and his conduct subsequently thereto, after he believed himself, and obliged others to believe, that he was the son of a god.—In the last class I would reckon all traditions and popular stories, which are more or less worthy of credit, as they can be more or less fortified by either monuments &c., known circumstances, or lastly, *probability*.

When the effect produced by a certain reported event is yet in existence, no man in his sober senses will doubt a fact so well authenticated.* For instance, it is said, that in the seventy-ninth year of the Christian æra, the city of Pompeii was destroyed or rather buried, by the volcanic ashes of Vesuvius. If any one even might have been inclined to doubt this, had it merely been reported, it is now rendered certain beyond a possibility of being disputed, as the buried city was actually discovered about a hundred years ago, since which time many streets have been re-opened. No man, therefore, can now doubt, that a similar fate has befallen, or may yet befall other places.—About a century ago an island was formed in the Grecian Archipelago, after a terrible convulsion of nature. This island yet exists, and the account of its emersion from the waves is consequently believed.—It will therefore be readily acknowledged, that the rareness and even improbability of a thing, can be no argument against its possibility, and whatever is authenticated and verified by *undoubted* effects must be received as true, no matter if the event be in accordance with the ordinary course of nature or not.

If then profane history is verified by the remains of antiquity, why should we reject the account which Moses has left us? Why will you, who deny the truth of the word of God, be more indulgent to the records of the Grecians and Romans, than to sacred history? Is there not a more noble monument of the historical truth of the Pentateuch, than Grecian marble, or Egyptian granite, namely, we ourselves, the Jews?—Answer me, are not the dispersions of Israel sufficient testimony of the existence of Moses, of the wonderful deliverance of the children of Jacob, and of their conquest of the Holy Land under the guidance of Joshua?—Will you believe that Sesostris reigned, Themistocles fought, Socrates and Plato taught philosophy,

---

* If therefore any thing is related to us, and we are assured that it had a mentioned effect, and it can be proved that this *effect* never took place; we may then safely and fairly consider the *whole story* a fabrication.

and Demosthenes spoke—and will you, can you deny that Moses lived? that through him the law was given? and that the history of the Israelites is faithfully narrated in the subsequent biblical writings?

"Well," some of you will say, "we grant the possibility, even the probability of the plain matters of fact in the Bible, but we will not admit the truth of the miracles; and as these are so much interwoven with natural occurrences throughout the Bible, they are enough to throw discredit upon the whole."

But if there is a God who created all things, and governs all, and sustains all by his will,—and there is a God! exclaims all nature—to whom all owes its origin—we must admit that miracles are within the scope of possibility; for, should not the Creator be able to order things differently, and yet preserve all in being, if He deems it proper? Since then miracles are possible, since we even see that *extraordinary* events occur daily; can we possibly *doubt*, that God could change water into blood for particular purposes, when He, in his unerring wisdom, thought it necessary towards the accomplishment of his almighty will? Could He not send frogs, or as some suppose, crocodiles, to plague the inhabitants of Egypt, when they refused to obey his will? Could he not let water flow out of a rock, when he determined to do so?

I admit, that God has ordained nature to *work so harmoniously*, that, to our impression, the slightest impediment would destroy the beautiful fabric. But does *that* change, or diminish, or circumscribe his *ability*, to order it otherwise? Can He not dry up every fountain? can He not split mountains asunder? can He not command the sea to produce habitable land in its vast and deep centre? and should He not be able " to give bread, should He not be powerful enough to provide food for his people?" Why then, let me repeat the question, will you not accept the Mosaic writings as the true chronology of times gone by? Will you reject them, because of their antiquity? Will you leave such a blank in the history of the world, from its creation to Herodotus? Forbid it science, forbid it reason, forbid it justice! Rather join with us and say:

" Moses is true, and his law is true !

CHAPTER IV.

THE PENTATEUCH.

In the foregoing chapters, I have endeavoured to show the plausi-
bility as least, first, of Moses's right to be acknowledged the author
of the Pentateuch, and secondly, of the claims of this book to be considered the true history of his time.—But how* did Moses know
what happened before his days?—To this, I answer, that he was not
only the narrator of his own observations, but also the compiler or
transcriber of existing historical materials. We have no means to
prove *positively*, that the Israelites had any writings before Moses;
but we can give various reasons, which seem to leave hardly any
doubt resting upon the matter.

In the first place, the greater part of the events in Genesis are
so circumstantially narrated, that it appears that those, who were
immediately concerned in them, were the historians of their times.

A second reason may be discovered in the peculiar phraseology of
at least two passages in Exodus. We read in Exo. xvii. v. 14 : "And
the Eternal said unto Moses, write this (the attack of Amalake upon
Israel) for a memorial *in the book*, and rehearse it before Joshua."—
The Hebrew words are the following : כתב זאת זכרון בספר (*Ketobe
zothe zickahrone Bassaypher*.) The word, *Bassaypher* signifies,
in the book, whereas *in a book* (Eng. Version) ought to have been
Besaypher; or, to make it more intelligible to an English reader, the
Hebrew syllable *ba* is the preposition *in* followed by the definite
article *the* (in the), and the syllable *be* is the preposition *in* with the
indefinite article *a* (in a).† If the passage, of which we are now

---

* If it is once admitted that the Pentateuch was written by inspiration, it
makes no difference, from what *other* sources Moses derived his information,
as the Holy Spirit was in that case his instructer, which would have prevented
him from committing any error; but as I direct my argument against unbelievers, I think it necessary to prove every thing, so as not to leave them any
opportunity for cavilling.

† I am indebted for this argument to the April No. 1826, p. 282, of the North
American Review.

treating, is rendered correctly, and which no Hebrew scholar can dispute, it is pretty evident, that, as God ordered Moses to write the attack of Amalake in *the book*, it must follow, (as no particular book is mentioned, either here or elsewhere,) that this expression must relate to a book well known to the then Israelites, and which book, moreover, must have been a record of their history *previous* to the promulgation of the law, as the battle with Amalake took place *before* that event, the most remarkable since the creation. The second passage is found in Exodus xxiv. v. 7, and is in the following words: " And he (Moses) took *the book of the covenant* and read it within hearing of the people, &c." This passage, however, is not so explicit as the preceding one, as it may refer also to the occurrences between the Exodus and the promulgation of the law on Sinai exclusively; though many are of opinion, that the *book of the covenant* here spoken of is that in which the covenants with the Patriarchs are recorded, meaning the book of Genesis; and this book must have contained the history of the world from the creation to the death of Joseph, and further, the first nineteen chapters of Exodus (the passage quoted being a part of the recapitulation of what occurred before the promulgation of the Decalogue). But as this cannot be well established, and as it is mere conjecture, though highly probable, I shall not insist upon it as a *convincing* argument.

But I have now to adduce reasons to show, that independently of every consideration of inspiration or prophecy, we have cause to prefer Moses's history to any profane history extant, and it may be added, that ever was or will be written.—For every historian, if he relates the history of an enemy, will delight to dwell upon his crimes, and place his misdeeds before the world in the boldest relief, and use every means to make him odious, and only put a limit to his acrimony, for the sake of his own reputation for veracity, and that he may not be charged with giving his picture too deep a colouring. If he speaks of a friend, or one whom he pretends to admire, he will always endeavour to gloss over the faults of the hero of his tale, or omit them altogether, if he possibly can. And if any man writes his own life, he never relates a fault of his own, except it be to gain applause for his sincerity, or he strives hard to excuse that to the world, which he, in his conscience, cannot justify. Is this true or not?

Not so Moses. From the commencement of Genesis to the end of Deuteronomy, he merely relates the facts, as they occurred, without at any time commenting upon them. He relates the history of Jacob and Joseph, those two prominent and exalted patriarchs, with the most bewitching simplicity; both are represented to ûs as they really were, without addition, without diminution. In some parts of their lives, any profane historian, had he been their biographer, would have attempted to justify their actions, and at least would have tried to prove them virtuous, though their actions might to some appear equivocal. But Moses does not do so; he gives us facts, lets us draw our own inferences, and justify or condemn actions according to the standard which he was the instrument of making known to the world; well knowing that the intelligent part of mankind would be indulgent to the few faults and occasional errors of these good men; particularly when he, at the same time, leads us to the mortifying reflection, that no one is entirely free from fault, and that the best occasionally transgresses; and if any one should now be disposed to vent his spleen against the bible characters, because they were not altogether perfect, he may be referred to reflect upon himself, and told to see if all is so pure within him, that he cannot err, before he can be permitted to be too severe upon the sins of otherwise good men.

We thus find him never giving a false or overcharged colouring to any thing he relates. In the affecting interview between Joseph and Benjamin every thing is told in so simple a style, that we are at a loss which most to admire, the delicacy of Joseph's feelings towards Benjamin, when he first sees him, or the sublime brevity in which the whole is presented to us.—That part, where Joseph makes himself known to his brothers, is in the same style of simple sublimity, if I may use the expression; "I am Joseph! lives my father yet?" These few words seem to proceed, so spontaneously, and so naturally, from a surcharged heart, and feelings raised to the highest pitch, that it is not probable that any passage can be found, either in ancient classics or in any modern production, that will in any degree equal the idea expressed by—I am Joseph! lives my father yet?

If we have seen Moses act and write so in matters where he was not himself concerned, we shall find him equally sincere, and equally regardful of truth, when he has occasion to speak of himself or his nearest relations. Though he had often opportunities to praise himself, or to sketch his own character in the most exalted manner, yet does he ever remain the simple narrator of facts, and speaks only once in his own praise, and that in a trait for which *alone* few men would think of praising themselves, namely the absence of all pride. (Numb. xii. v. 3. "And the man Moses was the meekest of all men upon the face of the earth.") What, the greatest of mortals to suffer himself to be slandered, and not resent the affront? What, does he suffer rebellion against *his authority*, without wishing the *ringleaders even* to be punished, save only then, when the well-being of Israel absolutely demanded this painful sacrifice?—Yes, it is even so. The man who was destined and appointed to be the leader of the Israelites shared all their toils, all their sufferings, and once only was sedition against his authority punished, and even then not through his agency; and his version of that event must needs be believed, since it is so circumstantially told, and it *occurred* before *the whole nation* of Israel.

Though he had undoubtedly acquired a great stock of knowledge in the sciences and the mechanic arts, yet do we not hear him boast of any of his acquirements; he only tells us in one part that his bodily strength remained unimpaired to his dying day, and in another he informs us, that he had an impediment in his speech, and this is all we know of the greatest of men!*—About his own actions he is very explicit, he throws no veil over them to hide their defects, and he has even the frankness to tell us, (Deut. ch. iii. v. 23—26,) that his earnest prayer to be permitted to enter "and see the good land, which was (to him) on the other side of the Jordan, the good mountain and the Lebanon," was not accepted, for the well known reasons several times recorded in the book of Numbers.

If we even search all books of antiquity, or modern times, we shall probably meet with none which is so impartially written as the Pentateuch; which presents both sides of a picture with the same faithfulness, as the Hebrew canon does; and where we have facts so simply given, and our judgment is more left at liberty to judge for itself.

This very carelessness of Moses about amplifications and excuses,

---

* Compare this with the lives of Hume and Gibbon, written by themselves.

proves to the candid mind, that his subject must have been a good one, and the cause he advocated righteous. For would any man, ushering a fable into the world as truth, take so *little* trouble to persuade the world to receive it, as Moses has done ? Would he not rather try to produce ingenious arguments, and well devised artifices, to make his laws palatable ? Did not the celebrated Lycurgus, I may say, *cheat* the Spartans into an acceptance of his code, (if any credit can be given to the Greek writers,) which otherwise would probably never have been tolerated, as the supreme laws of the land ?

But as there may perhaps be some other objections, of which I am, however, altogether ignorant, I will just state one instance of the great disinterestedness of Moses. The honour of priesthood was the greatest dignity among us, for under certain circumstances, the priest was even higher than the chief magistrate of the nation ; independently of religious distinctions and other privileges attached to that order.——If Moses now had been ambitious, or eager after power and glory, he would certainly, (*all along supposing he was not inspired*,) have assumed to himself and his descendants the highest honour. But did he do so ? No, he elevates his brother and his four sons, whilst he submits himself and his own children to Aaron's superintendence (see several passages in Numbers, particularly chap. viii. v. 5—26). No other conqueror, no other legislator ever acted in this manner. I will not say, that they did *assume all* honours and power, but it may be boldly asserted that no *one* conqueror or legislator ever *excluded* himself and descendants from honour, power, and riches !—It is well known, that the Levites had neither sovereign power, nor *immediate* property like the other tribes, since all their property was dispersed among all the tribes of Israel, and even then their possessions were limited within a mile on each side of their cities. Why then did Moses exercise this forbearance unless directed by a superior power, a power superior to *his* will, and to whose unlimited sway Moses, no less than every other member of the human family, was obliged to submit ? Indeed, it was his word Moses wrote, by his command Moses acted, and his almighty name was the watchword of Moses !

We have thus seen Moses proved to be the writer of the Pentateuch, seen him entitled to credibility as a historian in general, and also

4

seen him proved equal, if not superior, to any historian of ancient or modern times. I will then pause here and in the succeeding chapters endeavour to establish the truth of revelation, not alone by Moses's history, but also by our national existence as Jews, and as the representatives of the Israelites to whom the law was originally given, and the fulfilment of prophecies pronounced by Moses and his successors, the prophets and seers of Israel.—I must here also beg every one who reads these pages, to consult the passages in the Bible, to which l may refer, and take them in connection with the preceding and following verses, to see that the interpretation I may have to give, is consonant with the context, as l do not wish any thing to be taken upon my bare assertion. Should he in the succeeding part of this little volume find any thing startling at first sight, he will do well to reflect before he condemns my conclusion; at all events l hope to receive a fair hearing, not alone from Jews, but also from Christians and free-thinkers.

CHAPTER V.

THE HISTORY OF REVELATION—ADAM—NOAH.

I deemed it altogether unavoidable, before commencing to draw arguments from the Pentateuch, to prove at first, that it is highly reasonable to believe that its contents are true. Having accomplished this task, in the best manner I could, I shall now resume my original proposition, namely, to adduce proof in favour of the revelation given to Moses, and the subsequent adherence of the Israelites to the same, from his time until the present day.

In Chapter I. I have shown, that it is reasonable to conclude that God revealed himself to mankind, and have at the same time proved, that the contrary opinion would accuse the Almighty of injustice towards man.

But I hear the infidels and the wavering say :—" Most true, it would be unjust to suffer the world to be without a *rule of right;* but was it just in God to do, as you Jews assert him to have done, to give a law to you only, and that after two thousand years from the creation ?"

Before answering this question, I must state that I shall in the sequel adopt the Mosaic writings as universally acknowledged, and therefore argue from them without stopping to prove the correctness of every passage, having, as I conceive, already amply demonstrated the truth of the *whole*. Having premised this much, I have to state that the above objection would stand good, provided the assertion were true, that no revelation was known to mankind before Moses; but, it can be shown that the fact is otherwise. It is unnecessary to prove, that God is *capable*, when He is *willing* to communicate his commandments to mankind ; we Jews believe him not alone capable and willing, but also think that he has actually *done so*, and we shall continue in this our belief, till some one can *prove* that no revelation was given.—In support of our belief, we may cite the text of *our* Holy Writ, where this is so plainly written, as to leave no doubt upon our minds of the fact, believing at the same time, that the contents of Holy Writ are strictly conformable to truth.

The question arises then :—" Can it be proven from Holy Writ, that there was a revelation before Moses, and were there any inspired men, in his time, among other nations, besides the Jews ?"

To prove the affirmative, it is only necessary to give an abstract of the history of the world until Moses, to satisfy the greatest sceptic.

From *nothing* did the Almighty call *every thing* into existence, and He clothed the world in *light* by the word of his mouth, as Moses so beautifully saith : " And God said, let there be light, and there was light." After organising the mighty structure of the star-clad heavens, He on the sixth day of the creation created man, in the manner related in the second chapter of Genesis ; He formed his body out of the clay of the earth, but unlike other animals formed in the same manner, which are only endowed with instinct, He imparted to him a *living soul*, by which He made man an intellectual being. He gave him also a companion to cheer him during his hours of toil, and to share his prosperity.—Immediately after the history of their creation, we find God imparting his will to the *man* whom He had made, or in other words, He *revealed* himself to Adam. But oh, our sinful propensities; when we once give way to them, when we, to avoid hurting the feelings of those we love, rather *sin with them* than give them reproof!—Eve was tempted to taste the forbidden fruit of the tree of knowledge, and Adam ate, by her persuaded.—Adam and his wife were before in a state of innocence ; but now their innocence was past, they had offended God their Creator. Before, the earth spontaneously yielded them its fruit, and man needed only to apply himself to work, to gather that which was so bounteously offered him ; but now labour was decreed to him during his sojourn on earth.—Before, he only saw his wife happy ; but now he was obliged to see her often writhing under severe pain. Before, he could listen to the word of God with joy and elevation of heart ; but now it seemed to him the terrible voice of thunder, which splitteth cedars and maketh the wilderness quake. And this was not all, for even death—the dissolution of the body—that noble fabric of the Deity—became man's lot ; and not even the descendants of Adam were exempt from that dread decree, and a mortal father begat a mortal son.

But was the decree of God just, in punishing so trifling a transgression so severely ?—Yes! yes! It was not that the act in itself was so very heinous ; but the disobedience to the *only* command of God given to Adam constituted the offence. Man, by this act had lost his innocence, remorse must have visited him, for disobeying so just a God, and all his life would in consequence have been embittered. But death being destined to close at last his career on earth, and as he knew, that the living soul within him could *not die* with his body, he had an *incentive* to virtue—to regain that heaven by repentance and good deeds, which he had forfeited by disobedience. His life, before his fall, was free from earthly cares, indeed; but as he existed then as man—flesh and spirit—he could not enjoy *that* happiness, which he can be heir to in his present state, when he by the exercise of virtue, or repentance, when he has erred, deserves that happiness, which no eye has seen save that of God alone.—And the Talmud in accordance with this teaches, and inculcates by examples and passages drawn from the prophets, that repentance, *sincere* repentance, and good deeds are a shield against punishment, and guides to eternal life.—Adam had fallen, but did God forsake him? No, He, to use the language of man, sought him out, and asked of him: "Where art thou?" He did not at once upbraid him with his ingratitude, but called him first, to give him an opportunity of defending himself. But who can justify himself against Thee, O Almighty God? who trembleth not when Thou speakest in thunder?—Adam attempted to shift the fault on his wife, and she was indeed more guilty than himself, and her tempter more guilty still; and in the same manner was their punishment ordained,—thus giving a lesson to mankind, that, though many be guilty of the same offence, minor guilt should never suffer the same punishment with consummate crime. But great is the Eternal's goodness; while in justice compelled to punish, He at the same time took notice of the altered state of mortals—altered by their own fault—and provided them with covering, since the consciousness of guilt forbade them to appear any longer to each other, as they had done before, because their *ideas* and *desires* were no longer pure and unsullied. Adam was henceforward banished from the garden of Eden, to mourn in his toil and increased labour, over his fallen state; and the Cherubim were placed at the entrance of the garden, to guard with the flaming sword the road to the *tree of life*, and to prevent the re-entrance of man, till being purified by a holy life and submission to the will of his Maker, he be worthy *again* of a state of unmixed pleasure and uninterrupted enjoyment.

Though it is not stated in express language, it must nevertheless be inferred, that partial revelation, or to speak more intelligibly, a limited number of laws, were given to Adam and his immediate descendants. . For we hear God reproving Cain for the murder of his brother, and even speaking to him of sin, and of man's power to conquer his passions, and to do good, when he will. (Gen. iv. 7.) Cain was severely punished for his crime ; and would God have punished him if he had not known that the act he was committing was sinful ? Would *that* be justice ?—We are therefore forced to admit, that God had imparted some of the civil institutions at least to the first men, for their government.—In further confirmation of this point, we may adduce the example of Hannoch (Enoch), who is said " to have walked with God" (acted as He desired); and how could

Hannoch act so, if he had not been certified of the will of God?—Noah was to admit into the ark seven pair of all clean animals and two only of unclean ones; now what criterion did he have to distinguish between the two kinds, without revelation.

I am free to confess, that these inferences will not prove any thing positive, though they be ever so ingenious; but we have more solid ground to stand on in the ninth chapter of Genesis, where we see God giving laws to Noah and his children. The world had been overflowed; all men, save *eight*, had been swept off from the face of the earth; and when the flood had subsided, we see the Father of all, either kindly renewing the old, or giving altogether new commandments, for the regulation of the conduct of the children of Adam.

But when men again began to multiply, they soon forgot the God who had made them; ambitious of renown, they built a city and a high tower, resolved to dwell there, and thus prevent their being dispersed over the face of the earth, when God had decreed otherwise. To frustrate their design therefore, He changed their speech, so that no one understood the language of the other, and thus they were compelled to relinquish their building, and seek homes in the different quarters of the globe.*—Men soon after settled in communities, those descended from one man, or one family, in the same neighbourhood, and adopted such laws for their government, as suited their *fancy*. But they soon forgot—because they soon *neglected*—the word of their Creator—they no more remembered the dreadful scourge of the flood, being secured by God's own word against the recurrence of that calamity—they forgot that they themselves had been punished for their pride and arrogance; they became rebellious against God's majesty, and began to worship idols, and bowed to the work of their own hands. Some adored the sun and the whole host of heaven, whilst others even worshipped the crocodile, the ox, and the ibis.—A man distinguished himself in war, or slew a monster that infested a district, immediately the bards chanted his praise—he was made the lord paramount of his country-

---

*The very name of the city (Babel) is an evidence of the truth of Moses' account, for the Hebrew verb *Bahlole or Bole* signifies to *mix*, and this word is the root of בבל, where only the first letter is doubled. (See also Gen. chap. xi. v. 9.)

men—who, as his subjects, fell down in the dust before him—and his descendants declared him a god, and filled his altars with the blood of men; and thus tyranny spread at the same time with the growth of superstition.

Such a race was not worthy of receiving the pure and holy law of the pure and holy Eternal. What, are those, who, forgetful of God's first and solemn commandment to Noah, slay their fellow beings as sacrifices to their idols—are they, we say, fit to receive the word, which is as pure as the bright flame? Would such men, speak, philosophers! if you can, be a fit depository for the law of God?— Where then is the injustice, in God's not promulgating the *whole* law at this early period of the world?—

But let us turn from the sickening spectacle, where man is not much elevated above the brute, and let us look upon a brighter scene. When danger is the most pressing, help is frequently nearest; and so even was it in the person of our ancestor of glorious memory, who arose the messenger of truth and piety, when wickedness was spreading fast and threatened to shroud every thing in gloom.—Every one acquainted with sacred history knows, that I speak of the peaceful, unpresuming shepherd—Abram, who born of idolatrous parents acknowledged in infancy even, as tradition tells, the name of the Most High, and even suffered for the sanctification of the God of his salvation. He placed his trust in the Rock of ages— and, happy patriarch! thy hope was not misplaced, thy expectations were not in vain; for thy faith was recorded on high, thy sufferings were none of them forgotten, and amply wast thou rewarded, when the voice commanded thee to leave thy father's house; though to leave kindred and friends must have been painful to thy feeling bosom, yet was it sufficient compensation to thee, to have heard the voice of Him, who created the world by his word. Thou didst obey his word and wentest forth into a strange land, and great was thy reward!—May all thy descendants thus follow thee to obey God and to love Him, that they all may with thee rise from the ashes to everlasting happiness, in the presence of the God of Hosts. Amen!

CHAPTER VI.

When Abram was ordered to leave his father's house, he had already reached his seventy-fifth year; he had up to this time been childless; he nevertheless trusted in the word of God, by which he had been promised riches, children and a good name, the three greatest of earthly blessings. He at the same time received the promise, that he should be the object of blessing to all nations. Though, as has been said, he was at the advanced age of seventy-five childless, he had yet full confidence, that the God, whom he had acknowledged and worshipped from his youth, was *powerful, willing* and *ready* to keep his promises. Thus strengthened by the revelation he had received, Abram went forth into a land, whose name he had not even heard, for he had been told to go to a land, which God would show him. But soon it became manifest to him, that the country then inhabited by the Canaanites was the land of his destination, and the land assigned to him by Divine Providence as a temporary residence. If we enquire, what was God's motive in sending Abram forth as a wanderer? we will find the answer easy, when we consider the acts of Abram during his travels. In several places he erected altars for the service of the Most High, and there he taught the world to know its Creator and to render Him adoration. In other words, Abram was deputed to reveal in a country, where the terrible Moloch was worshipped, the sacred truths of the mysterious Father, who, unknown, invisible and incomprehensible to us, rules us, governs us, and provides for us. No doubt, Abram was successful; and we in fact find, that he had made friends among the chiefs in the neighbourhood of Hebron, then called *Kiryath Arbang*, and Aner, Eshkole and Mamray are mentioned, as men in league with Abram; and can it be believed, that his friends should have been ignorant of his opinions? and how could they, knowing his opinions, refrain from admiring and adopting them?

The Patriarch had not dwelt long in Palestine, when he was again obliged to leave this land of his sojournment, and pinched by famine, he went with his family to Egypt. Here he acquired large possessions, after which he returned again to the land of Canaan, and again proclaimed the unity of God.

In a few years afterwards, he rescued his kinsman Lot from his enemies, and brought back at the same time the captured property of the Sodomites. He then also received the blessing of the king of Salem, (afterwards Jerusalem,) ·Malkyzedeck, who was a priest to the *Most High God;* but he refused the rich presents offered him by the king of the sinful Sodom, though he had incurred great personal risk, in recapturing the prisoners and the property taken from the five confederated cities. Thus setting us an example, that good actions, to be really good and worth accepting, should be done without hope of emolument, and without a vain ostentation of disinterestedness, as we find that Abram permitted the king of Sodom to reward his followers, though he refused every thing for himself. ·

Abram's hope had yet been delayed, he was growing old, and yet he had no son to succeed him; but now, soon after he had recaptured Lot, he heard again the voice of God (in a vision) tell him, that he should have a son : and Abram believed it. But who can know the decrees of God—understand his ultimate views before they are accomplished? At the same time that Abram was promised a large and numerous progeny, he was informed that his descendants should be wanderers and slaves for four hundred years; yet he repined not, yet he feared not, for the fulfilment of the evil was a sure pledge of the ultimate fulfilment of the good.

Ishmael had been born since that event, and had reached his thirteenth year, when Abram, at that time ninety-nine years old, heard again the word of God revealed to him, saying : " Walk before me, and be perfect." His constancy was now again probed—his name changed to *Abraham*—and he himself commanded to *shed the blood of the covenant ;* he was also promised that the Almighty would ever be his God and Protector, and of his descendants after him, on condition that they, on their part, should observe the covenant of God, that is, to circumcise all male children when eight days old. This covenant was to be *perpetual*, and as we, the Jews, understand this *term* and the text in Genesis, was to be *unchangeable.*—God also promised Abraham a son by Sarah, precisely in a year from that

5

THE HISTORY OF REVELATION—ABRAHAM.

date. Sarah was then eighty-nine years old—but the decree was
fixed, and the child was to be called יצחק (Yitzchak) *Isaac,* commemorative of the *joy** Abraham felt, when he was assured of the
certainty of the event.

This eventful year had passed away, and Abraham and Sarah
were *rejoiced* with the birth of the long promised child, and it received the name which God had ordained.—Time again passed on,
and the word of God again went forth unto Abraham.—He was ordered to take the only son of his wife Sarah, his dearly beloved Isaac,
to the land of Moriah, to sacrifice him upon one of those mounts,
which yet surround Jerusalem. Abraham obeyed. "With tearful eye
and joyful heart," as the Hebrew poet so elegantly says, both father
and son prepared themselves to fulfil the imperious command of their
God. Did they repine? did they murmur? No—but calmly resigned to his will, they were ready to conform strictly to the precept they had received. The altar was built, the fire was kindling,
Isaac lay bound upon the wood, and the father—he who had given
him being—was grasping the knife to fulfil the last part of the mandate—when behold, a voice, the voice of a messenger from the Lord,
resounded with "Abraham! Abraham!" the knife drops by his side,
and he listens to the word of salvation then made known: "Stretch
not thy hand out against the youth, do him no harm, for now I know
that thou fearest God."

"Did not"—asks the Deist, "did not God previously know, how
Abraham would act? what need was then for that useless parade?"

True, *God,* the searcher of hearts, knew Abraham's mind, knew
also his entire willingness to obey *all* the *commandments known to
him;* but the world was to be convinced and instructed, and a great
deed was obliged to be done to accomplish this. Amidst all the
trials of Abraham, previous to this period, we do not find any, where
he was compelled to make any great personal sacrifices, which in
ordinary human foresight might not have been supposed to yield
him ultimately *worldly* benefits; and the unbelievers might therefore

* The Hebrew word צחק signifies to laugh, smile, play, feel joy, &c.; and it
is said, Gen. ch. 17, v. 17. "And Abraham fell upon his face ויצחק and felt *joy,*
and from this joy, felt by Abraham, emanated the commandment, to name the
child of promise יצחק from which the English *Isaac* is derived, in the same
manner as many other names, are from the original Hebrew.

have said, that Abraham's piety was not strong enough to enable him to obey the will of God, whose worship he taught, when his *all* was at stake. For this reason the command was given, that Abraham should offer up his son, him, whom he loved more than himself, whom God had previously declared should be the father of *the great nation*, who was also to be the *repository of God's covenant*. Who could *now* say with propriety that the doctrines of Abraham were preached for the sake of interest or self-aggrandizement? No one.—But also instruction was conveyed; first, that we should be always ready to sacrifice our own lives, when necessary, for the sanctification of God, rather than transgress the law; secondly, that we are to submit with the utmost resignation, to the decrees of Heaven, and that it is unbecoming in us to question the justice of God's dispensations; and thirdly, that God desires not, but on the contrary, detests that *one man* should sacrifice *the other*, pretending to bring an acceptable offering to the Deity.—It is, 1 presume, well known that the heathens then and afterwards thought (and this belief yet exists to the present day) human blood to be the most acceptable* offering to their idols; we find therefore that God by an *example* prohibited such a practice in his holy temple, which should never be defiled by murder and iniquity.

Was then, 1 ask, the *intended* sacrifice an idle pageant? Surely not. And God's blessing was also given both to father and son, that all nations were to be blessed in their descendants; which means, that through their descendants the word of God, which in itself is a blessing, was to spread over all the earth and make all mankind happy.—This promise has been fulfilled already, in a great measure. The sacred light of revelation was first lit up in the wilderness of Arabia, and from thence it has *commenced* spreading all over the globe. In every country some, at least, of the scattered *seed* of Abraham are to be found; their beautiful code of laws has been *partially* adopted in many places, and millions of human beings are drinking the waters of revelation, though they derive it from *differ-*

---

* There is a curious passage in Hoshea, chap. 13, v. 2, which proves how horrible the practices of idolatry were even in his time; for he says: "To them (the people) they (the priests) say: Those who sacrifice men shall (or are worthy to) kiss the calves," (in Bethel and Dan,) and this speaks volumes (even without any comment) in favour of the enobling virtues of revelation.

ent and *polluted* channels. Upon the *solid* rock of our law have the
followers of the Notzry and Mahomed built their systems, and though
in part erroneous, yet do these systems already acknowledge the
true God, his revelation, and his supreme rule.   May we not hope,
that the time will speedily arrive, when not alone the Nazarenes and
Mahomedans, but all the other families of the earth also will hasten
to the banner raised on the mountains, range themselves behind the
ranks of the true believers and exclaim :

The Eternal is the God ! The Eternal is the God ! ?

O happy time ! O blessed hour ! when our eyes shall behold the
restoration of Zion, the rebuilding of Jerusalem, and the temple on
Moriah, and the reassembling of the tribes of Israel !

CHAPTER VII.

THE HISTORY OF REVELATION—ISAAC.

Abraham had seen his son Isaac married to his brother's grand-
daughter, and seen him in possession of all earthly blessings : when
he was called hence, to shine in a world more bright than this, to
receive the reward for a long life of action and usefulness.   When
living, even the heathens called him " a prince of God," thus acknowledging his divine mission ; and dead—his memory has ever
been revered, both by his descendants and those who have joined
them.—After Abraham's death, Isaac followed his footsteps, and like
his father, he walked humbly before the Lord.   The first, who was
at eight days old joined in the covenant, he lived to an age of a hundred and eighty years, in the same manner, as unostentatious as
his father had done before him ; and though wealthy and much esteemed, he yet knew that all *earthly* pomp is vain, and that labour
is to man the sweetest of all employments.   Thus we find him engaged in agriculture, a careful husbandman and a kind neighbour,

even to those who had, without any good cause, offended, envied and even expelled him from their country. And as soon as they came to him as friends, he immediately forgot all animosity, and made the promises they desired of him. Who will not admire so benevolent a being, who forgets an offence, whenever the offender seems to feel contrition?

Isaac also followed his father in other respects, for he also erected altars and taught the worships of God : and to him was repeated the promise made to Abraham, that his descendants should be blest for Abraham's sake ; and thus we have already *one* reason, why the Jews were chosen to be God's people.

But even on the brightest summer's day, the heavens are often darkened with clouds, and so was it even with Isaac. His two sons, his only children, were at variance ; he himself had grown blind ; and to add to his calamity, Esau had married two women, who caused him and the meek Rebecca much heart-burning by their wickedness. His misfortunes did not rest here : on account of the blessing, which his younger son Jacob received, he was obliged to part with him, and many a year passed over his head, bereft of his child, who had to dwell among strangers. But at length the sky again brightened, and pleasure revisited the Patriarch's dwelling. Jacob returned from Mezopotamia with a numerous and blooming family, all children of righteousness, to cheer Isaac's declining years, —the brothers had been previously reconciled ; and thus, after years of trouble and affliction, the aged father had around him peace and contentment, and he also, like his excellent father Abraham, laid down his head in the grave, honoured and respected, happy in having fulfilled his task, and glorying in having proclaimed the wonders of the Creator of the universe.

CHAPTER VIII.

Was the constancy of Abraham tested by sufferings, was Isaac's love proved by his willingness to die, because he supposed his God required it? Jacob was no less tested, no less did he by his example teach that they who confide in God are never forsaken.—We have seen that Abraham received a revelation, and after him, Isaac; and as soon as Jacob became a wanderer from his father's house, we see him also receiving the promise of God of the future greatness of his progeny, when he, the son and grandson of wealthy men, who were so powerful, that princes even sought their alliance, was obliged to sleep in the open air with the hard rock for his pillow. Here we have another example, if any were necessary, that God is no respecter of persons, that to Him the rich and the poor are equal; that only the righteous, though poor and needy, is to Him acceptable.—We therefore find it recorded, that Jacob sleeping in the open air, upon that spot where Bethel was afterwards built, received a confirmation of the promise previously made to Abraham and Isaac, and that this prophecy should not be fulfilled in the person and descendants of his brother Esau, but in his own person and descendants.—When Abraham, besides Isaac had Ishmael and other children, when Isaac, besides Jacob had Esau; Jacob had not *one* among his numerous children, who was not acceptable to his God and Protector.

Like his father and grandfather, Jacob erected altars to the true God, and thus spread the light of *revelation* in the countries to the east and north of Palestine, which before had been made known to the west and south only. Though Jacob was obliged to live for upwards of twenty years amid a people, who knew not the worship of God, we yet see *him* constant in his faith; see him teaching his wives and children to love and fear their Maker; and not alone those who were connected with him by the ties of relationship, but also all others who were about him, acted as he himself had taught them ; for in chap. 35, v. 4, of Genesis* we read, that upon Jacob's requisition, all the members of his household delivered up whatever was in their possession, which in any manner could have been used for the worship of idols.

After a long separation from his father, Jacob was at last permitted to revisit Isaac's house ; but he was not allowed to remain there long undisturbed, for sufferings and troubles again overtook him, when he, as he thought, had sat himself down in quiet for the short remnant of his days. Thus giving mankind a lesson, which cannot be too often called to mind : " that not in this world must the righteous expect the reward of his good deeds, for he is here only in the outbuilding, where he is to prepare himself to enter the palace."† Also the following useful moral may be drawn from Jacob's patience and resignation, and his perseverance to *serve* God in all his severe and manifold calamities : " that man is not to serve God with a view of being rewarded, but to obey his commandments, and practise virtue independently of all views of emolument, gain, or honour,"‡ and " that in spite of calamities and reverses, we should never swerve from the path of right, for the practice of virtue will in itself be sufficient to kindle a light within, when even all around is gloom and darkness."§ Again—we often see the wicked prosper, and the pious suffer, for what serves virtue then, what avails piety, if with this life our existence were ended? But *this* is only the time for *action*, and when our body is enclosed within the grave, *then will the soul reap the harvest of its righteousness.*

Jacob had not been returned more than eight or nine years from his long exile, when dissention among his children became to him the fruitful source of the greatest mental sufferings, with which he had hitherto been afflicted. *Joseph*, being the eldest son of his beloved Rachel, was distinguished by his father by a *superior dress*

---

* Presuming that the greater number of my readers are acquainted with the Pentateuch, and as the major part of my arguments, unless otherwise stated, are drawn from this holy book, I hope to be excused, for not in *every instance* denoting the particular passage, from which these arguments are derived, as I do not wish to load the body of the text with long quotations and too frequent references, which must ever be tiresome and perplexing.

† Aboth, chap. iv,   ‡ Ibi. chap. i.

§ For further confirmation of this see Job, chap. i. and ii.

from the other children : this vexed them, and envy soon ripened into hatred, particularly when they found, that Joseph had the weakness to speak of their failings, which, to judge from their otherwise virtuous conduct, must have been trifling, to Jacob. From the short account contained in the 37th chapter of Genesis we can draw the following moral lessons; first, that it is dangerous for a father to have an *ostensible favourite* amongst his children, even when his preference is founded upon the *acknowleged superiority* of the favoured child ; secondly, that it is dangerous to be a tale-bearer, even if the tales relate but to trifles, for the *detection* of this failing is sure to be followed by the *detestation* of the slanderer ; and lastly, that we ought to be very careful, how we suffer envy or malice to approach us, for if we once give them a resting place in our bosom, we shall soon be hurried on to commit unjustifiable actions.

Jacob's other sons had been gone from home for some time to follow their occupation as shepherds, and Jacob determined to send Joseph after them to enquire about the welfare of his brothers and the well-being of the flock. No sooner had Joseph approached his brothers, than they determined to kill him, and to justify homicide by falsehood. But Reuben dissuaded them, but in his absence Judah advised to sell Joseph to a caravan of Ishmaelites just passing by. He was obeyed, and Joseph, then seventeen years old, was sold as a slave, and his father was left to mourn for him for the space of twenty-two years.

Joseph was in the mean time carried to Mitzrayim (Egypt), and sold to an officer of the Pharaoh,* by the name of Poteephar, who was so pleased with his new servant, that he made him his steward. How long Joseph continued in his new station, we cannot precisely determine ; but it could hardly have been above two years, when his mistress attempted to induce him to commit adultery, which Joseph refused to do, and gave as a reason, that he, by compliance, would " sin against God"; thus we have another proof, that some at least of the civil laws of our code were, even before Moses, known to the patriarchs, who were scrupulous in observing them.—When Joseph's

---

* Pharaoh or rather *Parngo* was the Hebrew name of the kings of Egypt, but was not the particular name of any one king; as at the present time the sovereign of the Turks is called the *Soltan*, or the emperor of Russia the *Czar*.

mistress saw that he would not be the slave of her desires, her love for him was turned into hatred, and she artfully accused him to her husband of an attempt to insult her, while he was absent. The master became enraged and threw Joseph in prison, where he lingered for many years a captive and a slave. But even in this apparently forlorn condition he was *not* without a friend, or altogether miserable; for the superintendent of the prison took, by the will of God, a fancy to Joseph, and gave him the appointment of an overseer of the prisoners' work.—Two years before his release he interpreted the dreams of two household officers of Pharaoh, who had been one year in prison. Joseph begged the one, whose dream he had favourably interpreted, to remember him ; but he forgot his companion in captivity, when he was prosperous, thus verifying David's saying : "put not your trust in princes." At the expiration, however, of the above mentioned time, when Pharaoh had a dream, of which no one of his sages could give the desired interpretation, his cup-bearer at last remembered Joseph, who was forthwith liberated from prison and brought before the King. Joseph's modesty and wisdom quite captivated Egypt's ruler, and he raised him (so was God's will) from a state of servitude to the second dignity in the empire ; and Joseph became the viceroy of the land. Though he now stood at the highest pinnacle of human glory, he yet sighed for his father, and his father's household, of whose fate he was altogether ignorant.—At length the severe famine, which raged both in the land of Canaan and Mitzrayim, compelled the brothers of Joseph to resort to the granaries, which he had provided for the approaching scarcity foretold by him to Pharaoh.—His brothers came before him, and bowed, or rather prostrated* themselves, before their brother, who immediately recognized them, though they had not the least recollection of him.

He sought a quarrel with them, called them spies, and would not, so he pretended, suffer them to depart, till one of them had brought Benjamin to him, who had remained behind with their father. He had them locked up for three days, and then permitted them to return, after having taken Simeon and bound him in their presence.—The

---

* This custom is yet observed, on approaching a king, in Turkey and other parts of the East.

6

reader would do well to peruse the whole transaction in the elegant language of the Bible, where we find *Reuben* reproving his brothers for the violence they had committed against the child (Joseph) and *them*, justifying the judgment of God and the punishment they then suffered for their inhumanity to Joseph. No wonder then that *he* wept, no wonder that he felt moved.

The nine brothers accompanied by Benjamin returned to Egypt after the lapse of a considerable time, and brought back the money, which they had found in their bags on their return home, to restore it to the superintendent of the magazines, to whose treasure they supposed it to belong.—When Joseph saw Benjamin he was obliged to leave the room and to withdraw into his private chamber, where his full heart was eased by tears; but he returned soon and dined with his brothers.—Before they were ready to depart, he ordered his superintendent, to contrive to put a silver cup, which had been on the table, in the bag of Benjamin, then to pursue them, after they had left the city, and when upon searching he should have found the cup, to bring Benjamin (as the supposed thief) back with him. The officer obeyed. But the noble brothers disdained to escape and suffer their youngest brother to remain behind *a slave;* and the magnanimous Yehudah (Judah) stept forward to offer himself in Benjamin's place. "For," said he, "thy servant (himself) has been a security for the youth to my father, saying, 'if I bring him not to thee, then will I have sinned against my father for ever.' And now let thy servant remain, instead of the youth, a slave to my lord, and let the youth go up with his brothers. For how could I go up to my father, without having the youth with me? I never could witness the distress, which would overwhelm my father."

Such generous self-devotion moved Joseph, his feelings were too strong almost for utterance, he ordered all strangers from his presence, and then *cried out:* "I am Joseph! lives my father yet?"

The children of Israel hurried away from Egypt, to tell their father that Joseph yet lived, and that he was regent over all the land of Egypt; but the heart once inured to sorrow does not even wish any joy to rob it of its sacred grief: it knows how short lived all pleasure is, and is fearful of some worse calamity yet to come, and then it can hardly admit any sudden gladness, because it is doubting its reality; and so did Jacob too remain incredulous, till he had seen the vehicles, which Joseph had sent for his accommodation. Then indeed was his joy unbounded, and from a full heart he spoke; "Enough, my son Joseph lives yet ; I will go and see him before I die."—Thus it came to pass, that Israel went with his whole family to Egypt; and in Beare Shebang (Berseba) *God revealed* himself to Jacob and told him, to go without fear to Egypt, for He would go down with him, and bring him also back again,—meaning : that neither Jacob's body nor his descendants should for ever remain buried in Egypt, but that both should be brought out again from that land.

Thus fortified by the word of God, our glorious ancestor arrived in Egypt, where he was soon locked in the embrace of his long-lost son; where he was soon taught to forget all his previous sufferings. Joseph, with the permission of Pharaoh, gave his family land, in the district of Goshen, where he supplied them with all the necessaries of life; and the children of the *true faith* became inmates of the land of the children of Cham.

Jacob had lived seventeen years in Egypt, when he found his end fast approaching ; he therefore assembled his children around him, and giving them his blessing and admonitions, he foretold that which should happen to them till the latest posterity. He prophesied of the Messiah, who is to descend from Judah, and thus spoke the dying saint :

" Not for ever shall the sceptre depart from Judah, nor the law-giver from his descendants, for Shiloh shall come, and unto him shall the nations assemble."

And surely the time *will* come, when unto the teacher, the prince David, all nations will assemble to worship the *only* true God, the Father of all, and shield of Israel. The sceptre has departed, and no more does the law-giver reside in Jerusalem ; but the sceptre must be restored, and the crown will return again to its former dwelling !—

When Jacob had blessed his children, he composed himself in his bed, and departed *this* life, to be an angel in heaven, and to shine foremost amidst the saints, whose resting place is at the foot of the throne of glory.

CHAPTER IX.

THE LEGATION OF MOSES.

In the foregoing pages it has been proven to the conviction of any man, who feels no abhorrence against being convinced, that a revelation existed before Moses, and though the law, we now have, be the most perfect, yet could not the Syrians, Babylonians, Egyptians, and Canaanites excuse their gross wickedness, *by pleading igno-rance* of the divine will; for they had ample means of acquiring a knowledge of the laws given to the patriarchs, if they had but desired it; for wherever Abraham, Isaac, and Jacob went, they taught the word of God. And even if they had not done this, their rectitude, *chastity,* and hospitality ought to have been admired, and not alone admired, but also imitated. Instead of this, all the horrors of murder, human sacrifice, and incest, were practised by these nations to an almost incredible extent. Who would believe, that mothers carried their children to the valley of Moloch, and stood by while the poor innocents were roasted alive on the heated arms of the brazen image? Can it be credited, that the crocodile received the babe out of the arms of its mother? Would it be believed, if the fact were not, alas, too well authenticated, that the women were often the wives of their own sons?—I will not mention the images of incest, for the *brief* catalogue of crime is already revolting enough, without any further addition.

The days of happiness and tranquillity for the descendants of Jacob were over; and Joseph—who before he died, had ordered his remains to be taken away from Egypt, whenever it should please God to conduct his people to the promised land—was scarcely dead, scarcely had the last clod of earth rung upon the coffin of the last of the patriarchs: when the new king of Egypt forgot the kindness of Joseph, the benefits he had heaped upon the inhabitants of the country under his dominion, in having saved them from the desolating famine.—The Israelites had greatly increased in numbers since the arrival of Jacob, and the tyrant of Egypt feared them as inimical to his government, *falsely* thinking of them, like many rulers in later times, and even in the present day, think of us, their descendants, that they could have no community of interest with the other inhabitants of the country, amongst whom they resided. His fear soon made him look around him for remedies, or rather, preventives, against the too rapid increase of the hateful people within his dominions, though the land on which they resided, had been given them *as an inheritance*, by the especial *command* of his predecessor.—By labour then did the new king endeavour to check the growth of the Israelites, and at the same time to break down their high-mindedness, for he thought, that as *slaves* they would cease to be dangerous to the state, and *useful* in building cities, monuments, and other public edifices, independently of other manual labour, which he compelled them to do. But the tyrant's aim was frustrated, and the more the Israelites were oppressed, the more they increased. Seeing his designs so sadly disappointed, he became furious, and ordered the midwives to murder all the male children of the Hebrews, as soon as born. But these heroic women, regardless of any mischief that might happen to them, did not obey the king's cruel mandate ; and when he discovered this, he commanded *his own people* to throw every male child of the Israelites into the Nile.

But vain are the efforts of man against the decrees of Heaven ! In the midst of this calamity was born by Yochebed, the wife of Amram, of the tribe of Levi, *that* child, who at the age of eighty years, rescued, under the peculiar guidance and providence of God, his fellow-believers from the yoke of slavery.—After Yochebed had concealed her infant for three months, she found it impossible to hide him any longer from Pharaoh's blood-hounds, and with sorrow she was compelled to place him in a box, and expose him amidst the reeds of the Nile, for she preferred leaving his *rescue* to the hand of *Providence*, rather than begging his life of *men*, whose hearts were steeled against mercy.—The box was providentially discovered by the king's daughter, who, feeling compassion for the helpless innocent, determined to save him. When the child grew up, she adopted him, and called him Mosheh (Moses,) from a Hebrew word, which denotes *drawing* out, as we also read in Exodus: "And she called him Mosheh משה, for (she said) 1 have drawn him (משׁיתיהו) out of the water.

When Moses was grown, he went out one day to see his brethren work, and he saw an Egyptian beating an Israelite; Moses, who perhaps found *no other chance of saving the Hebrew's life*, slew the Egyptian and buried him in the sand. Egypt was now no longer a safe residence for Moses, for soon did Pharaoh hear of what he had done, and intended to kill him; but Moses escaped. He now, who had been reared in a palace, had been the adopted son of the princess of Egypt; became the servant of the chief of Midian (a district in Arabia), and so much was Jithro pleased with him, that he gave him his daughter Zipporah for a wife, by whom he had afterwards two sons, of whom one was called Gershom, the other Eleazer.

The above mentioned king of Egypt was dead, and yet the pressure was not removed under his successor from Jacob's children, and bitterly did they groan under their heavy labour; but their Father in Heaven heard their cries and determined then to save them.

Moses, *so he himself tells us*[*], was tending the sheep of his father-in-law, and drove the flock far into the wilderness, and arrived at the mount of God in Horeb. The wonderful appearance of a thorn-bush being on fire, without being consumed, attracted his attention, and he steppped forward to see "why the thornbush was not consumed?"—But hark! his step is arrested, and a voice calls out: "Come not hither! take thy shoes from off thy feet, for the place thou standest upon is holy ground." The Eternal then proceeded to tell Moses, that he was the God of Abraham, of Isaac, and of Jacob, the God, in times of old adored by the patriarchs, with whom he had made a covenant; He had therefore resolved to redeem their descendants from their servitude in Egypt, and bring them into the promised land, and that He had destined Moses to be the messenger to Pharaoh, and to be the leader of the Israelites after their redemption.

Moses, hearing himself appointed to such a high station, modestly declined the honour, on account of his supposed inability. But God told him, that He would assist him; and to *prove to Moses the truth*

---

[*] Here I must beg the reader to refer to the third chapter of Exodus, where the whole account of Moses's mission is so beautifully given.

of his mission, He gave him a *sign ;* that namely, *when the mission should be in part accomplished, by the liberation of the Israelites from thraldom, they then should worship God upon that mountain,* (Horeb). Here our law teaches us a lesson, of which we ought never to lose sight, " that prophecy cannot be verified, but by the accomplishment of the prediction, and *no miracle, however striking, can establish the truth of what any man, pretending to be inspired, says,* if the *event* accords not with the prediction."

When Moses felt thus convinced in his own mind, he asked by what name the God of their ancestors should be announced to the Israelites ? And God answered אהיה אשר אהיה, which ought to be rendered : " I am the unchangeable Eternal Being, who ever will be ;" and He commanded Moses to tell to the Israelites, " The Ever-Being אהיה has sent me to you."—Moses was yet diffident, yet afraid, that the people to whom he was sent would not believe him, if he did not show them *miracles,* to convince their senses. And he was gratified, for God gave him power to work certain miracles.— But Moses would not yet consent, and offered his want of eloquence as an excuse ; God, however, spoke to him as follows : " Who gave to man a mouth ? who maketh him dumb or deaf, or well endowed with hearing and seeing, or blind ? is it not I, the Eternal ?" Thus far Moses had been right, in not grasping too eagerly at power and distinction ; but when he had seen that it was God's will, that he *himself,* and no other should be the messenger, he ought to have raised no more objections ; for when he yet refused, so he himself tells us, he was rebuked by God, who then assigned him his brother Aaron as *spokesman,* and thus gave him a partner in the work of salvation, which otherwise, as we have every reason to believe, would have been accomplished by Moses alone.—The following moral lesson is clearly deducible from the whole narrative : " we ought never to be eager to claim honours, but when we find ourselves capable to do any thing serviceable to mankind, or to the cause of virtue and religion, or if we see things done wrong by others, which we could do better ; then it becomes our duty to come forward, and offer our services ; to hold back then would be *false delicacy,* but not *modesty,* and we deserve punishment if we suffer mischievous errors to exist, which we by our exertions could perhaps remove."

Moses having received his commission from his Maker, wandered

back to Egypt, having previously taken leave of Jithro, and being
assured, that he would expose himself to no danger by his return to
a land, where he was once threatened with the scaffold.—Aaron,
who was rejoiced at Moses's elevation, met him on the road, and
they, after their arrival in Egypt, assembled the elders of the Israelites; Moses performed the miracles before the people, and Aaron
related to them the message, with which Moses had been charged.
And the people believed.—Although heavily oppressed, they yet
well remembered the *promise* given to *Abraham*, and *the manner* of
Moses's prophecy convinced them, that he was the chosen messenger
of the God, whom their forefathers had worshipped.—After having
made known the word of salvation to their brothers, Moses and Aaron
repaired to Pharaoh, and in the name of the Eternal demanded the
release of his people. Pharaoh refused and said: "Who is the
Eternal, that I should obey his voice, to let Israel go? I know
not the Eternal, nor will I suffer Israel to depart." The obvious
meaning of this answer is, that Pharaoh said, that the *Eternal* was
a deity unknown to him, and as such he would pay no respect to
his commands.—Like the miser, who clings more firmly to his ill-
gotten treasure, when he finds that his enjoyment of it will soon be
over; just so did Pharaoh order, that the Hebrews should be compelled to do harder work, and their daily task not be in the least diminished, when he discovered by the determined manner of the *exiled*
Moses, that his dominion over the children of Israel was soon to
terminate; for even Phaoraoh must have felt assured that no man,
much less one, who had been *obliged* to leave the empire, would
boldly step up to the king and make such a monstrous demand, if he
had not the power to make his threats of vengeance good.

Pharaoh perhaps intended to stifle, by harder oppression, the
incipient desire for freedom just excited in the bosom of a degraded
people; he also endeavoured, but in vain, to resist the power of the
Most High;—but he was soon taught to know, that he himself was
but a man, a weak, powerless mortal; that the gods, to whom he
looked for support, were things, in which there is no power to help,
and—that there is *none* like our God.—His rivers were turned into
blood; frogs came in masses to plague him and his equally guilty
people; vermin and wild beasts came to destroy them, and pestilence
swept off their cattle; their own bodies were afflicted with dangerous

ulcers; hail and locusts were sent to destroy every tree and every plant which grew in the field, and at last there was darkness, which lasted for three days, and was so intense that no one could see the other.—As long as the plague lasted, Pharaoh seemed to relent and willing, that the Israelites should leave the country; but no sooner had the evil been removed by Moses's praying to God *for his enemies*, than Pharaoh and his ministers forgot their promise, and yet kept Israel enslaved. Nine plagues had already, in this manner, passed over Egypt, many times had Pharaoh refused to keep his promise; but now his proud spirit even was to yield, and he, who but lately spoke with contempt: "I know not the Eternal," was now destined to feel the full weight of his wrath, and to acknowledge that *his will* must be obeyed. Pharaoh had but just forbidden Moses ever to come to him again, under pain of death; when Moses was notified, and ordered to tell him, that that very night the greatest distress should overtake all Egypt, neither king nor slave should be spared, and that not even the cattle and the idols, which the Egyptians worshipped, should escape. For Moses was ordered to announce, that just at midnight, when every one should repose in security, every first-born of each family, in the whole land of Egypt, was to die, and that even the king's first born, his presumptive successor, should perish, and that then the bereaved parent would be willing to allow the Israelites to depart, to worship God the Eternal, who had chosen them to be his servants.

CHAPTER X.

THE EXODUS.

It was in the beginning of the month of Abib,* that Moses and Aaron received the first commandment promulgated to those who went out of Egypt. It is well known, that the Egyptians, although they are so highly celebrated for their learning and skill in various arts, were silly enough to worship beasts, and amongst the rest the bull (Apis) and the ram; for it is, I suppose, known to most classical scholars, that *Jupiter Ammon* was represented with a *ram's head.*— As has been already related in the preceding chapter, the time of Israel's redemption was fast approaching, and Moses and his brother were then commanded to tell the whole nation of Israelites, that each family should provide themselves with a *lamb*, which should be in their possession as early as the tenth day of the month, but not be killed till the afternoon of the fourteenth. The Egyptians never ate meat, for beasts were their gods; but now the Israelites, who had been their slaves for many years, selected the *idols* of their *masters* as sacrifices to the God of Abraham, Isaac and Jacob, thus showing the Egyptians, that the descendants of the patriarchs were no longer afraid of them; whereas before this time the Israelites were not permitted to kill animals in the presence of the Egyptians, (see Exodus, chapter viii. v. 22).—The Hebrews were also commanded, to sprinkle the blood of the paschal lamb upon the door-posts; " to what purpose? did not God know where the Hebrews lived, without this mark?" Certainly, but the commandment was given to test the faith of God's people. Those who, fearful of offending their task-masters, omitted to obey the will of God, were not deserving to be spared, when these suffered; but those who, firmly relying upon the promise of their God, obeyed his word with alacrity, were indeed worthy of being spared. Thus was the blood a true mark of

* Now commonly called Nissan. The months of the Hebrew year have, since the return from the Babylonian captivity, been distinguished by Chaldean names, and the Hebrew ones have not been in general use since that time.

discrimination to the *Israelites themselves*, between him, who confided in God, and him, whose faith was weak and wavering.—They were also commanded to be dressed as if prepared for a journey, while eating the passover-lamb; with their clothes well fixed, their sandals on their feet, and their sticks in their hands, and to eat the meat hastily; thus was it indicated to them, that immediately after the eating of the offering, they should be ready to leave the land of their oppressors. They were further commanded that they themselves, and their remotest descendants, should eat unleavened bread for seven days, from the fifteenth till the twenty-first of the month in the evening.—The passover was also to be eaten with bitter herbs, in commemoration of the *bitterness* of the sufferings of the Israelites in Egypt.

The above commandments were strictly observed; and when the night after the fourteenth day had set in, the Israelites were celebrating the *first Passover*. The blood of the sacrifice *graced* the door-posts of the habitations of the Hebrews, when just at midnight the avenging God went forth over the land of Egypt, and slew every first-born of man and beast in Pharaoh's dominion. " We are all dying," resounded through the land, and when the tyrant's first-born dropt dead at his father's feet, *even he* relented; he called Moses and Aaron, begged them to leave his land, and craved their blessing. The Egyptians, who before could not bear the idea of letting their servants go, now drove them fairly off, would not give them time to bake their bread, and gave them gold, silver, and clothing, any thing to be rid of such dangerous inmates. And was Moses, who was seemingly the author of all this misery, hated by them? No, he stood high in the estimation and affection of Pharaoh's ministers, and the people of Egypt; for all acknowledged that he was the servant and messenger of the true God, and that by his will and permission alone Moses was enabled to do these great things.—The people of Israel, therefore, who had been slaves for many years,* were in this manner freed from their oppressors, and they went out openly and unmolested, to meet their new destinies under a leader beloved by his own fellow-believers, and respected even by his enemies.—They were destined for the conquest of Palestine; but the Eternal did not

---

* This event took place, according to the Rabbins, in the four hundredth year after the birth of Isaac, and as I believe 430 years after Abraham had left *Ur Casdim*, which is, I think, the time mentioned in Exodus, chap. xii.

wish to lead them through the country of the Philistines to the immediate acquisition of their inheritance; He preferred to let them pass through the wilderness of Arabia, to teach them more fully, that they were altogether dependent upon his support.—He sent a *pillar of clouds* to go before them by day, to point out the road they were to travel, and by night, he illuminated their path with a *pillar of fire*, so that they were enabled to travel by day and night.

When the terror of Pharaoh and his people had a little subsided after their late calamity, they repented their having dismissed the Israelites, and all went out in pursuit of them, to bring them back to servitude.—The Egyptians overtook the Israelites, as they lay encamped along the shores of the Red Sea. They, who had been redeemed but a few days ago, saw column after column of their revengeful pursuers arrive; and how should they be able to withstand this well armed host of horsemen and charioteers? Behind them were their enemies, and before them they saw the agitated waves of the Arabian Gulf; there was therefore no possibility of retreating, no advancing; the danger was pressing, and six hundred thousand freemen saw no alternative between *death* and *slavery*. The very idea was maddening, to think that their wives should be swept off by the flood—or that the necks of their tender children should bend under that heavy yoke of slavery, under the pressure of which they had themselves so long groaned.—In their anguish, they called upon their God to assist them, and He heard their prayer.—It is true, that some began to grow faint-hearted, and accused *Moses* as the author of their present distress; but let those, who may be disposed to think our ancestors so very blameable for their want of confidence, only reflect how they themselves would have acted under equally trying circumstances.*—But Moses stood unappalled in this emergency—he, the man of God, knew no fear, and he inspired his affrighted brethren with a share of the confidence he himself felt. Secure of a happy issue, he ordered the Israelites to stand quiet, and in the spirit of prophecy he assured them, that they should never again see the Egyptians in the manner they beheld them that day.—

* Let me not be misunderstood, as being the apologist for the rebellious spirit manifested so frequently by the Israelites; since my only aim is to draw the attention of those saints, *in their own opinion*, who accuse the Jews of want of faith, to themselves, and to reflect if they are in the least more virtuous, in despite of their boasted sanctity.

All the nation became silent—all clamour was hushed, whilst Moses prayed to God, who had through him so often before manifested his power.—And soon was his prayer answered from Heaven; he was ordered to stretch his staff, with which he had performed the other miracles, over the sea, and behold! its waters were divided, and were *congealed*, and stood up like two walls, to the right and to the left. The tribes of Yeshurun boldly advanced into the dry chasm of the ocean, and passed through unharmed. Their pursuers, being baffled in their intentions, and disappointed of their prey, hurried onward after the retiring Israelites; but soon they discovered, when it was too late, their inability to accomplish their purpose; against their will they were dragged forward, and they arrived in their turn in the middle of the sea. Moses was again commanded to stretch his hand over the sea, and all the Egyptians were at once overwhelmed in one confused and sudden destruction; for the sea ebbed down again to " the gate of tears,"* and buried under its mighty waves the whole host of Pharaoh, and *not even one* was left to carry home to his countrymen an account of the terrible catastrophe.—The destruction was complete; and when the Israelites saw the corpses of their enemies thrown upon the seashore, they all acknowledged the great power of their mighty Deliverer, and as our legislator expresses in a few words: " And the people feared the Eternal, and they believed in the Eternal and his servant Mosheh." When Moses and all Israel saw the great deliverance, and when they felt that they were now and for ever free from Egyptian thraldom, they composed that elegant hymn, which must ever remain an example of chaste and elevated poetry. In which after rehearsing the great deliverance, by which they had been saved from slavery and from death, they speak in terms of confidence of the fulfilment of the yet remaining unaccomplished promises of God, and conclude with the following beautiful sentences:

" Thou wilt bring them, and Thou wilt plant them in the mountain of thy inheritance, in the place, O Eternal, Thou hast prepared for thy residence; the sanctuary, O Lord, which thy hands have founded!—The Eternal will reign for ever and ever!" May this be his will, and may all flesh speedily be brought to acknowledge Him alone, and to the observance of his precepts. Amen.

* The straits of Bab-el Mandeb, which form the outlet of the Red Sea.

CHAPTER XI.

THE ISRAELITES AND REVELATION.

In the foregoing, I have briefly narrated the history of the Israelites from Abraham, the founder of the nation, to their deliverance from the Egyptians. We will therefore pause here a little, and examine the following question : " Is it reasonable to suppose that God revealed himself to the Israelites? and is it compatible with the dignity of the Creator, to make a nation or a set of men, just released from slavery, the depository of his will ?"

No one will deny, since denial is useless and unnecessary, that the Israelites were a nation just released from slavery, that they were ignorant and idolatrous; yet this admission does not in the slightest degree invalidate the assertion of Moses, that these Israelites were chosen as the depository of God's will and law. Let us but examine the object of religion, the intended influence and scope of the revealed word of God, and no solid objection can be raised to the Bible having been given to a people who were ignorant and unused to a worship different from the rites of the heathens, amongst whom they had hitherto resided. For religion is intended to fill our minds with a proper idea of God and his attributes, and in consequence, to raise our thoughts to Him, inasmuch as we are dependent upon his bounty for our daily subsistence, nay to his kindness for every moment of our life.—The more we feel our dependence upon God, the oftener the subject is brought before us in its full force, the greater the benefits are we receive from his goodness: the more must we, of necessity, be alive to his mercy, the greater will be, must be, our desire to merit the continuance of his supreme protection, by gratitude towards Him—by the observance of his precepts.—The Israelites had been for nearly two hundred years compelled to do the most degrading work, and they were even inhumanly beaten by those very persons, whose ancestors owed every thing to the Hebrew Joseph. (See above.)—At the same time the promises made to Abraham, and reiterated to the succeeding patriarchs, were not forgotten by the Hebrews. But year after year rolled on, and their toil was not diminished, the appointed time was drawing to a close, and they were *yet* slaves. At length, Moses, the son of Amram, communicated to them the joyful tidings that God had taken cognizance of their deplorable situation, and that even then at the moment he was speaking, the decree of their redemption had gone forth.—If now the additional pressure of the last acts of Pharaoh's tyranny had continued long, the Hebrews would probably have derided and scorned him (Moses) as a deceiver, who had mocked them with hopes of deliverance, and was even the proximate cause of additional hardships. It was not, however, the will of God, that his faithful servant should be considered in this light.—No sooner had Pharaoh announced his determination of still more tightening the chains of the captives, than Moses was sent to him, to demand again and again the release of God's first-born, namely, our nation. Pharaoh still refused.—Punishment after punishment was inflicted upon the king and his Egyptians, whilst the Hebrews remained unharmed amid the desolation around them. At length, by that dreadful scourge, the last the Egyptians suffered at home, the king was *compelled* to comply with God's will and dismiss Israel, and when he attempted to force them back, we have seen already the entire destruction which befel him and his army.—These things were not done in a corner, they were not done before a few men; but before the whole Hebrew and Egyptian nations, all of whom *saw and (therefore) knew all*, that we are told did happen.—The *Egyptians*, therefore, were convinced that the *Eternal* is a God, who cannot be offended with impunity; and the Israelites were taught, that He keeps his word, and that He rewards those who love Him, to the thousandth generation, and besides—that He was *their* glory and *their* God, who had done all those wonderful things, which *their own eyes* had beheld.

In this manner were the Israelites convinced, that their *sole* dependence was the favour of God, for by his assistance alone were they redeemed from that captivity, of which in spite of their numbers they had been unable to free themselves by *their own exertions.* Their mind was therefore in a proper state to receive lasting religious impresions. They owed every thing to God, they had seen his *power*, and *felt* his *forbearance;* and can any man devise a state of society, where more lasting impressions could be made by the divine

law, than that in which the Israelites were, when going out of Egypt?
Here every thing tended to draw them to their Maker—the ties of
the covenant had been renewed, and new obligations of obeying God's
word had been laid upon them, and all they could do, to requite the
many favours they had received, was—to devote themselves to the
service of God.—It is true, they murmured several times, when they
wanted bread and water, and God gratified them.—They frequently
sinned, and they were punished; but soon they acknowledged the
justice of the decrees of Heaven, and were forgiven, because they repented. And to this day the law is respected by us, its very pages are
considered *sacred*, and our greatest praise is to have *observed its precepts*, as far as lies within our power. The impression was made *three
thousand* years ago, and it is as *fresh at this moment*, as it was on
that day, when, after the Israelites had seen the power of God anew
displayed, by giving them *water* out of the hard rock, they went out
under the guidance of Joshua to repel the attack of the Amalekites.
They were unused to arms, yet did they fight bravely for a whole
day, under the eye of the *youthful hero*, who led them on against an
enemy, whose very trade was war; for they confided in God, and
hoped that He, who had led them out of Egypt, would vouchsafe to
defend them against the attack of a barbarous horde—and they were
not deceived in their expectation. Moses ascended a hill, where he
prayed with uplifted hands (Talmud Roshe Hashanah, chap. 3, §. 8,)
for those who fought, and they conquered by the name of God, to
whom their hearts were raised during the battle!

Does any man want the objection at the head of the chapter refuted by more *solid* arguments? I think not—for what has been
said already must convince every reader, that the very state of society considered objectionable to the account of Moses relative to the
law having been given to the lately freed Israelites, was of all others
the most favourable, and infinitely preferable to a state of affluence,
where the mind of nations, equally with that of individuals, is alas,
too often, and too much, engrossed with worldly affairs; and nations
and individuals thus circumstanced are too little inclined to think of
the decrees of their God, whose creatures they are, and to whom they
are indebted for that very affluence which makes them think so
highly of their own power and wisdom, and so *lightly* of their God
and Creator.

CHAPTER XII.

THE DESCENT ON SINAI.

The last notes of the song of thanksgiving had died way along the shore of the Arabian Sea, the shout of triumph over the conquered Amalekites was hushed : and Israel lay encamped in the wilderness of Sinai. The whole neighbourhood of Mount Horeb is described by late travellers as strikingly sublime, and the mount itself, though not quite so elevated, as some others in the neighbourhood, as having, nevertheless, a wonderful effect by its several and distinct summits, one more elevated than the other. At the foot of this mountain, our ancestors encamped, at the commencement of the third month ;* they had therefore arrived at that spot, where it had been foretold to Moses, (see above, chap. ix.) the Israelites should worship God, after their leaving Egypt.

It was therefore, here, that Moses was called for the first time before the whole congregation, to receive the annunciation of God's will. He was commanded (Exodus, chap. xix, v. 3—6): " Thus shalt thou say to the house of Jacob, and tell the children of Israel : you have seen what l have done to Egypt, and that I have borne you on eagle's wings, and brought you to me. And now, if you will obey my words and observe my covenant, then you shall be to me a people more dearly beloved than any other nation, for all the earth is mine. And you shall be to me a kingdom of priests, and a holy nation." Let us understand this message well, for then we shall easily discover upon what terms the Almighty promised to befriend us, and under what circumstances we were to be the dearly beloved people.—Previously to this moment the Israelites had been told, that their redemption from slavery was to take place, not on account of any

* The month in which they were relieved from Egypt being, by God's command, instituted the first of the ecclesiastical year. See Instruction in the Mosaic Religion, page 124.

8

thing they themselves had done; but solely, because of the covenant
with Abraham, Isaac, and Jacob, and the promises made to them.—
The Israelites, being now free, were told : first, that it was *God*,
and *not Moses*, by whose power they had been redeemed ; further,
that the Almighty had subsequently—like the eagle that protects its
offspring from danger—protected them, and delivered them from
flood, from famine, from thirst, and from the sword ; and lastly, that
if they would now agree to the conditions, which *He* would propose,
then should they be entitled to the continuance of his protection and
fostering care. Although God could, after his goodness to them,
have, according to human notions of gratitude, *demanded* their obedience ; yet did He lay before them his *intentions*, for their acceptance or refusal. Thus teaching us, that we should never presume to
dictate to a person, indebted to us, any thing which might by chance
be disagreeable to him, but that we ever ought to gain his compliance by gentle persuasion.—Well then—God proposed to the children of Israel, that they should receive his *peculiar* protection and
love, in case *they would obey his commandments* and *observe the
terms of the covenant*, to be proposed to them.—He also justifies this
preference of them by saying : " All the world is mine," meaning,
since you choose *voluntarily* to observe my statutes, no *nation* has a
right to complain of my favouring you more than others, for all nations are equally mine, and all shall ultimately be deserving to be
called by my name ; but since I must make a beginning with one,
to promulgate my law in *the first instance* to them, it is but just and
fair that I, who am the maker and master of all, should be left to
choose *that** people, which I, in my superior wisdom, think better

---

* The prophets frequently refer to the existence of the Israelites, as an argument in favour of the existence of God, and Isaiah (chap. 43,) calls upon all nations, " to bring instances, where any of them could foretell things, which were
to happen, and to produce analogous events to our history, from theirs ;" and
then he proceeds (v. 10): " You are my witnesses, and my servants, whom I
have chosen." (v. 12) " And you are my witnesses, speaketh the Eternal, and
I AM GOD." Here then the prophet rests the truth of the law, and the proof
of the existence of God, upon the existence of the Israelites ; and to us it really
appears, that the existence of the Jewish nation proves that there is a superintending Power, and that this Power has chosen this people for some ulterior purpose, which is known to Him alone. Let us endeavour to account for our
national existence as we will, a moment's reflection will be enough to convince

fitted and more deserving than any other, to be the depository of my statutes, till the rest of mankind be also fitted to adopt *my will* as their guide, and *my law* as their code.

Can any philosopher step forward and assert, that the Israelites were not better fitted, than any other people, then or even now existing, for this great purpose of God? They were already unconnected with any other nation, they had no home, but *that one* they expected to acquire by the assistance of their God; they had therefore to make no great personal sacrifices by secluding themselves from the rest of the world: when, on the contrary, it would have been a most difficult thing to reform a people, whose manners were once settled, and this difficulty would have been not a little magnified, when this very change of manners must have set them up as a mark of hatred to all the surrounding nations, whose manners had been formerly similar to theirs, and with whom they had lived in friendship.—Independently of this reason, the Israelites were already better acquainted with *revelation* than any other people, and their manners were probably not so corrupt.—Moreover, the Israelites were prepared to receive the law of God from feelings of gratitude towards Him for the signal favours they had received, which was, as has been shown, another powerful reason to entrust the law to them.

To return to the subject under consideration,—the Israelites were promised happiness and *salvation*,—for God said, they should be *a holy people*,—if they would on their part abide by the conditions proposed, and observe the duties required of them. Let it be well observed, that God here plainly says, that the *righteousness of a man is sufficient to ensure his salvation*, for he does not even hint in the slightest manner at a saviour, or to speak more clearly, at a mediator between God and man. According to this definition, which can hardly be controverted, we may safely rest our hope of salvation upon our obeying the will of God and upon our observing his precepts, and we are not to expect to be saved through any being, save the *Eternal*, for He alone is *our* Supporter, *our* Saviour and *our* Redeemer.

No sooner had Moses delivered the message of God, than all the

us, that the biblical account is the most rational, nay, the only probable one of the origin, progress, and fall of our nation, the once powerful Israel, but now the humble and much despised Jews.

people unanimously (not together) answered. " All that the Eternal has spoken we will do." When Moses had carried back this reply to God, he was further notified, that He would come to him in a thick cloud, that the people might hear, when He spoke to him ; and God at the same time, promised Moses, " that in him they should believe for ever." Thirty centuries have already elapsed, since our great and good leader was taken from us, (at a time when his strength was yet unimpaired) ;. and *his* mission is yet believed divine, and its truth defended by the Jews. Does not my writing this imperfect defence of our law in part verify this prediction? Can any denier of the truth of prophecy assert, that *this prophecy* has not been fulfilled to the letter? What right has he, then, to deny the authenticity of *at least this one* prediction?

When the people had declared their willingness, nay their eager desire, to *see their King*, as the Rabbins figuratively call the desire of hearing the word of God proclaimed without any mediator, not even Moses, the latter was ordered, to prepare his brethren for three days previous to that glorious day. Perfectly clean, perfectly free from all earthly desires and pollution, should they meet their God, and receive his *holy* and *pure* law, in holiness and purity. The mount Sinai was to be the place, whence the law was to be proclaimed, and on that account Moses was commanded to fence it round, so so that no one should approach the sanctuary of the Lord, and death would have been the punishment for the violation of this interdiction.

At dawn of the appointed day there rested a dense cloud on the mount, and the terrible thunder rolled, and the bright lightning flashed, at the coming of the Most High in his glory. The trumpet —a trumpet not blown by mortals, but sounding by the will of the Almighty—called forth with its loud blast the people of Israel. And they trembled, whilst Moses led them out of the camp and placed them at the foot of Sinai ; for the mount emitted flames fiercer than the destructive volcano, and shook to its very base.—It could not have been an ordinary earthquake, not a common eruption of a burning mountain ; for then, in the ordinary course of nature, the approach to the base of the mount would have produced instant death. But, no ! it was the glory of God, in whose presence there is safety, which produced this effect, and therefore did the Israelites, led by Moses, advance with a trusty mind and a firm step, though with a quaking heart, for who fears not when God speaks?—After Moses had placed his brethren in proper order, he ascended the mount; but he was ordered to go down* and give warning a second time, that no one should pass beyond the barrier which Moses had drawn round the mount. And here we have another moral lesson, "that it is not enough, that a father tell his children, and a superior those under his charge, only once of their duty; but that they ought to repeat their instructions so often, that they cannot be forgotten, or else the father and guardian have neglected their trust, and they are answerable to God for sins committed by their charges through ignorance.—

When the Israelites were at length fully prepared, the all-powerful God spoke as follows:

1. " I am the ETERNAL *thy* GOD, who have conducted thee out of the land of Egypt, from the house of slavery.

2. Thou shalt have no other gods before me. Thou shalt make thyself no image, nor any likeness of aught in heaven above, or on earth below, or in the waters beneath the earth. Thou shalt not bow down to them, nor worship them; for I the Eternal thy God, am a watchful† God, who am visiting the sins of the fathers on the

---

*The intelligent reader is requested to read with particular attention the nineteenth chapter of Exodus, and he will discover, that Moses was not in all probability on the mount Sinai during the promulgation of the Decalogue, for it is not mentioned, that he re-ascended, till after the promulgation, and we have therefore another proof that Moses had no agency in imposing a law of his own invention upon the Israelites.

It is but justice to say, that I am indebted to Mr. Jacob Mordecai of Richmond, for this remark.

† It is really astonishing, with how much avidity every difficult passage, nay every obscure word, in the whole Bible is seized by infidels, and explained by them in such a manner, as to make its meaning absurd, and thus they attempt to defend their infidelity, saying, that they cannot believe such nonsense, as they pretend to say they have met with in the holy scriptures. A stronger instance can hardly be found, than the assertion, that according to the Jewish Bible, God is a *vindictive Being*. God pardon me, for even penning this blasphemy! And where do they find this? In the Decalogue they say, where it says: He is a *jealous* God. But if I may venture an opinion, I would explain the words אל קנא in the following manner: The Israelites had seen the goodness of God manifested to *them*, ever since Moses was first sent to them, and though they had already shown themselves dissatisfied on several occasions, yet had

children, on the third generation and fourth generation, of those who hate me ; but am doing mercy unto the thousandth generation of those who love me and keep my commandments.

3. Thou shalt not bear the name of the Eternal thy God in vain, (not use it without necessity, nor at an untruth,) for the Eternal will not suffer him to remain unpunished, who beareth his name in vain.

4. Remember the Sabbath-day to keep it holy. Six days thou mayest labour and do all thy work ; but the seventh is a day of rest in honour of the Eternal thy God ; then thou shalt not do any manner of work, neither thyself, nor thy son, thy daughter, thy man and thy maid-servant, not even thy cattle, and the stranger who is within thy gates. For in six days did the Eternal make heaven and earth, the sea and all that is in them, and refrained from work on the seventh day ; therefore did the Eternal bless the Sabbath-day, and declare it holy.

5. Honour thy father and thy mother, that thy days may be long upon the land, which the Eternal thy God giveth thee.

6. Thou shalt not commit murder.

7. Thou shalt not commit adultery.

8. Thou shalt not steal.

---

they never been punished, except we consider the attack of Amalake as a punishment. But now God told them what was their duty, and that it was obligatory upon them to do what they were certified to be right: and as they now knew, what God considered as right, they should be punished for transgressing the precepts of the law, or in other words for *doing wrong ;* and therefore did God continue : " I am קנא אל" a God, who am ever watchful and remembering all that happens, and therefore *ready* to punish, where punishment is due. If this explanation is correct, it follows, that God, according to our Bible is *not* a vindictive Being, but a just Judge, who, as such, punishes all sins against his will, because they are offences against the standard of right. " But does not the Hebrew word קנא *always* mean *jealous*, in its common acceptation ?" No, for we find in Numbers chapter xxv. 11 v. בקנאו את קנאתי: which is very properly translated, " because he was *zealous* for my sake." See also the succeeding chapter, and Instruction in the Mosaic Religion, page 37, note ; and I may add here, that when the within was written, this book was not in my possession, which is another proof, that all who study the Bible with candour and honest zeal will generally agree with each other in their conclusions, although they are divided by time and space. And is this not a beautiful commentary upon the truth of the Mosaic revelation ?

9. Thou shalt not answer as a false witness against thy neighbour.

10. Thou shalt not covet thy neighbour's house. Thou shalt not covet thy neighbour's wife, nor his man-servant, nor his maid servant, nor his ox, nor his ass, nor any thing else which belongs to thy neighbour."

The foregoing precepts are technically called : *the ten commandments* or *the Decalogue,* and are the foundation of our whole civil, moral and religious code.

When the Israelites heard these precepts announced from on high, they were filled with fear and apprehension. For the voice of the Eternal had not been heard by any other people before them, and they had therefore beheld and heard that, which no mortals ever before had seen or heard. The Israelites had desired to be convinced with their own eyes of the truth of Moses's mission, and they had wished to hear the word proclaimed by God himself. They had been gratified, they had seen the glory of God, as He proceeded from Sinai, and shone unto them from Sayir, and sent his beaming light forth from Paran, and came with myriads of saints ; and they had received from his right hand the law as pure as fire, as they lay prostrate before him. (Deut. xxxiii.)—Being therefore now convinced of the truth of Moses's mission, they begged of him, to receive, by himself alone, the commandments, which God might ordain for their government, and that he should teach them afterwards, what he had learned ; for they themselves were in fear of losing their lives, should they witness again the great fire, which was yet burning, while they were speaking to Moses.—But he wished to induce them to persevere in receiving themselves the other commandments, and he therefore answered : " Fear not, for only to prove you did God come, and that his fear might be upon your faces, that you may not sin. When Moses however heard from God, that the request of the Israelites was pleasing to him, he then, but not till then, consented to be the instructer of the people and to tell them all, which he should hear announced by God.

In this manner became Moses the messenger of God to the people of Israel, and their messenger to and interceder with God. Can it be believed, that a man thus honoured should promulgate laws of his own, should teach aught but the word of God? The man chosen by God and confided in by the Israelites could not have acted so ;

whatever he taught was the word of God, and all his thoughts were for the safety of the Israelites, and when they sinned and deserved utter annihilation, he offered himself to die, that they might escape. Much had he to encounter, many difficulties had he to overcome; but he at length succeeded, and the descendants of Jacob confided in him when alive, and wept for him when he was dead. Shall any man in the present age dare to slander such a good, such a pious man, call his words untruths, and his miracles deceptions? Can it be possible, that his contemporaries, who saw him act, who heard him speak, should have confided in him, if he had been a deceiver? And that they *did believe* him, is evident, from our existence as a distinct nation. For it cannot be denied by any human being that *we exist now*; nor, that we did exist in the days of Tacitus; nor, that we existed in the days of Ezra, nor previous thereto; if we then proceed to trace our origin backwards, we must, and so must even the most obdurate doubter, arrive at the days of our blessed legislator, as the time of our first becoming a nation, with peculiar manners and distinct laws. If this is true, (and there exists not the man, who can disprove it,) then it is also true, that it would argue the grossest ignorance of human nature, to believe, that one man *unaided* should have been able to impose upon two successive generations, and that he was *unaided*, cannot be denied.—Let us therefore rather believe, that Moses was sent by God, (the ability of the Creator to do it cannot be doubted,) to work those miracles, and that it was the word of the living God which Moses taught!

CHAPTER XIII.

Having in the preceding chapter enumerated the precepts contained in the Decalogue, I hope to be excused, if I pause in my argument relative to the divine origin of our law, and proceed to explain the Commandments themselves; for I can assure my readers, that if they once understand the true bearing of the Mosaic institutions, they must confess either that Moses, more than any other man who ever lived, united in himself the philosopher, legislator, and governor, and that as such, he is entitled to be imitated and obeyed *from our own free choice;* or that his wisdom and power of mind were given him for the special purpose mentioned in his books, by the immediate inspiration of the Most High, that he merely *copied* the words spoken to him, and therefore, Moses's laws (not Moses himself) are to be obeyed implicitly, without our enquiring at every turn: " Can I understand the reason of this or that particular precept?" For since they are all and every one the *emanations* of the will of God, they *must* be obeyed, though we be ignorant of the reasons the Almighty had in giving these, to *us* mysterious, laws. This point will be more clearly illustrated in a subsequent part of this work, and I shall therefore commence, without further preface, with the explanation* of the Decalogue.

PRECEPT I. *I am the Eternal thy God, who have brought thee out of the land of Egypt, from the house of slavery.*

Most, if not all Christian commentators, think this verse only a kind of preamble to the Decalogue; we Jews, however, take it to be the first commandment. Its meaning is this: " You Israelites have been in Egypt, and you were taken thence by a Power superior to man. *I am that Power, I am the Eternal;* do not believe that there are more persons in the Deity than *one;* no, *I am* your

---

* For a more particular elucidation of the Decalogue than is here given, see " Instruction in the Mosaic Religion," page 39 and seq.

9

God, indivisible and all-powerful. Acknowledge *me* alone and none esle.—Therefore,

PRECEPT II. *Thou shalt have no other gods before me, &c.*

Since I have told you that there is no God besides *me*, it is unlawful for you to worship any thing else, no matter what *its strength, beauty, or wisdom* may be. But some one of you may think: " True, I will not worship any other being, but the Eternal God; but can I do wrong, if I make myself a symbol, to remind me always of his power ? I will make an image to represent God, and this image shall admonish me of the greatness of my Creator; I will look at the sun, and prostrate myself before him, and adore the *Creator* by worshipping the most powerful *creature;* the earth, through God's bounty nourishing all mankind, shall be to me the emblem of his goodness, and the pure flame, the emblem of his purity."—Therefore do I command you, not to make yourselves any personification or representation of the Deity, for I am incorporeal, you know not *my* essence (Deut. iv.); and *under what figure* will you represent me, since you have never seen me ? And then you will sin if you prostrate yourselves before images and creatures, or pay them religious adoration. No image can represent me, the light of the sun is darkness compared to me, and the fire is impure compared to my holiness.— But do not imagine, that because I am good, deviations from my commandments will have no serious consequences; do not deceive yourselves with such specious self-delusions, for I am careful of my honour, and you will be punished if you act wrong; and if the son follow the sins of the father, if the grandson or great-grandson imitate his ancestors' apostacy, each will be punished, not alone for his own sins, but receive also a share of the punishment his progenitors have incurred for their wickedness. But do not think, that the punishment for vice will be in a greater degree, than the reward for virtue; no—for I will do good even to the thousandth generation for the virtuous actions of their ancestors, if they obey my words. You will therefore be convinced, that though I will punish vice, I am yet benevolent, and that I rather reward, than punish; since the punishment for sin will be continued only, to the *fourth,* whilst the *thousandth* generation will be benefited by the virtue of the ancestors.

PRECEPT III. *Thou shalt not bear the name of the Eternal thy God in vain, &c.*

When you are called upon to testify to the truth of any thing, be very careful how you *call upon me* to be a witness to your actions; no falsehood can I allow, nothing but truth will satisfy me, who am the God of truth. Do not mention my name upon frivolous occasions, for I am holy, I am your God, your Father, your Protector, you must venerate me even in your words and thoughts; do not therefore mention my name, except when it becomes necessary, either to asseverate any thing, the truth of which can be established solely through your oath, or when addressing me in prayer.—I cannot suffer any levity with my name, and will therefore punish every one, who impiously uses it frivolously or falsely.*

PRECEPT IV. *Remember† the Sabbath-day to keep it holy, &c.*

I have commanded you to acknowledge me your God, and to abstain from idolatry; and I now further command you to set apart the seventh day of every week for my service and your recreation, as I abstained from work after I had created the world. But if you should ask, what proof have we, that that Being who speaks to us now, is the author of all? then will I advise you to remember, that you have been slaves in Egypt, and that *I conducted* you thence. Your redemption was brought about, as you remember, by my changing the regular course of nature. The river was filled with blood, instead of water; the land that formerly smiled with plenty, and was as lovely as Eden, was visited with hail and locusts, in a manner unheard of before; and the country, where the sun always shines bright, where a cloudy day is never known, was shrouded for three days in impenetrable gloom. After you had left the land of your affliction and had arrived near the Red Sea, you saw nothing *before* you, but death in the troubled billows of the ocean, and

---

* The Jews never pronounce the name of God as it is written, and only the priests were allowed to do so when they blessed the people, and the high-priest during the sacrifices on the Day of Atonement. (See *Yoma* and the Musaph of Kippur.)

† In the commentary on this precept, I have endeavoured to unite the original Decalogue (Exo. chap. xx.) with the recapitulation of it by Moses in Deut. chap. v.—But these remarks are not my own discovery, since I am indebted for them to my esteemed instructer, Rabbi Benjamin Cohen, to whom I owe also several other remarks, of which I have made use without acknowledgment.

naught *behind* you, but destruction from the countless host of Egypt; when all of a sudden the sea divided and piled itself up in two solid walls.—Who wrought these wonders? It was I the Eternal, who have also redeemed you to be my people. Who, I ask you, can change nature, but nature's Lord? Who again is nature's Lord, but nature's Creator? You must therefore acknowledge, that I your God, who changed the natural course of events in Egypt, (and of this you were all witnesses,) am nature's Lord, am nature's Creator. I created the earth you stand on, the sea which surrounds you, and the wide expanse of ether, in which the innumerable systems are fixed and sustained by my will alone, in six days: I spoke, and all that you see rose into existence; but when I on the sixth day had finished my creation, by making *man*, I ceased and made nothing more; for on the seventh day, after all had been produced from nothing, I added not the least to the system I had approved of on the sixth, (Genesis i. and ii.) and I now fix it as a day of rest to be held sacred, and to be strictly observed by the last descendants of your nation, in remembrance of the creation of the world and your redemption from Egypt.

I moreover do not command the heads of families *alone* to rest, but each member of your families, even your servants, nay even your cattle—every thing shall rest on my Sabbath-day; the voice of the oppressor shall then be hushed, and the sigh of the bondman shall not be called forth, but calmness, peace, and content shall, on that day, reign amongst you.—You have no right to call this commandment hard and oppressive, to be compelled to rest one day out of seven; for I allow you six days, to do every thing you have to do; I do not restrain you from doing any lawful work in all this time; but having been employed six days in pursuits for the promotion of your interest or amusement, you must dedicate one day to my service. On that day you must visit the places where you can receive instruction in my laws, that you may know how to serve me. You are also to abstain from labour, that by a suspension of your daily toil, you may acquire fresh strength for renewed exertion in the coming week. On that day your servant shall have leisure to think, as well as his master, of their common Maker, and breathe more freely than he can do on those days when he is engaged in his toilsome task. Your rest shall be quiet; no noise or shout of revelry must be heard in your streets, and not even slight work, which requires no exertion, is allowed to be done. Remember it is the Sabbath! Do not speak about business, make no bargains even by word alone, and do not arrange plans of labour for the coming week; but abstract yourselves altogether from your usual occupations, devote this day entirely to me, your God, and let the weekly day of rest be a symbol to you of the day of bliss of the righteous, after they have thrown off the covering of clay, when there is no care, no toil, no grief, no tears, no master, no oppressor; but where all is security, peace and joy!

PRECEPT V. *Honour* thy father and mother, &c.*

When hitherto, O children of Israel, I have spoken to you only of things relating to my own service, I have now to reveal to you the *duties from man to man.* The first of human beings, who claim the attention, regard, and honour of each of you, are his father and mother. Be careful in your behaviour towards them, honour them while living, and do not slander their memory when they are dead; and although they are then not present to punish you, yet have I given the judges amongst you power to punish with death that ungrateful son, who curses his father or his mother.—Do not think this punishment too severe, for he who can forget his duty towards his father and mother, will soon neglect his duties towards God and his fellow-men, and he does not, therefore, deserve to live.—Do further treat both your parents alike. Though your father may chastise you more than your mother, remember he is your father, that his chastisements are intended for your benefit, to bring you by gentle and well-timed punishment to an acknowledgment of your errors and failings, and that, by correcting them, you may become better and more worthy members of society, than if he, by ill-timed indulgence, be blind to your errors, and from *mistaken* affection fail to correct you. Be also careful of paying proper respect to your mother's commands. Though she may not always inflict punishment when you deserve it, do not on that account grow indifferent about obeying her; consider she is your mother, and therefore, entitled to your obedience no less, than your father. In short, *honour* your

---

* In Leviticus, chap. xix. v. 3, it says : " Each of you shall fear his mother and father, and observe my Sabbaths," for an explanation (the same as is given above) see the commentary of Rabbi Solomon Yarchi, on this passage.

father, although he chastise you, and fear your mother, though on account of the benignity of female disposition, she be often too indulgent towards your failings.

I have said that you should be punished for disobedience to your parents; but there is also reward destined for you, if you observe this my commandment. Though I have said that father and mother are to be obeyed, yet must you never think yourselves at liberty, to violate any of my commandments, because your parents desire or even command it: no—they, no less than you, are *my creatures* and *my* servants.—You, it is true, owe in a measure your life to them; but they and you live solely by my will, and equally with yourselves they are bound to serve me. If therefore, your father tells you to violate, for instance, the Sabbath, you must disobey *him*, because obedience to him in that case, would be disobedience to your God!

Precept VI. *Thou shalt not commit murder.*

Not alone towards me and your parents have you certain duties to fulfil, but also to your other fellow-mortals. Whatever has been assigned by my providence or permission to your neighbour, or even to your enemy, must be sacred in his possession. In the first place: You shall take away no man's life, unless he aim at yours, and in that case only when be has expressed his intentions so fully, that there is no doubt of his willingness to do so, whenever he has an opportunity, and then only, if his death is the only means of saving your or another person's life. At all events it is your duty to apply to the judges, rather than to procure justice for yourselves by your strong arm and violence. You are not allowed to maim any person or do him any bodily mischief whatever.—You are not permitted to lay violent hands upon yourselves, your lives are in my keeping, for I have placed the soul in your body, and *as men*, therefore, you *can have no right* to appear before my judgment-throne uncalled; but through whatever sufferings you have to pass, you must remain on earth, and bear your misfortunes with fortitude; for know, that there is sufficient reward in my power to pay you for your patience in enduring, and resignation in suffering! Even in this life, you see that I often reward constancy and patience; and *can I not* repay him a thousand-fold, who suffers with patience and dies resigned, because he thinks that by so doing he is serving me?

PRECEPT VII. *Thou shalt not commit adultery.*

Since the object of the promulgation of my commandments is to secure in the most ample manner the security and peace of society, I enjoin upon you to abstain from every act, which in the most remote degree could injure the security and peace of the domestic circle, or which could lead others to ruin, or bring them in the way of sin.—You have heard, that the safety of your neighbour's life and limb is dear to me; but his home also must remain uninvaded by the arts and wiles of the seducer. Permit him therefore to be gladdened by the partner that has been assigned to him to share his earthly toil, and who is the solace of his hours of woe, and the attentive mother of his children; and rather rejoice, that your brother is so blest. And reflect, how miserable he would be, if he discovers that she, in whom he so fondly confided, has been untrue to her duty, and bestowed her embraces upon a stranger.—Think how perhaps he may become infuriated, and aim at the heart's blood of the destroyer of his peace; and that even, if the husband should not succeed in his revenge, I the all-seeing One do not slumber, but will assuredly send destruction unto him who is regardless of my precepts.—Further you must know, that on no account can you be excused for incontinent conduct. You have no right to lure any female from the path of virtue to gratify your unholy desires, for all departures from the rules of the strictest morality are odious to me. And O consider, the state of misery to which the fallen, weak-minded and confiding woman is exposed! Spurned by friends, neglected by her lovers, and an object of derision to every stranger, her very touch is pollution, her breath is like the pestilence! and she is rendered so only to gratify the consuming passion of the ungodly lover of pleasure; and only when too late she curses herself and her immolator, when she sees herself forsaken and despised, and dying prematurely, without the voice of comfort to breathe consolation to her, when racked by sickness and overwhelmed at the idea of appearing in judgment before my awful throne!—Let it therefore be your constant study, ye children of Israel, to show to all the world the example of a holy life, which I demand of you, and that you are deserving of the name I gave you, when I said: "Israel is my first-born."

PRECEPT VIII. *Thou shalt not steal.*

Whatever property any man has acquired is to remain his, unless

I, for reasons known to me, deprive him of it, or he himself voluntarily resign it. You have no right to take even the smallest trifle, which is not strictly and honestly your own. I have given a man riches, and who should have the right to take it away from him by force or stratagem, without offending me? Does not the thief say by his actions, that he knows better than myself, your God, how to distribute my bounties? But let not the rich man by carelessness or design withhold from the poor labourer his wages, even for one hour; the poor man deserves to possess that, for which he has worked, and to withhold it, therefore, is theft.—Let every man, who may be appointed to the exalted station of *judge* amongst you, be careful, how he decides in disputed affairs laid before him for his decision. Let him be careful to scan the evidence on both sides, and decide impartially, unswayed by bribes, favour, partiality, compassion or prejudice. Let him decide on the mere abstract question, "who is right," and let him consider, that he is in a measure my representative on earth, and he must therefore, *like myself*, be strictly adhering to what is right without the slightest deviation; for if through neglect or precipitancy a wrong verdict should be given by him, he robs the party, against whom the wrong decision is made; and the man who has been appointed a guardian of the rights of the people, and a defender of the oppressed, is no better than a prowling thief or a high-way robber. Again, if the poor man come before a judge with a complaint, he is to give an attentive hearing to the cause, though the matter, for which the poor man seek redress, be but a trifle! and let him consider, that, what is to the wealthy man a trifle, may be of great service to the poor; and further, that I, the Eternal God, watch with as much solicitude over the most abject wretch, as over the king on his throne, and the judge shall for this reason also, consider the *trifle* of the poor as of equal importance, in point of right, with the immense treasures of the rich man.

PRECEPT IX. *Thou shalt not answer as a false witness against thy neighbour.*

Some one of you may say: "I will not murder my neighbour, I will not seduce his wife, nor will I steal his property; but he has offended me, and since he is sued for a certain sum of money, which in fact he does not owe, but if I give testimony against him, he will be obliged to pay it; I will not let this opportunity pass without making him feel my resentment." Let me admonish you all, not to rob your neighbour in such an indirect manner, though no ultimate benefit may result to you from such conduct.—If a man is upon his trial for any crime, for which, if convicted, he is to suffer bodily punishment, do not speak any thing as a witness against him, which in any manner might be adverse to truth. On the contrary, when you are obliged to give evidence, consider that you are standing before your God, that every action, every word, of yours will be noticed, never to be forgotten; say nothing which is not strictly true to the best of your knowledge ; but it is also obligatory upon you, to say all you may happen to know, though it might injure your friend and benefit your enemy, for it is *your* duty to speak out, and to show favour to no man ; but let truth be ever your guide, and fear not the consequences, for the more painful the duty, the greater the sacrifice of personal feelings is : the greater must your merit be, the greater also will be your reward!

PRECEPT X. *Thou shalt not covet &c.*

I have already told you, that you must not injure your neighbour by conduct ; but in your own thoughts even you are not to meditate him any injury, much less attempt to execute your thoughts ; for you are not permitted to covet that which is not yours. Do not *desire* to possess any thing belonging to any body else ; for if once you give full sway to your desires, if but once you contemplate the means of satisfying your wish, you have already committed the sin of trespass by half. You will not long remain satisfied with desiring ; but you will soon contrive means of getting the desired article in your possession. Do therefore guard yourselves against covetousness, and you will not have to struggle hard against temptation to sin. Let your expectations be moderate, and less will satisfy you ; desire little, and you will be content with the humble lot I may assign to you ; envy not your neighbours, and you will be happy, if *they* are happy, and feel heart-felt pleasure, if all around you are affluent, honoured and beloved. And think not, that you will suffer any loss by so doing ; for your own *peace of mind* will be accompanied by the respect, love and gratitude of all good men, and by the good will, grace and satisfaction of your Maker ! "

10

CHAPTER XIV.

THE JEWISH COMMONWEALTH.

It will be self-evident to every one, who but glances at the Deca-logue, that its precepts are the foundation of the whole Mosaic law. If we search through all the statutes of this code, they can be traced , to one or more of the precepts of the Decalogue ; and thus it will be seen, that though but ten commandments were made known to the Israelites without a mediator, it may yet be said that all the re-maining civil, moral, and ceremonial ordinances are contained and comprehended in them, and it may therefore be maintained, that to a certain extent the *whole* law was communicated to the *whole* Is-raelitish nation.—As an illustration of this let us consider the duties towards God, as we find them detailed in Deuteronomy, in connection with the *first precept.*

If it is once solemnly impressed upon our minds that we owe our being and our preservation to the Almighty Creator, who liveth for everlasting, and who reigneth through all eternity, we must be im-pressed with feelings of awe at his greatness, with sentiments of ad-miration at his wisdom, and with gratitude for his kindness and mercy. All this will lead us to adore and love this great Being,[*] who shows us kindness[†] when we act righteously ; defends us from danger and injury, when we are menaced ;[‡] and forgives us our transgressions, when we repent of our errors.[||] Have we thus es-tablished the love of God in our hearts, we will naturally desire to do something, by which we can manifest our love, and to let our feelings be displayed in our actions. But as we can neither injure God by our misconduct, nor benefit him by any thing we can accom-plish, since He is so far elevated above us in power and beatitude : we can do nothing else in requital of his goodness, we can show our love in no other manner, save by listening with profound attention to his instruction,* which is contained in the revelation He has given, and regulating our lives by the records of his will.

This idea is beautifully illustrated in the tenth chapter of Deuteronomy, commencing at the twelfth verse. There is not perhaps in the whole Bible, though full of passages strikingly grand for their beauty and force, not another passage more calculated to awaken religious awe in the soul of man, than the one we are speaking of. It places before our eyes the relative position which man bears to his Maker in the strongest light. God is exhibited as the greatest conceivable being, in possession of the immensity of space, and of every thing animate and inanimate contained therein; man among this infinity is almost nothing; and still he is told, that his case, his life, and his wants are objects of importance to the Deity, from whom nothing is hidden, be it ever so insignificant. Further, that obedience, love of God, and justice and kindness towards others, are deeds which will propitiate the favour of the infinite One, and that this exhibition of piety is a thing desired of man. Who will not now be willing, so to say, to oblige the Creator? who would withhold obedience, when man can gain so great a prize by it? But I need not comment on a passage so very lucid in itself, and will present it therefore entire to the reader, and let him compare it with the idea advanced, that through the whole Bible the same chain of thoughts and precepts is continually kept in view.

Moses had been reminding the Israelites in a preceding part of the address he held to them a short time before his death, of the many benefits they had received from God, and how often He had pardoned their sins; and then proceeded to say :

" And now, O Israel! what does the Eternal, thy God, ask of thee, but to fear Him, the Lord thy God, to walk in all his ways, and to love Him, and to serve Him, the Lord thy God, with all thy heart, and with all thy soul ; to observe the commandments of the Lord, and his statutes, which I command thee this day, that thou mayst fare well.—Behold the heaven, and the heaven of heavens belong to the Eternal thy God, also the earth, and all that is upon it. Only in thy ancestors did the Lord find pleasure, and He therefore chose their descendants after them, namely *you*, from all the nations, as you see this day. Lay then aside all wickedness of heart, and be no

* Deut. chap. x. v. 12.

longer stubborn and disobedient. For the Eternal, your God, is the
God of gods, and the Lord of lords ; the great, the mighty, and the
terrible God, who respecteth no face, and receiveth no bribe; who
righteth the orphan and the widow, and loveth the stranger, to give
him food and clothes. And *love you the stranger*, for you yourselves
have been strangers in Egypt.—*The Eternal thy God thou shalt
fear, Him thou shalt serve, to Him thou shalt adhere, and by his
name thou shalt swear ;* He is thy Glory, and He is thy God, who has
done for thee these great and wonderful things, which thy own eyes
have seen."

If we mortals now only considered how much we owe to God,
that He not alone gave us existence, but *also a law*, to make *this
existence beneficial* to ourselves: should we not of our own accord,
and even without the certainty of punishment for transgression, be
diligent in the study of his law, careful in the observance of his statutes, in short dedicate our whole life to his glory ? And how are
we commanded to act ? To imitate God in his acts of mercy, as far
as we can. Is He merciful ? so shall we be too—Is He good to all
mankind ? so shall our love to the human race be universal, and not
confined to any particular sect—Does He show us benevolence without any possibility of remuneration ? so ought our charity to be, proceeding from feelings of love, pity, and goodness of heart, but should
never be practised for the sake of fame or reward—Does He teach
the world how to act rightly ? so shall we also be ever ready to dif-
fuse the knowledge of truth and of our holy law; *in fine,* to be
loving God and be perfect means to practise universal charity !
How then can the freethinker, or even the *atheist*, ridicule our law
as superstitious and injurious to society, when he sees the love of
the stranger and the protection of those who need our protection,
enjoined at the same time with the observance of the ceremonial
law (*statutes of God*) ? Let me tell him, that we think not *that* man
good, who says his prayers at the appointed time, is a regular attend-
ant at the place of worship, but is unmindful of the duties *towards
man ;* but *only* him we call a good and pious man, who *besides* being
a devout observer of the laws relating to the *worship of God alone,*
is also a *philanthropist,* and protects the orphan, is kind to the widow, comforts the distressed, is charitable as far as lies in his power
to the poor, and is liberal, and just, and forgiving to the affluent.—I

cannot stop to quote passages for every part of the foregoing assertions, since the Mosaic law is so replete with exhortations and injunctions on these points, that they are to be met with in almost
every chapter; it is moreover my hope that every one, who reads
this defence, may be induced to read the Pentateuch through with
profound attention, and long quotations can be of but little use, not to
say tiresome, to most readers.

If we take the foregoing in connection with the five last precepts
of the Decalogue, it will be apparent, that our law is very careful
in guarding the rights of every person of the community, from the
chief of the nation down to the humble stranger who has no permanent dwelling. The rights of every individual are so well defined,
that no misunderstanding can take place.—When we yet had a
government of our own, every man was in fact upon an equality with
the most exalted of the nation, and the governors were raised to
the dignity they possessed only by the choice or consent of their
fellow-citizens. The Israelites exercised the right of meeting in
primary assemblies, without permission of government, and of discussing public matters, also of petitioning their governors for the redress
of grievances, long before a republican constitution of that kind was
known amongst other nations. (See 1st Kings, chap. xii.) Every
Jew was eligible to any office he was capable of filling, with the
exception of the service at the altar, and the watches in the temple,
and singing whilst the sacrifices were offered. But even here the
Israelites proper had a share, as well as the priests and the Levites.
For besides the twenty-four divisions of the two latter, there were
representatives chosen from among all Israel, who, being likewise
divided in twenty-four companies, were obliged to stand by, whilst
the sacrifices were going forward These men were selected from
the most wise and virtuous, and were called אנשי מעמד (*Anshay
mangamahd*).—Although none but the male Levites were allowed
to sing the psalms in the temple, yet were the Israelites, and even
females, permitted to accompany the singers with instrumental
music. So that even in the temple worship and the sacrifices, each
of the three divisions had their particular rights assigned to them,
which were on no account *to be invaded or usurped by the other.*

It has been intimated, that the institutions of the *republic* of the
North American confederacy are of *modern* invention; but this can-

not be admitted as altogether founded on fact, for the Mosaic code was evidently intended to form a republic of *freemen*, who were all *equally* entitled to protection from the government. The government of the Jews was in the strictest sense of the word a government of *laws*, and not of arbitrary rule. It is true, *our constitution* is *not* the work of the people themselves ; but then it has that advantage over every other yet invented, that its laws have never, to this very day, required the slightest amendment or repealing, as it is well known, that the wisdom of every precept it contains has been proved by the experience of every age. It is almost needless to compare our laws with those of the other nations of antiquity, for none of them ever enjoyed any *rational* liberty ; and besides it is, if I do not err, universally admitted, that *truly* free governments have only been formed among nations, who enjoyed, at least to a certain extent, the light of revelation. And the late French revolution proves, more than any argument I can adduce, that *no nation can be free*, which has not a proper respect for the Mosaic code; and the virtuous republic of Switzerland as clearly demonstrates, that a people truly regardful of the word of God must ever be free, for a *thorough knowledge of it is* the *best* safeguard any nation can devise for the upholding of its liberty and the crushing of tyranny, whenever it should dare to rear its dreadful and blighting head.—But without religion liberty soon degenerates into phrensied licentiousness, and instead of a government founded on reason and equal rights, despotism and the spirit of faction will govern the land with a bloody sceptre and unrelenting oppression !

Though properly speaking it does not belong to a defence of our law to describe our judiciary system ; yet can I not refrain from inserting a few particulars in relation thereto.—Money matters were decided by arbitrators, chosen by the parties themselves, each appointing one, and these two selecting a third ; and these three, thus chosen, pronounced judgment ; but appeal could be taken, or rather contested points of law and equity could be carried before the *high-court* or Sanhedrin of seventy-one in Jerusalem. In matters of corporeal punishment, or trials for life and death, the number of judges was twenty-three, and if there was but a majority of one vote for finding the criminal guilty, he was forthwith to be set free, as a division of *thirteen* to *ten* was necessary for the conviction and con-

demnation of the accused. If a man was once condemned, his sentence could be revised to save him from death ; but if a man was once
acquitted, though there should afterwards have been found the most
positive evidence of his guilt, he could *not* be tried again for the
same offence.[*]

We thus find some of the provisions of the laws of the American
republic practised already three thousand years ago.—Every contested point of law of whatever description, civil, criminal, or ceremonial, was finally decided upon by the Sanhedrin, and their
decision was to be *strictly obeyed*. (See Deut. chap. xvii. v. 11.) To
establish any cause, it was necessary to produce at least *two* lawful
witnesses, who were obliged to testify as to the fact, that they had
seen it, and forewarned the person who committed the act, previously
to his doing so, or admonished him to desist while engaged in the
supposed crime. They were interrogated separately, so that one
should give no clue to the other; in this way any discrepancy in the
testimony must have been easily detected, in which case, if the difference was a material one, the accused was acquitted. In case the
witnesses could be convicted of having offended against the ninth
precept of the Decalogue, they were to be punished with the same
punishment the person by them accused would have suffered if he had
been convicted; and no pardon durst be extended to false witnesses
(Deut. chap. xix. v. 21).—No man could act as judge, if he had
seen any crime committed, or in money matters, if he was capable
of giving testimony for or against either party ; even the president
of the Sanhedrin, emphatically called *the judge* (chief justice), could
not sit on the bench, but was obliged to give his evidence before the
inferior judges ; so that every case must necesarily have had a fair
hearing, and every man accused of crime an impartial trial.

1 have said that no rational liberty was enjoyed by any heathen
people, and thinking that some proof may be required of me for this

---

[*] Exodus, chap. xxiii. v. 7, we read : ונקי וצדיק אל תהרג כי לא אצדיק רשע
"And him, who has been once declared innocent and righteous, thou shalt not
slay, for *I* will not suffer the wicked to go unpunished." This verse is understood by us to refer to a person, who has been tried and acquitted, as it would
be unnecessary to forbid the murdering of the innocent and righteous in general;
besides the conclusion of the verse is a strong argument in favour of the above
given translation.

bold and unqualified assertion, I shall take the liberty of comparing a few points of Solon's laws, which are, I believe, the most liberal of the ancient systems, with those of Moses, whose fate it has been to be so much cried down and denounced. Every liberal man will agree with me, that it is dangerous to entrust one class of men with particular privileges over any other class of the same community, or to use the figurative language of a great philosopher and statesman* now dead, " to provide the backs of one class of the community with saddles, that they may be ridden by the more favoured class."—If Solon's laws had this tendency, then I hope, that their superiority over our laws will no longer be asserted by any man, whose boast it is to be the supporter of universal liberty and equality of rights.

I shall not waste much space and time in investigating the subject at any great length, but shall content myself with picking up a few facts, as I find them related in Gillies' Greece (vol. ii. p. 93 and 94). He says, the Athenians were divided into four classes according *to the property they possessed,* and that the lowest class, though they had a right to vote in the popular assemblies, yet could never become members of the senate or Areopagus, or hold any magistracy whatever. Now let me ask, what great use was the power of voting to the *commons,* when the *senators* had the extraordinary authority of deciding what business should be laid before the popular assemblies? And had they not the right of convoking these very assemblies? Then again the senators had the power of passing laws, which were in force for a whole twelvemonth, without ever consulting *the people* at all about them; they possessed the chief part of the *executive* power; their president had the custody of the archives and treasury; the senate alone could build ships, equip fleets and armies, and seize and confine state criminals; and to crown all, *they could examine and punish several offences, which were not prohibited by any positive law!*—I am not disposed to pursue the subject any further, not being engaged in writing a disser-

---

* The late President Jefferson in his letter to Mr. Weightman. Since the text was written, however, the author of these pages has seen a statement, that these emphatic words had been originally employed by *Richard Rumbold,* who was executed for a participation in the Rye-house plot, under James II. of England, in 1685. Having quoted the words under an impression that they were original with President Jefferson, this correction was considered necessary.

tation on the Athenian laws; but let me respectfully ask all Americans, who have so justly a great horror of all *ex post facto* laws and constructive treason, how they would like to have their representatives in congress invested with power to examine and punish offences not prohibited by any particular law?—Away then with the cant of these men, who prefer Solon's laws to Moses's code,* solely because Solon was a *Greek* and Moses a *Hebrew,* and claimed no merit for those excellent laws, made known through him, because he said, and said truly, that they were not the fruit of his own invention, but the expression of the will of God ! I had thought, that the world had grown too liberal and too enlightened to act so foolishly from ignorance ; to what cause then are we to ascribe that silly praising of the Greek and Roman legislators and the rancorous abuse of the Jewish code ? Is it malice ? Hatred towards the Jews and aversion towards their laws ? Though this may *perhaps* be an excuse to individuals belonging to other nations, what can be said in exculpation of those our own people, who act the parricide by ridiculing Moses and despising his code ? It must be considered equally improper, as for a person to be *pleased* with every thing *abroad,* and to *find fault* with every thing *at home,* solely because it is at home. And it may be likened to the conduct of fretful and too much indulged children, who spurn every endearment of *their own mother,*

---

* Fault has been found with the Pentateuch for containing so many penal statutes, where life was the forfeit. This objection can weigh nothing in the mind of the thinking. For when a law is known and well understood and its practice uniform, the criminal cannot blame the law, but only himself for disregarding it; and then the punishment of death was only against crimes of the deepest die; and if it is wrong to punish such crimes with death, it is equally wrong to punish them with imprisonment ; and are criminals to run at large unchecked by the arm of the law ?—Besides this, the practice of the Jewish code, was any thing but sanguinary, as will appear from Maccothe, chap. i. §. 10, where it says : "A Sanhedrin which slays once in seven years is called a *destructive* one ; Rabbi Elazar son of Azariah said, once in seventy years; Rabbi Tarfone and Rabbi Akiba said, if we had been in the Sanhedrin, no man would ever have been executed. Thereupon, said Rabbi Shimone, son of Gamaliel, men such as these would have caused the increase of murderers in Israel." This characteristic extract must convince all, how great the clemency was, which was exercised in our courts ; so much so, as to cause one of our greatest men to say, that this lenity, if carried further, would have emboldened criminals through the impunity shown to others, who had been on their trials.

11

but are pleased to excess with the most useless and trifling toy from the hands of *a stranger*.—But is such conduct becoming men and *philosophers*, who say they search for truth? Shame! shame! remember that you have not all the wisdom and all the knowledge to yourselves, and you would therefore do well to draw some lessons from *that* book, which confessedly contains the best code of laws, ever devised for the government of mankind.

CHAPTER XV.

THE BIBLE AND PAGANISM.

It has of late grown fashionable among some of the learned men, to assign a high moral character to the Greek and Roman mythology; and even the Guebers have come in for a share of the *whitewashing process*. It has always been believed, that the latter were the worshippers of the sun and fire; but wonderful to relate, it has been discovered, how long ago I know not, that they did not worship the fire as a deity, but only prayed to it as a *symbol* of the Creator of the sun and fire, in the same manner as the Roman Catholics yet have image-worship amongst them, in which images are only considered as remembrancers of God's power. How far the Guebers were actually acquainted with the attributes, which revelation ascribes to the Creator, I indeed cannot tell, for my knowledge of antiquity (and I confess it without the least hesitation) is very limited. But it appears to me very strange, that the opinion should have been general for so long a time, that the Guebers in reality worshipped the fire, and this at times, when they were masters of Persia, if the contrary were true. Moreover we are told by Mr. Rollin and others, that the Persians believed in a *good* and *evil* god, and consequently, their idea of the Creator could not have been that

which the Jews, or even the philosophers themselves, call rational.
The Hindoos also are praised for the simplicity and antiquity of their
faith, and we hear a great deal concerning their sacred books.
However, according to a late writer, (Mrs. Graham's* Letters on India,) they believe : " That the creation of the gods is coeval with
that of the world ; and when the *Supreme Intelligence* called the
universe into being, he delegated to the gods the creation of mankind, and the formation and government of all mundane objects.
Brahma, the creating energy, with Vishnu, the preserver, and Siva,
the destroyer, were the greatest of the deities." There is a good
deal more about the Indian deities in the letters referred to, but
what has been quoted already, is sufficient for our purpose. From
the extract just given, it appears, that if it even be admitted, that
the Indians believe in a Supreme Intelligence, and consequent Creator
of all, they have nevertheless a very crude notion of the government
of this world by this Supreme Intelligence. We Jews believe, that
God created the world, governs it, and preserves it ; that there is no
power independent of his will, that every power, even that power
superior to man, is accountable to Him, and to Him alone, praised be
He for everlasting ! This belief presents to our idea an *adorable*
Being, who, though superior in *intelligence*, *power*, and *happiness*
to aught which exists, yet disdains not to watch over the welfare of
his creatures. The *enlightened* Indians, on the other hand, believe
that the creation of the world was intrusted to mere *creatures* (for
their gods are [as above] creatures of the Supreme Intelligence), of
which *creating* creatures, one is the *creator*, the other the *preserver*,
and the third the *destroyer ;* a pretty trio, truly ! The *creator* (see
the sequel of Mrs. G.'s letters) Brahma has withdrawn from the
government of what he made himself; and the *preserver* Vishnu, is
hardly capable of saving things from the destructive power of the
destroyer Siva, who, strange to tell, is also considered as the *repro-
ducer*. There may be, no doubt, a hidden and rational meaning to
all this, which appears evidently a strange mixture of truth and fable; but it is useless to extract the beauties of heathenism in this
place, and, however instructive it might perhaps be, I am compelled
to resign the task to those, who so much admire the system of the

---

* Her account is confirmed by others ; I quoted her book as the only accessible one to me, when this work was written.

Brahmins, and though delighting in the obscure allegories of Indian mythology, reject as unwise the obvious beauties of the Mosaic and prophetic writings. And if even they should succeed in making matters appear rational, we Jews would still continue to point to the book of our blessed law-giver, and exclaim: " Look at this wonderful work." We also must ever continue to prefer the doctrines and religion taught therein to any other system, since the Mosaic code is so much more explicit, than the law of any other nation, and as religion, to be useful, should be intelligible and accessible to the ploughman, who cultivates the soil, no less than to the philosopher and public teacher, to whom, alas ! worldly interest is frequently the sole monitor to induce them to practise outward piety.

That the Brahmins have also what they term sacred writings, which however have evidently no divine origin, proves nothing against the authenticity of the Mosaic writings, which also claim a divine origin ; as the very excellence of the latter, their great simplicity, the sublime conceptions contained therein with regard to the Deity, prove, beyond a doubt, their pre-eminence over the former, and consequently, Moses may have been a truly inspired man, and writing by divine direction, if even no other man ever was ; and in fact, the very claim any thing sets up to divine origin can only be tested, by its agreeing or disagreeing with the standard of the Pentateuch. So well were the authors of the sacred books of the Israelite convinced of this, that they in no place seek to hide the existence of *false*, or *pretended*, prophets. We are even told that there existed in one assembly more than four hundred deceivers and but *one* who was a prophet of the Eternal. Besides, as the great miracle of the promulgation of the law was no doubt made known to the inhabitants of the East by the ships of Solomon, which traded to Ophir, it is highly probable, that some deceiver, residing there, conceived the plan of offering something to his countrymen which they should obey as an emanation from Heaven, and so it may have happened, that truth in the first instance was made the instrument for the propagation of falsehood. As I have said before, my acquaintance with matters of antiquity is not sufficiently extensive to enable me to determine the age of the writings of the Brahmins ; I however do not recollect ever to have read or heard, that it could ever be assumed, that they were of as early a date as the Pentateuch, and it may therefore be actually as I have suggested. Nevertheless, I offer my own hypothesis with extreme caution, and I hope not to be called presumptuous, for daring to venture offering an opinion, which may perhaps have never been suggested before.

The Greeks and Romans, too, had a religion, acknowledging the existence of God, and claiming an obedience to the divine will. But how different was this from the law which has been given to us. Of the Creator they had but a confused idea, and Ovid, one of the most learned Romans, said in one of his poems :

> "Sic ubi dispositam, *quisquis fuit ille deorum,*
> Congeriem secuit." *Metam.* i. 32, 33.

Meaning, that a God, *whoever* he might be, ordered the chaos, as Ovid describes. The poet was well convinced that the gods, commonly worshipped by the Romans, were unable to produce the world, and order every thing as it exists ; hence his uncertainty, and his " quisquis fuit ille deorum," yet he knew not what to call him, or what station to assign to him amongst the immense number of the deities acknowledged by his countrymen.

Jupiter is generally called *pater omnipotence ;* and yet he also appears to have been obliged to submit to inexorable *fate,* and thus the greatest deity of the Romans had a superior power to direct him, whose decrees could not be disobeyed. For thus says Virgil, (and he had certainly the best means of information on all subjects connected with his belief,) in the first book of the Æneid :

> —— "Trojæ qui primus ab oris
> Italiam, *fato* profugus, Lavinia venit
> Litora." 1—3.

Again :

> "Parce metu, Cytherea, manent immota tuorum
> *Fata* tibi." 257—8.

All the supreme power of Jupiter, therefore, seems to have consisted in his knowing, more than any other god, what the fates had decreed. Homer, in the begining of the eighth book of the Iliad, introduces Jupiter in the act of consulting the fates, to whom they had decreed the victory, and thus even he was compelled to consult a mightier being than himself—chance or fate—to enable him to know how to act correctly.—Here are the words of Homer as translated by Mr. Pope :

> " But when the sun the height of heaven ascends,
> The sire of gods his golden scales suspends
> With equal hand; in these explored the fate
> Of Greece and Troy, and poised the mighty weight.
> Pressed with its load, the Grecian balance lies
> Low sunk on earth, the Trojan strikes the skies."

Independently of this mystery, there are many other considerations to compel us to consider the Greek and Roman religion immeasurably beneath ours; for their deities were, even by them, not viewed in a very favourable light, and both Homer and Virgil have given us some specimens of the life of the *immortals*.—The greatest praise Homer ever bestows upon Juno, is his calling her " white-armed, or large-eyed, (ox-eyed rather,) elegant Juno," and the like; and Virgil, in the first book of the Æneid, describes Venus:

> " Dixit, et avertens rosea cervice refulsit,
> Ambrosiæque comæ divinum vertice odorem
> Spiravere; pedes vestis defluxit ad imos;
> Et vera incessu patuit dea." 202—5.

Here no one finds the gods known by any thing but their superior beauty, white arms, large eyes, broad neck, handsome hair, a long robe, and to sum up all in the *strongest possible* manner, the very gait proved the goddess! Wonderful! And this is all, for no superior intelligence, no power beyond that of mortal men, is ever displayed! But how great is the difference between Virgil's story of the recognition of Venus by her son, and the simple, yet sublime, account of the angel's appearance to Manoah and his wife, where he (the angel) went up in the flame just ascending from the altar, and did wonders, which Manoah and his wife witnessed. (See Judges chap. xiii.)

What kind of life was led by the Grecian gods, according to the poets, may be inferred from some of the concluding lines of the first book of the Iliad.—Vulcan is there represented, as pouring out nectar, first to his own white-armed mother, and next to the whole multitude of the gods; but the lame smith did not get much reward for his pains, for

> " Vulcan with awkward grace his office plies,
> And unextinguished laughter shakes the skies."
>
> *Pope's Transl.*

There was, moreover, continual strife between Juno and Venus; Jupiter and his wife frequently quarrelled, and some hard names were given from one to the other; the father of the gods was very jealously watched by his spouse, and he was hardly allowed to let a visiter come to him, without exposing himself to an altercation.

Now see the difference between the Bible's and the Greek writers' account of the Divinity. For the God of Israel is always represented, throughout the Jewish canon, as a great, immaculate, and perfect Being; whereas the Greek and Roman gods had all the vices of the Greeks and Romans themselves. Jupiter was confessedly very viciously inclined, and practised vice whenever he could; and the story of Venus and Mars is certainly not very creditable to them or to the circle of gods, among whom such conduct was not alone tolerated, but even approved. Homer's gods are ranged against one another in battle, and Mars, the brutal god of war, receives a wound from Diomede, and the god retires to Olympus, and complains to father Jove about the wickedness of the Grecian hero.

What must have been the state of religion amongst the people, when they were told the like of their gods, images of whom were stuck in every nook and corner of their houses? Is it a wonder that the Greeks and Romans at length fell to the lowest state of moral depravity? Is it not in this manner easily accounted for, that the very temples of Vesta, Minerva, and Diana became at last places of prostitution?—It may be, and there is hardly any doubt of it, that *originally* there was some reasonable foundation for the mythology of the ancients—it may be that all the tales about the lives of the gods were only allegorical allusions to some acts, committed by men—it may be that the multiplicity of gods among them, was only emblematical of the universality of the Almighty's providence—it may be that the light of revelation originally given to *Adam* and *Noah* was never altogether extinguished, and that it continued to emit now and then a luminous ray, though ever so feeble—all this, and more may be said, and said with truth; but that does not in the least controvert what has been said above; for if we even admit that *heathenism was truth disguised*, it must nevertheless be self-evident, that this disguised truth could have been known to the priests only, perhaps to the *Pontifex maximus* alone; but the multitude, those upon whom religion ought always to exercise its chief and best influence, did, (as may be boldly asserted) know nothing of their gods, save, and *only that*, which was taught them in Homer and other similar books.

We therefore find the baneful influence of paganism upon the morals of the people to be so dreadful and almost surpassing belief; we find the Greek and Romans in their very acts, of what they called religious exercises, practising the most odious profligacies; they were corrupt, but they did justify this corruption by the practices of their gods. I could, if I but would, transcribe some of those practices, but I will not stain my paper with their recital, and must therefore refer the curious to the works of Homer and Virgil themselves. Having said thus much I must beg every learned unbeliever to point out to me *one single* passage in the whole twenty-four books of our canon of a similar tenor. And for all that, these learned infidels can ask with an air of exultation: "Who can prefer the psalms of David to Homer?" O there are many that do, and they are at the same time ready to admit, that they never could praise Homer half as much as he is generally praised. For this very good reason; Agamemnon, Menelaus, Achilles, and Ajax Telamon are complete ruffians, uttering perhaps at times some pretty phrase, which they never could have spoken, and Odysseus is one of those dishonest politicians, those crafty intriguers, the like of whom so much *disfigure* the pages of modern history. There can indeed be but little objection to paint *vice* and *barbarity* in their true colours, provided they are held up to our *detestation :* but not such is Homer's aim; every epithet intended to express greatness and preeminence, from *godlike* down to *quick-footed*, is lavished upon these heroes, and thus *he seems* at least to approve of the conduct of the *barbarians*, whose deeds he recounts. And then, there is hardly a *good* character in all Homer, if you except the noble Hector and the wise Nestor.— The Greeks had further as *many gods* and *demigods* as they had ancient kings, modern heroes, and—trees in their forests! What kind of religion is that, where the augurs looked at the flight of birds, and the haruspices inspected carefully the entrails of the slaughtered ox, before an army could march, or before a battle could be fought?—How much more elevated is the idea, that through prophecy alone, made known to the high-priest by *holy* inspiration, the *Israelites* marched out to attack their *invaders.**

* The reader will please to refer to Essay III. for a further account of the practices of war amongst the Israelites, where he will find some arguments to prove that war was not an *occupation* of theirs.

After our ancestors had come in sight of the enemy, the priest, who always accompanied the army, but never fought, was to speak as follows (Deut. chap. xx.) : " Hear, O Israel, you approach this day to battle against your enemies ; let not your hearts faint, fear not, tremble not, and be not cast down, because of them ; for it is the Eternal, your God, who goeth with you, to fight with you against your enemy, to save you" (from danger) ! When the priest had finished his address, the officers made the following proclamation : " Whoever there is among you who has espoused a woman, built a house, or planted a vineyard, or who is fearful and faint-hearted, let him return home." In this manner every one, who by some worldly cause was particularly attached to life, every one, who was naturally a coward, every one, who, from the compunctions of a sinful conscience, felt himself unable to enter into the front ranks of the fight, fearing that he should die in battle in punishment of his sins—all these, I say, were admonished to go and return home, for *not the multitude* gain the victory, but those who, though few in number, are men, whose " knees have never knelt to Baal, and whose mouth has never kissed him." (See the account of Gideon's battle, Judg. chap. vii.) Our religion was thus intended to prove to us that to be victorious we must first deserve to be so ; and to conquer the heathens, we should by superior virtue and greater reliance upon God deserve his assistance.

In fine, whatever hidden, and to Jews unknown, beauties the Greek and Roman rites may have had, *our* religion would stigmatise as superstition, and as such all the ceremonies of the Roman augurs, Tuscan soothsayers, and Greek oracles were prohibited to us. (See the 18th chap. of Deut.)—I hope to have, in the few foregoing words, said enough to demonstrate, that without even calling in the aid of revelation, our religion is, upon grounds of human reason also, more sublime, more sacred, than the creeds of all nations of antiquity taken together.

I have heard it said that it is highly probable that Moses borrowed his doctrines and laws from the Egyptians, with whose customs he was intimately acquainted. But this assertion, though generally and very confidently brought forward, can be refuted by a single passage from Leviticus, a book, allowed even by the most malignant critics, to be of undoubted antiquity. We read (Lev. chap.

12

xviii.) : " And the Eternal spoke unto Moses as follows : Speak
unto the children of Israel and say unto them, 1 am the Eternal
your God. You shall not do such things as are done in the land of
Egypt, in which you have resided; nor shall you act after the manners of the land of Canaan, whither 1 am bringing you, nor shall
you walk in their ordinances."

Here Moses speaks as explicitly as possible, prohibiting the imita-
tion of Egyptian customs; how can any man, who wishes not to be
considered a *maniac*, then say, that Moses at the same time copied
Egyptian customs and forbade their execution? The idea is too
absurd, and must, therefore, be rejected by every fair-reasoning
man ; and where is the man who, after this, can deny that Moses's
law is altogether original, and altogether unconnected with any
code either known before or after him?

I have said that the Psalms of David are preferable to Homer; and,
to exhibit the justice of the preference, I shall transcribe the following two passages, the first from the eighth, and the other from the
eighteenth psalm :

" O Eternal God, our Lord, how powerful is thy name in all the
earth ! who placest thy glory above the heavens. Out of the
mouth of babes and sucklings Thou hast established thy reign, to
confound thine opponents, to quiet the enemy, and him who seeketh
vengeance. When I look at thy heavens, the work of thy hands,
the moon and the stars which Thou hast founded ;—what is man,
that Thou rememberest him? and the son of Adam, that Thou
regardest him? And Thou hast made him a little less (gifted) than
angels, and hast crowned him with glory and honour. Thou hast
given him dominion over the works of thy hands, and hast placed
all things under his feet ; sheep and oxen—all, and also the beasts of
the field, the birds of the air, and the fishes of the sea,—and he
passes through the ways of the ocean ! O Eternal God, our Lord,
how great is thy name in all the earth !" Psalm viii.

" In my distress I called upon the Eternal, and prayed to my God,
and He heard my voice out of his temple, and my cry came before
Him—to his ears.

" And the earth shook and trembled, and the foundations of the
mountains were loosened, and they quaked, for He was angry.
Smoke rose out of his nostrils, fire blazed out of his mouth, coals

were kindled from it. And He bent the heavens, and went down, and a cloud of darkness was under his feet. And He rode upon a Cherub, and flew along, and rushed by upon the wings of the wind. And He shrouded himself in darkness, around his pavilion ; dark waters, clouds piled upon clouds ! From the light before Him passed through his clouds hail and coals of fire. And the Eternal thundered in heaven, and the Most High let his voice resound ;—hail and coals of fire. He sent forth his arrows, and scattered them ;—and mighty lightning, and confounded them ; and the channels of the waters were seen, and the foundations of the universe laid bare, from thy call, O Eternal, from the breathing of the breath of thy anger !" Psalm xviii. v. 6, &c.

The extract from the eighteenth psalm is particularly strikingly grand. He (David) describes the power of the incomprehensible God, whose word is sufficient to prostrate all before Him in ruins ; He is shrouded in darkness, but light, or rather intense brightness, (נגה) is immediately around Him : there all is light, all is glory, all is gladness ; only to man, whilst he is yet mortal, is the Deity clothed in the thick cloud, that rests at his feet. But the flashes of the lightning, the rolling of the thunder, the rattling of the hail, the scalding streams of lava, the burning coals from the volcanos—all proclaim to us his might and his power. He but speaks and the earth trembles ; He but breathes and mountains are split in twain. But does it cost Him any effort, any great exertion ? O no, all this happens מנשמת רוח אפך " from the breathing of the breath of thy anger ;" by which the Psalmist means : the ease with which a man breathes is well known, and thus easy is it for our God to do this mighty work. Here then we have a picture of the power of the Almighty, we see his great omnipotence displayed in glowing colours ; and we are told that all his desire is that we should be good, obedient to his will, submissive to his dispensation, that *we ourselves* should be made happy, that we may be worthy to enjoy " delights at his right hand for ever :" and can a stronger reason be addressed to the human mind ? can any thing more strongly impel him to obey the will of his God, made known to him for his own happiness alone ?

Has Homer any passage to equal the foregoing in sublimity ?— Virgil, indeed, attempts a description of Jupiter's power, and says :

———" ille flagranti
Aut Atho, aut Rhodopen, aut alta Ceraunia telo
Dejicit."   *Geor.* i. 331—3.

Virgil must needs employ a *telum*, for neither he nor any other heathen had any conception of God's power being manifested by his *word* alone. God, according to our ideas, however, has no need of any materials in his government of all the world, for He, (as our prayer so elegantly says) : " Reviveth the dead with his word !"—And, though the translation given above is not at all to be compared in brevity and closeness of diction with the Hebrew, it is yet sufficient to prove that a person may be a *very good man*, and *yet dare* to prefer *David's Psalms* to *Homer's Iliad*, or even to *Homer's Odyssee*.

I shall now close this chapter with a translation of a portion of our daily prayers, and beg those of my readers, who are Greek scholars, or who possess a translation of the first book of the Iliad, to compare it themselves with the prayer of Chryses addressed to his Sminthean Apollo.

" Thou art mighty for ever, O Lord, Thou revivest the dead, art powerful in helping us, and causing the wind to blow and the rain to descend.—Thou maintainest the living with kindness, and revivest the dead with great mercy, supportest the falling, healest the sick, loosenest the bonds of the captives, and preservest thy truth to those who sleep in the dust. Who is like Thee, Lord of strength, and who can be compared unto Thee, O King, who slayest and bringest to life again, and lettest salvation spring forth !"

Here the unbelievers have something nervous, concise, and energetic, where the wonderful deeds and the great kindness of our Maker are enumerated in a few forcible words, without any ornament whatever. And since they so much admire every thing that is *not Jewish*, they ought to ransack their classics to produce parallel or even superior beauties to the foregoing.—But they cannot !—Well then, let them admit, that not alone is Moses's *law* superior to any ancient or modern *constitution*, but also that *our style* of writing, both in the Bible and our regular prayers, is as far above what has been written by profane poets and prosaics, as light is preferable to darkness !

CHAPTER XVI.

THE PHYLACTERIES.

If by *superstition* is understood a belief or confidence in things, having no existence in reality, or existing only through fraud or ignorance : then it can be boldly asserted, that we Jews are not superstitious ; but that, on the contrary, we abhor superstition as being contrary, and in opposition, to our religion.—If by *bigotry* are meant an inveterate adherence to error, and a persecution or a tendency to persecution of others who have firmness enough to resist such errors, or to oppose the enforcing of it, when presented to them for acceptance : then can we again assert, that we are no bigots ; for our religion is not founded on error, as has been proved, and besides this we wish to burden no one with our opinions, who admits them not of his own accord.—But if by superstition are understood, a veneration of God, belief in revelation and hope of future reward for virtue—and by bigotry, an adherence to opinions *so well* founded, and a determination to resist all innovation, no matter by whom recommended : then hail, superstition ! welcome, bigotry ! If philosophers have determined to stamp such *virtuous* resolutions with the *odious* names of bigotry and superstition, we must needs be prepared to bear these opprobrious titles with content and resignation ; and I venture to assert in the name of our whole nation, that not twenty good Jews could be induced to relinquish their opinions, merely because these opinions have received harsh names from unbelievers. And if I could be convinced, that Jews could be base and cowardly enough, to be swayed by mere abuse without argument, I should be sorry to be considered a member of their community. But, thank Heaven, I know my brethren better ; and though they may deviate, though they may live *for a time* forgetful of their duty ; yet will they always cherish with fondness the idea of their having been born members of the nation despised and trodden under foot ; and examples are not rare, where even apostates called in the brethren to their dying bed, after refusing the attendance of any other !

But some one may ask, " have not the Jews superstitious customs, for example, the cloak they wear during prayers, the phylacteries, holydays, the blowing of the cornet, and the palm branch ?" This question may at first sight appear to throw very great difficulties in the way of a defence of our religion ; but a candid enquiry must soon convince us, that the above ceremonies are by no means superstitious, although their true intent may not be altogether obvious to a prejudiced and superficial enquirer.

Let us commence with the Tallith, or *cloak*, used during prayers. We find in Numb. chap. xv. v. 37, the following commandment : " And the Lord spoke unto Moses as follows : speak unto the children of Israel, and bid them to make themselves fringes (ציצת) at the corners of their garments throughout their generations, and that they put upon the fringe of the corners, (*borders* Eng. vers.) a string of blue, תכלת."—In Deute. chap. xxii. v. 12: " Thou shalt make thee fringes upon the four corners of thy vesture, wherewith thou coverest thyself." The reason for this commandment is given in Numb. chap. xv : " That by seeing these fringes, we might remember all the commandments of the Eternal and observe them, and not follow blindly the evil desires engendered within us, by the beholding of the eyes and the desiring of the heart." Our Rabbins give the following explanation : ת* is 400, צ is 90, and י is 10, and in consequence the numerical value of the word ציצת, is 600; there are also on each of these fringes *eight strings* and *five* double knots, thus the number of the word itself, together with that of the strings and knots, amounts to *six hundred and thirteen*, this being the whole number† of the commandments in the Mosaic Law. If even we reject this explanation as too fanciful, there is yet no reason to laugh at the fringes, since, as we are always covered with clothes, they seem to be well adapted (it being once so understood) to act as monitors to us, when we are going to do any thing unlawful ; and it is the object of the precept, that the sight of the ציצת shall withhold us, by addressing our senses, from offending against our religion,

---

* Every Hebrew letter has a numerical value, for instance א is 1, ב 2, ג 3, &c.

† See Instruction in the Mosaic Religion, page 109, note.

and *they* are to tell us, when every other voice* is silent : " Beware !
remember the commandments of thy God !" And is this symbol,
though simple, not far superior to and much more rational than the
idols, statues, and marks of other nations ?

In former times the Israelites wore the fringes upon the corners
of their cloaks ; but since our dispersion, and because it has become
dangerous for us in many places to be *known as Jews*, we wear
under our clothes a four cornered garment, to which the fringes
are attached ; and in the synagogues or other places of worship we
make use of a square, or rather, oblong cloak, to which they are
fixed, and this garment or טלית (Tallith) is worn during public worship by day, but not at night, except at certain occasions, which it
would be needless to detail here.—When the purple colour (הכלת)
was yet known, we were obliged (see above) to have one of the
strings of each fringe of this colour, but since this colour is no more
known, we are unable to comply with this provision of the law to
its full extent ; and the fringes we make use of are, therefore, composed of eight white strings only.

The phylacteries תפלין (Thephillin) are improperly supposed to
be considered by us in the light of *amulets*, as has been lately
asserted by an English writer, who also quite *liberally* (as liberally
as most writers concerning us, who are either deists or Christians)
supposes, that they were for a similar purpose as the Greek, Roman, or Arab amulets. The *learned* writer was, no doubt, misled
by the term *phylacteries*, derived from the Greek verb *phylasso*, *I
watch* or *guard ;* but the תפלין are *not* phylacteries, a name which
properly belongs to the קמעה, a cabalistical instrument. But since
there is no word in the English, Latin, or Greek, synonymous with
the Hebrew word *Thephillin*, I shall drop the term phylacteries
altogether, and in the sequel make use only of the proper word.—
There are two kinds of Thephillin, and both consist of *extracts
from the Law*, written upon parchment. They are commanded to

---

* And thus teach the Rabbins : Whoever has ציצת on his garments, תפלין
on his head, and a מזוזה on his door, will not easily be misled to sin. For to be
engaged in acts of religion, and having things pertaining to religion constantly
near us, will act as a check, whenever the mind should desire to enter the way
of sin, and be as it were a silent rebuker in all matters of dereliction from our
duties.

be made* in Exodus xiii. and Deuteronomy vi. and xi. (which see).
The two kinds of Thephillin are : the *Thephillin shel Roshe* and
Thephillin shel Yahd, or in English, Thephillin for the *head*, and
Thephillin for the *hand ;* they (as well as the Tallith) are used during the morning prayers, but not on the Sabbaths and festivals,
though the Tallith is worn on these days also.—The Thephillin
themselves are *four* paragraphs from the Pentateuch, namely, Exod.
xiii. v. 1—10 ; 2d, Ibid. 11—16 ; 3d, Deut. vi. v. 4—9 ; 4th, Ibid.
xi. 13—21. In the Thephillin shel Yahd these paragraphs are
written upon *one* piece of parchment, and fixed in a small case
made of the same material; on one side of which is an opening,
through which a leathern thong of about two yards long is passed ;
on one end of which are a knot and loop of a peculiar form, through
which loop the other end of the thong is drawn, and the whole
Thephillin can thus be fixed upon the arm.

The Thephillin shel Roshe have the same paragraphs, but written upon *four* different pieces of parchment, and are fixed in the
order above mentioned, in a parchment case with four divisions. A
thong is fixed to the *Thephillin shel Roshe* in the like manner as to
those *shel Yahd ;* yet so that they may be worn round the head.
On one side of the case is stamped a *Sheen* with *three* heads : on the
other a *Sheen* with *four* heads.—The knot on the *shel Yahd* forms
a ׳ (Yod) the one on the *shel Roshe* a ר (Dahleth) and, as said, the
case of the latter is stamped with a ש (Sheen), these three letters
combined read שרי, an attribute of God synonymous with the English
Almighty.

The last kind of the commonly so called phylacteries is the מזוזה
(Mezoozah) and consists of the two paragraphs from the sixth and
eleventh chapters of Deuteronomy mentioned above, written upon
one piece of parchment, which is rolled up from the right to the left.
The word שרי together with three other words, (which, however,
stand higher up, by themselves,) is written upon the outside ; it is then

---

* See Instruction in the Mosaic Religion, pp. 115 and 116, where the
other regulation concerning the Thephillin can be found.—I have been thus
particular with the explanation of Tzitzith, &c. that any one may see their
whole intent, meaning, nature, and object, and thus judge for himself whether
there is any superstition connected therewith, or whether they are more correctly to be regarded as proper religious observances.

put in a reed, a tin, or other case, and fixed on the door post in every *proper* room, so that the name שדי (being visible through an aperture left in the case) may be seen by every one entering the apartment, and be thus ever reminded of the greatness and power of the *Almighty*.

"But what can be the meaning of all this?" This will easily be plain to us if we but read the passages cited above; we will there see that the Thephillin were ordered for a twofold reason: first, as a *monument* of our redemption from Egypt; and next, that the laws of our God may be continually before us. For we read in Exod. chap. xiii. v. 16: "And it shall be for a token upon thy hand, and a mark of remembrance (frontlets, Eng. vers.) between thine eyes, for by the strength of (his) hand has the Lord brought us out of Egypt."—And in Deut. chap. vi. v. 8, after having said, in the preceding verses, that the law of God should be always in our mouth, that we should converse about it in whatever place or situation we might be, Moses continues: "And thou shalt bind them as a sign upon thy hand, and they shall be as frontlets between thine eyes." The Mezoozah, also, is very plainly commanded in the ninth verse of the sixth chapter of Deuteronomy. The object of God in giving these ordinances was probably this: "I have forbidden you to raise yourselves monuments of sculptured stone or molten metal; but I will give you a *nobler* monument—my *law* shall be this monument; passages commemorative of your redemption shall be your *daily garment*; so that the recollection of the events connected with this redemption and the promulgation of the law shall never cease; they shall also be a sign of my perpetual power, of my constant providence, and of my unceasing watchfulness over you; fix, therefore, these chapters upon your doors and gates, that you may be always mindful, whenever you lay Thephillin and see the Mezoozah, that I, the all-powerful, who formerly released you from slavery, am yet able and willing to watch over you, protect you, and again redeem you—by whatever trouble you may be afflicted—when the time shall have arrived which I have appointed as the termination of the punishment you may have to endure for your transgressions against my will—and that I may again show you wonders, as I did in those days when you went out of Egypt."

13

CHAPTER XVII. '

THE FESTIVALS.

" Were the Hebrew festivals like those of the heathens, times of general licentiousness, and for this reason superstitious and injurious; or were they dedicated to the honour of God and the improvement of the people, by inciting them to virtue, and in consequence, reasonable, useful, and even necessary ?"

To answer this enquiry, we have but to consult the institutions of Moses themselves, to pronounce in favour of the usefulness of our festivals.—The first in order that presents itself, is the *Passover-feast* (פסח Paysach), or the annual celebration of the redemption from Egypt; it commences on the evening after the fourteenth, which, according to our mode of reckoning time, is the commencement of the fifteenth day of Nissan or Abib, the fifteenth day of this month being always the first full-moon-day after the spring equinox ; and all the subsequent holydays are (at present) regulated by the Passover.—I have said that this feast is the annual celebration of the Exodus ; we have thus again, in our institutions, a confirmation of the truth of the Mosaic *history*. For this reason. The Passover was instituted to celebrate a certain event, and the reason stated to those very persons, who ought to have known if the reason assigned by Moses was founded upon truth or not, i. e. they ought certainly to have known (for this is the reason given,) if they themselves *had been* slaves in Egypt *or not*. Suppose a man were to arrive in this or some other city, and tell the inhabitants thereof: " You must celebrate annually the victory which you gained over the enemy, who besieged your city for so many weeks," when, in point of fact, no such enemy had been seen, nor such a siege had taken place. What does every one think would be the fate of such an imposture ? Either the impostor would be laughed at, as a madman, or, if he should be attended to, it would argue the greatest ignorance and the most unaccountable credulity in those who chose to obey such an

impudent impostor.—But the Jews did keep the Passover in commemoration of their redemption; is there not now every reason to
believe that that event actually did take place?

But to return to the subject under discussion:—The feast was
annually ushered in by sacrificing, on the fourteenth day of Nissan,
the *passover-lamb*, in the same manner (with some slight exceptions) the first one had been prepared in Egypt.—The feast itself
was celebrated *seven** days, commencing with the fifteenth day.

---

* After the return of the Israelites from Babylon, a great number of the
brethren yet remained behind, and they regulated their months and festivals by
the messages they received from the great Sanhedrin at Jerusalem, where the
commencement of every month was ushered in by the chief judge's saying:
מקדש החדש " the month is sanctified," (meaning this day is the first of the
month,) after competent witnesses had been examined relative to their having
seen the new moon. (See Mishna of Roshe Hashanah.) At first telegraphs were
used by the Sanhedrin, to make the result known to all the captivity—as those
living out of Palestine were called;—but when, on a certain occasion, the
Samaritans counterfeited the signals, and deceived those at a distance, the Sanhedrin came to a resolution not to employ the signals any longer; and from
this time forward they sent out messengers, who travelled with the utmost possible expedition. Those living at a great distance from Jerusalem, could not
always be certified of the first day of the month before the holydays set in;
and they celebrated, therefore, for each day of holy convocation *two* days,
instead of *one* day, as originally commanded in the Pentateuch. For instance,
they reckoned the month of *Adar* at twenty-nine days, (as it is commonly, we
may say always,) and taking the thirtieth day as the first of Nissan, they
commenced *Paysach* on the fifteenth day from that date. But as they did
not *exactly* know if the Sanhedrin had commenced Nissan with the *thirtieth*
or the *thirty-first* of Adar, they continued to withhold from work also on the
sixteenth day after the twenty-ninth of Adar, so that they kept, at all events,
the first day of Paysach on the proper day, which would not have been the
case if they had only kept the fifteenth day after the 29th, when the first of the
month had not been until the 31st of Adar. Thus it originated, that they
celebrated eight instead of seven days of Passover, two instead of one of the
Pentecost and New Year, and the Tabernacles nine instead of eight days. The
Day of Atonement alone, on account of the inability of most persons to fast two
entire days, was celebrated on the thirty-ninth day after the first of Elul; for
this month was never known to have had more than twenty-nine days, but, as has
been said already, they were obliged to wait for the messengers of the Sanhedrin to be assured of this fact. After the calendar was fixed, and so organised
on scientific grounds, that those in Syria and the adjacent countries were no

The first day was a day of holy convocation, that is to say, no work was done except the preparing of food ; the law was read publicly, additional sacrifices were offered, and the whole *male* population of the Israelites was assembled to worship at the temple in Jerusalem. The seventh was also a day of rest ; and during the whole feast of the Passover unleavened bread was eaten, to remind the Israelites that their ancestors had been hurried out of Egypt in so great a haste, that they could not prepare their bread even in the customary manner.—On the second day of the Passover, being the sixteenth of Nissan, an omer-full of new barley was offered in the temple, with appropriate sacrifices and ceremonies; and from this day it was lawful to eat of the new fruit, and this day was considered the commencement of the harvest.

The time of rejoicing had now arrived, and hill and valley were covered with the ripening treasures of the husbandmen. This was the time of general activity throughout Palestine, and whilst the highminded daughters of Israel were superintending the household, the male population applied themselves to the labours of the field. The reaper's song was heard throughout our land, when they bound in sheaves the rich blessing of God which fell in rows before their sickles. The poor, the widow, the orphan, and the houseless stranger, were permitted to gather all that had fallen down accidentally, been forgotten, or left purposely for them. No one dared to dis-

---

longer obliged to wait for messengers from the Sanhedrin to fix the first day of the month on the proper day : the Israelites living out of Palestine continued, upon the recommendation of the *Beth-Din*, assembled in *Tham*, to observe the additional holydays ; not, however, thinking them commanded by Moses, but as commemorative of the state of the captives previous to that time. The *second* and *last* days are considered as mere prolongations of the preceding ones, and the same chapters are read for the conclusion of the reading of the law (מפטיר), as on the original days.—That the Sanhedrin had the right to recommend the observance of this custom, I cannot doubt, (see Deut. chap. xvii. and 1 Kings, chap. viii. v. 6.) and since the Israelites, in all their dispersions, have acted accordingly for seventeen hundred years, the custom has in a manner become law, and it would accordingly be wrong to abolish the custom of our ancestors, for the sole reason that some merchants sustain a trifling loss by the observance of *six* additional holydays in a whole year.

N. B. The narrative part of the above is drawn from the second chapter of Talmud Betzah.

turb them, but they shared, without being made to feel it, the blessings bestowed on their more opulent neighbours.

Fifty days from the fourteenth of Nissan had passed away, and again the streets of Jerusalem were filled with the gladsome shout of the men of Israel, as each company came with music, and the ox with gilded horns, bringing the first fruit of their delightful land to the temple of their God. For the sixth day of *Sivan* had arrived; and the Israelites therefore were assembled before the altar of their God, on the day on which the law, under which they so happily lived, had been proclaimed to their ancestors as they stood trembling at the foot of Sinai! O days of happiness, days of joy, you have indeed passed away, and Israel linger in a land not their own. No more in the vineyards on Israel's mountains are the daughters of Zion seen to dance, and the sons of Levi no longer chant the songs of praise on thy hill, Moriah! Woe to us, that we have sinned! woe to us, that in the land, where the glory of God once shone, the stranger lives forgetful of our God's power, and the Eternal's glory!

On the first day of the seventh month is the commencement of the civil year; the day, on which, as our wise men teach us, the Most High holds judgment over all the inhabitants of the earth, and apportions to each man his annual share of prosperity and woe. O dread day, when mortal man is to be judged by his Maker! what good deeds has he done to justify himself in judgment? can the sinful worm yet speak loudly then, when he contemplates the fearful distance between him and the HOLY ONE of Israel? Therefore did God command us to blow the cornet on that day—to let the *signal* trumpet be heard—to call up the latent energies of his people, to exhort them to a speedy and sincere repentance.—There is also another reason for the blowing of the cornet. In the eastern countries it is the custom to receive the king with music, particularly wind-instruments; we therefore blow the cornet to show, that we acknowledge the Creator, on the day on which the world was created, *our* King, amid the fervent prayer of the people and the sound of the trumpet.—The Day of Atonement at length approaches, and we go to the temple of God, and abstain from all earthly food and drink from evening to evening, and only live in the contemplation of God, his greatness, his kindness, and his mercy! and happy are we, if we come well prepared, well fortified in faith and firm reliance upon God's mercy—happy, if we have forgiven all our enemies sincerely and truly—happy, if our frail body alone separates us from the Deity! If we come thus before Mercy's throne—the purity and whiteness of our garments a true emblem of the purity and sacredness of our souls—if the voice of the שופר (cornet) has had its intended effect upon us—if the nine days of preparation have not been misspent : then may we be assured, that on that day all our sins will be forgiven, and that, cleansed from our iniquities, we shall stand pure and unspotted before the Eternal!

When the temple yet stood, the high-priest walked on that day into the holy of holies, whilst the cloud of incense filled the place, where the ark of the covenant was, and here he sprinkled on that day alone the blood of the sacrifices, and here he also prayed a short prayer for the welfare of the people. Before he killed his sacrifice and that of the people, he confessed his sins and the sins of the congregation, imposing at the same time his hands upon the heads of the animals, and when he pronounced the name of the Eternal, all the priests and people, who were standing by, fell upon their faces and exclaimed : " Praised be the name of the glory of his kingdom for ever and ever !"—But, no longer is our temple standing—no longer are the descendants of Aaron graced with the sacerdotal robes—and the holy of holies is no longer the dwelling place of the ark ! The fat of oxen is no more seen burning upon the altar—no longer are its sides sprinkled with the blood of the sin-offering—and the incense no more curls upwards under the hands of the Cohen ! Mayest Thou, O holy God, receive our prayers—the offering of the contrite heart—in the place of the offerings of beasts, and let our lips* pay for steers which, in days of yore, were led to thy temple in atonement for our sins !

The year had terminated, and the sun had entered *Libra*, and thus produced the autumnal equinox ; the grapes hung in rich clusters along the vines, and the golden fruit glistened among the dark foliage of the fruit trees. Here and there autumn had already

* This is a quotation from Isaiah, and plainly means, that since the captive Israelites can no longer offer up sacrifices, which could only be done at the place chosen by God; the prayer which we offer up, the words of our lips, may be as acceptable to God as the steers once burnt upon the altar.

changed the hue of the leaves, and some lay scattered under the trees, which they had graced during the spring and summer. Every husbandman was busied with gathering in the bounteous blessings of his God, to provide himself sustenance for the coming winter. The heart of man was raised high, when he contemplated the manifold blessings showered upon him, though unworthy he might be. Gratitude would naturally then fill his bosom, and he would feel more inclined to obey the will of God, because of his great kindness to him.—In this time of general joy, on the fifteenth day of the seventh month, were we commanded to celebrate the feast of Succoth or Tabernacles. On the Day of Atonement our sins had been forgiven, and immediately after we were commanded to build *tabernacles* סכות for our residence during the first seven days of the feast. Though the chill of autumn had already arrived, yet was it our duty to prove ourselves worthy of having our sins forgiven to us, by placing entire confidence in God, and obeying his will to the letter, though it might be a little inconvenient to our bodily ease, and we were obliged to dwell in booths for seven days in the *chilly* time of year, to commemorate that He caused our ancestors to dwell in booths, when He brought them out of Egypt.—The dwelling in tabernacles was therefore a symbol of our placing ourselves under the shadow of God's protection, and withdrawing from the cares and enjoyments of life.—This feast was also a time for all the *men* of Israel to meet at the city God had chosen for his residence, and the first and eighth days were, like the Passover and Pentecost, days of holy convocation and suspension of labour. (All the ceremonies, except the sacrifices, relatives to the holydays are yet observed by us at the present time, as commanded by Moses.)

On the first day of the feast of Tabernacles we were to take the fruit of the citron-tree, the palm-branch, the myrtle and the willow. These four productions of the vegetable kingdom were in old times, and are even now, used in the following manner: the palm, the myrtle, and the willow, being united in one bunch, are taken in the right hand, and the citron in the left, and thus held, they are waved three times each towards the east, west, north, and south, upwards and downwards, in certain parts of the prayers. " But what is the meaning of this?"—Let us consider the shape and formation of these various products, and we shall find them symbolical of ourselves.—

The palm branch is tall and erect, and its leaves are branching out from it on both sides; it is like the stature of man erect, it is like his back-bone, from which the ribs branch out on either side; the oval myrtle leaf is like the eye of man—and the willow like his lips compressed—the citron is pointed like the man's heart; all these are taken for the worship of God, and thus shall our body, our eyes, our lips, and our heart all be united in the worship of God.

Or perhaps they may be symbolical of the nation of the Israelites. The citron is a fragrant fruit and delightful to the taste; the palm bears fine fruit, but has no fragrance; the myrtle has fragrance, but a bitter taste; and at last, the willow has neither taste nor fragrance. Thus are amongst Israel, men of good learning and good works—men of good works without learning; men of learning without good deeds; and at last, others who have neither learning nor virtue. But although one is superior to the other in virtue and learning, yet do we find that God commanded us to join the citron, the palm, the myrtle, and the willow, thus showing, that however exalted we may be, though our brother be ignorant and sinful, yet shall we not cast him off; but unite him with us in the bonds of love, and induce him to worship, no less than we do, our common Creator.—We wave the four kinds mentioned to all the four corners of the compass, towards heaven and downwards to the earth, to indicate that we acknowledge God, " who formed the corners of the world, made the heavens, the earth, and all that is in them;" we wave the palm-branch* in our prayers, to thank God for his bounty with the plants he has given us for our use and sustenance; we hold up the palm-branch and pray Him to continue his kindness to us, and to save† us from evil, and to give us prosperity in all our doings!

When we have dwelt seven days in the tabernacles, when on the seventh we have laid by the palm, the myrtle, the willow, and the citron, when we have said the last grace in the Succah (tabernacle): we are yet to celebrate another day more, a closing day of festiviy to

---

* For the sake of brevity, and on account of the size of the palm-branch above the others, the expression has become common amongst us: to say grace over the לולב (Loolab, the palm-branch), when in fact the citron, the myrtle, and the willow, are also understood.

† אנא ה' הושיעה נא אנא ה' הצליחה נא : Psalm 118, v. 25.—This psalm is read during the feast of Succoth.

the honour of God. Then we pray for the blessing of timely and abundant rain, and a year of plenty, of cheerfulness, and of peace; that we may all have as much as we stand in need of, without our being obliged to beg for our bread from a brother or a stranger, but receive it immediately from the Supporter of all!

Some of our wise men have compared our festivals to the three stages of the human life. Passover is our youth, when all before us is yet happy expectation, and when we enter the rugged path of life with a buoyant heart and smiling countenance; we only look at the surface of things, and seeing amid the *fine flowers* and *verdant hills* no obstacle to our onward march in virtue and worldly prosperity, we dream not of disappointments we may have to encounter, and of trials that await us.—Next comes the Pentecost, the middle age of man, when we have been already obliged to *work under a hot sun;* we have perhaps been often overcome by faintness in our daily toil, we have heard the thunder roll over our heads, and seen the lightning rend the green forest trees—to drop the figurative language, we have, as we grow older, been forced to undergo many fatigues and disappointments to procure an honest livelihood; we have seen our best hopes foiled, and we have discovered how firmly we have been forced to withstand that temptation, which has drawn so many others around us from the path of virtue.—At last comes the feast of Tabernacles, when the autumn begins to scatter the *yellow leaves* round the tree; the time when age is already encroaching upon our strength of body and vigour of mind; when our hairs begin to grow white, and we are at last thinking of enjoying the fruit of our labour through a life mixed with sorrow and gladness—and we begin to look forward to the winter, to the grave, which must at length receive us, and which, when it closes over us, hides all our cares, all our earthly joys—and leaves the soul free to enjoy that blessing, to deserve which she has so nobly acted here below, in withstanding sin, subduing the passions, and dispensing good to all around us! O happy old age!—when with such thoughts and feelings we see death approach; and we need not then fear *the temporary dissolution,* which must for ever join us to our Father in heaven, in bliss, joy, and everlasting peace!

CHAPTER XVIII.

THE SACRIFICES.

It will be easily discovered in reading the preceding chapter, that the festivals, and the ceremonies attending them, are not founded upon superstitious usages ; but that they are intended to preserve to the latest posterity the memory of *those events*, which are recorded as the cause of their being instituted. Thus was the Passover instituted to celebrate annually our redemption from Egypt ; the Pentecost (שבועות Shahboongoth), the promulgation of the law from Sinai, and the Tabernacle-feast, that for forty years our almighty Redeemer caused our ancestors to live in tents by Him provided, and that He, through all this time, held his protecting arm over them, and provided for all their wants, and supplied them with the necessaries of life. The first day of the seventh month is, as has been mentioned above, the New-year's-day, the day on which all the world is judged ; and the tenth of the same month is the Day of Atonement, on which sins sincerely repented, faults positively amended, and injuries done to our neighbours atoned for by full reparation having been made them, will be forgiven by God to those who seek his forgiveness.

But some may say again : " We will admit that the festivals can be construed to mean very pretty things ; but what have you Jews to say in favour of the sacrifices ? Can any man seriously believe that the blood of an animal can operate as a forgiveness for his sins —or rather, can it be taken, according to your opinion, as a full expiation for *offences* committed ?"

To answer this query properly we will now proceed to investigate, according to the truths laid down in the Pentateuch and the prophets, the *view* of the offerings, and *how* and *when* they were required.—First : " Did the Jews believe that they could be forgiven when they sinned wilfully, at the same time promising a sacrifice in atonement of this sin ? And : Granted the Mosaic law did not countenance such a practice, had not the Jews degenerated so much at the commencement of the reign of the Emperor Tiberius, as to deem such unhallowed conduct justifiable?"

We must, unhesitatingly, answer both questions in the negative; for the Mosaic law did *not* teach that a man *might* sin, and bring an ox as an atonement; nor did the Rabbins and Pharisees, at the time of Tiberius, teach any thing like it, but just the contrary. And although it has often been asserted, that at various times, if not throughout their whole existence, the Jews looked upon the blood of animals as the only thing requisite to obtain atonement for any sin committed : the contrary will be apparent, if any man will but candidly examine the passages from our writings I am going to adduce in support of this assertion.

In the book of Leviticus we find no where that wilful sins could be expiated by sacrifices alone; on the contrary, we read in Numb. chap. xxxv. that no expiation could be made by a murderer, except with his life; analogous crimes were punished without accepting bail or mainprize (Levit. chap. xxiv. v. 21.); and (ibid. chap. xxvii. v. 29.) we find that no man *condemned for a crime** (not *devoted* as incorrectly rendered in the Eng. vers.) *could be redeemed*, but was absolutely *to die.*—What, then, was the object of the sacrifices? how were they brought? and on what occasions?

* The Hebrew word which I, according to the interpretation of our Rabbins, have translated as above, is חרם‎. The same word is found in Exod. chap. xxii. v. 19. זבח לאלהים יחרם‎, &c. which must be translated : " He, who sacrifices to any other deity save the Eternal alone, shall be *condemned* to die," and cannot possibly be rendered by *devoted* with the signification it apparently has in the English version of the twenty-seventh of Leviticus. The intention and meaning of this passage is this : in the commencement of the chapter on *valuations* it appears that every person of every age, of both sexes, has his *particular and fixed price*, if any one should destine the value of such persons for the service of God. At the end of this chapter, therefore, we are told by our legislator, that to give the value of a *criminal* in the treasury of the temple, would be of no avail to save his life, for that it was forfeited notwithstanding such a price. " And was such an exception necessary to be made?" Certainly, for many nations used to take *pay* from a murderer even, to save his life; and amongst the Germans the price for murder was *less* than that for horsestealing. It was, therefore, necessary that God should prohibit, in the most explicit terms, any such demoralising practice amongst that people chosen by Him as his peculiar treasure.

In studying the book of Leviticus we shall discover that sacrifices were *national* and *individual*. The national sacrifices,—i. e.
those for the whole congregation—were either the daily burnt-offerings תמידים, the additional sacrifices מוספים for the Sabbaths and
festivals, or *sin-offerings* חטאות, when the whole congregation had
acted contrary to a principle of the law ; as, for instance, if the Sanhedrin had given a wrong decision upon a question of law referred
to them, and all the Israelites had acted according to this erroneous
decision, but contrary to the will of God, as laid down in the law.
(Lev. iv.)   The אנשי מעמד spoken of above in chap. xiv. attended
at these sacrifices, as the representatives of the people, except at the
national sin-offering, where the Elders, who were the cause of the
sin, themselves attended and imposed their hands upon the head of
the victim ; and on the Day of Atonement the high priest was
obliged to do the same with the goat destined as the offering for the
whole people. (See. Lev. chap. iv. v. 15. and ibid. xvi. v. 21.)

Private or individual sacrifices were either brought when a man
had, through ignorance, offended against one of the principal negative precepts, the offering in this case was called חטאת *sin-offering ;*
or when he had wronged his fellow man, or committed one of the
other sins enumerated in Leviticus, for which a *trespass-offering*
אשם was to be sacrificed ; or when he had escaped an imminent
danger, for which a תורה i. e. *thanksgiving-offering*, was brought ;
or at last offerings which a man voluntarily obliged himself to bring,
which were of two kinds, שלמים peace and עלה burnt-offerings,
though the latter were frequently offered as an atonement for *evil
thoughts*, when a man had not accomplished the intended sin or trespass.   It is useless to explain the various kinds of sacrifices, which
were either of horned cattle, sheep, goats, birds, or fine flour, and
in one instance barley meal, (Numb. chap. v. v. 15.), as these can
easily be found out by turning to the law book itself; I shall therefore proceed at once to explain the reasons and purpose of the sacrifices.

God is just and merciful to all his creatures, for He maintains all
through his infinite kindness, and has, as we have seen, given them
a law, which, if obeyed, must lead a man to happiness.   To obey,
therefore, the will of God, is nothing more than to show our gratitude to Him by following the rules which He has marked out for

our happiness, and, in consequence, we shall be made happy, if we are, in every sense of the word, religious.—To disobey the word of God is *ingratitude*, and we therefore, by our own actions, discard happiness and choose misery and punishment. If a man sins wilfully he can blame only himself for misery he may draw upon himself by his acts ; and ' if these offences be committed against the peace of society, he will be punished by those entrusted with the management of public affairs, and who are, therefore, guardians for the time being, of the public welfare—that is, the happiness and peace of society.—But if he should transgress, not the laws of *men*, but the statutes of *God*, should he not in this case *also* deserve punishment? Shall the laws of God be transgressed with impunity, when those of men must be obeyed to the letter? Certainly not, and whatever may be said about the cruelty it would appear in the Deity to punish man hereafter for sins committed in this life ; yet will every thinking man see, upon a moment's reflection, that God cannot be blamed for that, which man by his own wickedness and wilful folly draws upon himself, when he had the power to avoid the evil.—But for *wrong* actions done unknowingly or in ignorance man cannot, with any degree of justice, be punishable to an equal extent with sins committed wilfully. Yet a wrong action, a sin, has been committed, and the *harmony* of right has been disturbed ; and then man should always be watchful, always consider the bearings of all he engages in, and should, moreover, make himself acquainted with his duty ; he ought, therefore, to make atonement for his sins, he ought to show that he is sorry for having offended his God, who maintains him and watches over him. He was for this reason obliged to bring a sin-offering to the temple door, lay his hand upon its head, and kill it, or have it killed, as a sin-offering. (Lev. chap. iv. v. 33.) The meaning of this is : that the offerer, who wished to be forgiven, was to ask of God the forgiveness of his transgression, whilst imposing his hands upon the head of the victim, and then have this animal killed, with a view that it was intended for this particular occasion. No foreign thoughts were to obtrude during the sacrifice ; but the sinner's attention was to be riveted to the ceremony ; and he was to consider, that as he himself had laid his hands upon the head of the beast, thus had he himself deserved the imposition of hands by the witnesses of his crime, previous to execution, (Ibid. chap. xxiv. v. 14.) ; as the blood of the beast was flowing, thus had he deserved to be dealt with, and so on at every stage and ceremony during the sacrifice. If a man truly penitent, thus prepared and so doing, came before the altar of God, can it be doubted that the sacrifice was obliged to work a reformation in him? And again, can any man gainsay that he ought to have been forgiven, if he was sincerely sorry for what had past, and acted for the future as he had determined during the moment of *holy* enthusiasm?

As has been said above, if a man has sinned it is absolutely necessary that he should make an atonement of some sort or other. If he commits theft or otherwise wrongs another person, it is but just that he should make restitution to the full extent of the injury he has done. But though he thus satisfy his neighbour, yet he has also offended his God, for every breach of duty against the peace of society is an offence against the law of our God, whose object, in promulgating it, was the happiness of mankind, as has been already sufficiently established in the foregoing.—Any man, therefore, who had been guilty of such a sin, as just mentioned, was to bring a *trespass-offering* in expiation, and its treatment was in almost every respect similar to that of the sin-offering.

When the traveller in the pathless desert had felt the keen blast of the poisonous Simoom, when he had expected to perish amidst the endless sand, for want of water, for lack of food: it was his duty, after he had reached the residence of men, to return, publicly, thanks to his God, and to bring to his altar the תורה (Todah) the *offering of thanksgiving*.—When amidst the storm of the battle-field he had sunk overpowered by fatigue, and been led away captive, and had long lingered in hopeless captivity in the land of his enemies: he was also to testify his gratitude when he had returned to the bosom of his family.—When a man had been thrown upon the bed of sickness, all his bones had ached, when he loathed food and a speedy death had been impending over him: when he recovered he was bound to proclaim, before all, the mercy of his Deliverer from death, and with his thanks bring the offering as ordained.—When the seafaring man had encountered a furious storm, while the waves dashed the frail bark to and fro, when the master had exhausted all his skill in vain, and expected, in mute despair, the wreck of his ship: when then God's mercy had been manifested to him, and the storm abated, and the sea calmed, and he had been permitted to enter the port of his destination in safety—he was obliged to praise God before the assemblage of people, and to repair to the altar with the sacrifice.*

We have thus a brief view of the object of this sacrifice; but who is bold enough to call it superstitious, when we must admit, even without the aid of revelation, that we are bound by mere common gratitude, when we have escaped from danger, to return thanks to Him who is the disposer of our fate; and how can our gratitude to Him be better shown, than if, by a public acknowledgment of his mercy, we induce others, who may have strayed from his ways, to love, to fear, and to adore Him?

When, at last, a man saw himself blessed and all around him cheerful, he brought a peace-offering, of which all his friends were usually invited to partake. This sacrifice, the firstlings and the annual tithe of the increase of the flocks, were permitted to be eaten for the space of two days and one night, but all the other sacrifices, those I mean, which were eaten either by the priests or the offerers, were not allowed to be eaten after midnight of the first day, and whatever was left after this time, was to be burnt. (See various passages of Leviticus relating to the sacrifices.) It is well known, that it was unlawful for any Israelite to sacrifice out of the precincts of the temple, and the tendency therefore of the frequent offerings was to bring the people often to the house of God, where an interchange of opinions and acts of friendship could and did take place. And the greater the individual happiness of the Israelites was, the greater must have been the benefit arising from those meetings, for when a man is happy himself, and actuated by motives of true religion, he will always be glad to rejoice when others are happy, and he will try to do all in his power to promote general satisfaction around him.

Though the private burnt and peace-offerings are spoken of in the law, yet were we never commanded to bring such offerings; for in this, as in other acts of virtue, the Almighty never intended to force our inclinations, but left it altogether to our own free choice to bring

---

* These four cases are described in the 107th psalm, with the usual energy of the sacred poets; and all those desirous of being kindled by an ardent devotion to the great and merciful Supreme, may be safely referred to this psalm, as they must rise from its perusal with a mind filled with a holy reverence of God's majesty.

such sacrifices or not.   He even tells us (Deut. chap. xxiii. v. 23)
that we should commit no sin, if we made no vows at all ; but, on the
other hand, He most strenuously exhorts us to keep strictly to our
vows, for their violation is highly offensive to Him.

We have thus seen briefly exhibited the nature of the sacrifices;
but it may be asked :   " Did not the Jews think themselves absolved
from sin by *the mere sacrifice of beasts* and *a pretended* reformation?"

That such opinion may have taken root amongst our ancestors, I
cannot *positively* disprove, though it is highly improbable ; but this
I can say with the utmost confidence, that if they ever thought so, it
was contrary to what they had ever been taught by the prophets.—
The first *lesson* on this subject we find in 1 Samuel chap. xv. v. 22.
Samuel had orered Shahool (Saul) to go and slay all the Amalekites
and to suffer not even a beast to live. Shahool did go and conquered
the Amalekites, but took the best of the cattle along with him ; and
when the prophet enquired of him at their meeting after his return,
" about the voice of the sheep he heard," he answered him frankly,
that " they (the sheep) had been brought from the enemies' country,
and that they were intended for sacrifices." Hereupon Samuel said,
and I beg every Jew and every stranger to our faith to consider
with attention his words : " Does the Eternal find as much pleasure
in burnt-offerings and sacrifices as in hearkening to the voice of the
Eternal?   Behold, to hearken, is better than a fine sacrifice, and to
obey better than the fat of rams !   For disobedience is equal to the
sin of witchcraft, and refusing to comply is like idolatry and image-
worship." This speech of Samuel is too plain to be misunderstood,
for he is here correcting an error into which Saul had fallen, and of
course it must be conceded, that sacrifices were *not* according to the
Mosaic law and the opinion of the good amongst the Israelites the
only thing necessary for the absolution of sins.—This position is incontrovertible ; but since the truth of the prophets has been so
frequently assailed, since their motives have been so often misrepre-
sented, since their doctrines are so little understood : I shall give
concurrent evidence from three others, according to our belief, inspired writers, namely, Ahsaph, Isaiah, and Jeremiah, in accordance
with Samuel's address, and thus force even the most obdurate to admit, that the assertion in the commencement of this chapter is
correct.

First, as to Asaph; the opinion of the holy bard is found in Psalm l. v. 7, &c., where he speaks in the person of the Deity : " Hear me, my people, whilst I speak, Israel! whilst I testify against thee : I AM GOD, THY GOD ! Not for thy sacrifices will I reprove thee, nor need thy burnt-offerings be continually before me. I will not an ox from thy house, nor a ram from thy enclosures; for mine are all the beasts of the field, the cattle on the mountains by thousands; I know all the birds of the mountains, and all that moveth upon the field is with me. When I hunger, I need not tell thee, for mine is the universe and all that is in it.—Shall I eat the flesh of the fattened sheep? and drink the blood of the rams? Offer up thy thanks unto God, and then pay the Most High thy vows. And call on me in the day of affliction, and I will help thee out—thus only thou honourest me !"* Here the Psalmist plainly tells us, that not sacrifices alone are agreeable to God, for " when He hungers He need not tell us, for all the world is his ;" but his chief delight (if I may so express myself) is, that we *show* ourselves grateful for his kindness by our actions, and honour Him by word and thought !

Isaiah (chap. i. v. 11,) exclaims in the bitterness of his heart : " To what use serves me the great quantity of your sacrifices, says the Eternal, I am tired of the burnt-offerings of rams, and the fat of fattened sheep ; I no longer desire the blood of oxen, of sheep, and of goats. And when you come to appear before me—who asked it of your hands to tread (the floor of) my courts? Bring no longer your insincere† meal-offerings, for it is incense of abomination to me," &c.

Again, chap. lxvi. v. 3, he says : " He who kills an ox, slays a man ; he who sacrifices a lamb, breaks the neck of a dog ; he who brings a meal-offering, sacrifices a swine ; he who burns incense, bringeth as it were stolen property as a present ; they also chose their own ways, and their soul delighted in their abominations."

* This translation is chiefly according to Yarchi's commentary upon the fiftieth psalm, which see.

† The Hebrew words שוא מנחת are rendered " vain oblation," which does not, according to my opinion, express the prophet's meaning ; for he intended not to say, that the *oblations in general* were *vain*, but that they were disagreeable to God on account of the wickedness of the people at that time ; I have therefore thought proper to translate these words " insincere meal-offerings."

15

In the 57th chapter, Isaiah explains what kind of fasting *can* be agreeable to God, from all which it appears, that no *outward* show *can*, according to the opinion of Isaiah, tend to operate as an expiation for sins.

Jeremiah confirms the assertion of Samuel, Asaph, and Isaiah, in the following words : " For I did not say to your fathers, nor did I command them, on the day when I carried them out of Egypt, any thing about burnt-offerings or sacrifices. But this matter commanded I them, as follows : " Hearken to my voice, and I will be your God, and you shall be my people, and you shall go in all the ways which I will command you, that good may be done to you." (Jeremiah vii. v. 22 and 23).

There are other passages in the Bible to prove that the Jews did not think slaying an animal sufficient for an atonement if not accompanied with sincere repentance, and amelioration of the former course of life of the sinner, if the offence was against God alone, or reparation of the injury done to man—before a sacrifice could be supposed to be acceptable to the Deity.

Instead now of the Jewish sacrifices being a superstitious rite, like those of the Romans, Greeks, and other nations, they were on the contrary intended to draw forth the finest feelings which grace human nature : in the first place, love and gratitude to God ; secondly, restitution of property, unlawfully obtained from our fellow-men ; and lastly, they were eminently useful to make ourselves better men, and more fitted to receive the blessings of the Most High, whose forgiveness we always implored by the act of sacrificing.—Another noble feature does this law of sacrifices present to our view. After our legislator had detailed in the first chapter of Leviticus the regulations to be observed at the sacrifice of an ox, of sheep, and goats, and of pigeons : he next laid down, by the order of the Almighty, the rules for the sacrifice of a handful of meal, the *offering of the poor*. Here we find also many regulations for, and a description of the various modes in which the poor man could bring his humble offering ; thus showing, that the poor man's pittance will be no less acceptable to the Father of all, than the rich man's magnificent present ; as we are also taught by our Rabbins : " No less he who gives little, than he who gives much, will be acceptable, provided he steadily direct his heart and thoughts to the honour of Heaven."

Some *canting* heathen may perhaps whine about the cruelty of our priests in sacrificing *innocent* animals, and refer with exultation to the Brahmins, who never even eat meat. But this objection, if it be really urged, is really too nonsensical almost to deserve the least notice; since, however, I wish to proceed step by step, I shall endeavour to break its force by a few words. Well then, philosophers, if you yourselves will abstain from animal food altogether, I would be compelled to admit this your argument of some weight; but it is hardly probable that you are resolved to sacrifice this much to your principles of universal benevolence, for all of you are too fond of what good things this life affords to act so; but even if you did, that could be no reason why *we* should abstain from that which our law allows us. All the brute, vegetable, and mineral creation was made subservient to man: is not this true?—To proceed: in the first ages of the world, namely, before the flood, animal food was not allowed to man, and it was only first permitted to Noah. (Genesis ix.) Since then animals may be slaughtered for our own use, could we make a nobler use of this permission, than to dedicate them to the service of our Maker?—" But the Brahmins?"—But let me ask *you*, do they not burn widows alive upon the funeral piles of their husbands? Do they not sacrifice men to their idols? Is not in fact their religion, if religion it be, more like brutality than wisdom?—I may therefore freely assert, that the objection on that score against the sacrifices is of no force.

We must now investigate the last part of the introductory question, namely: "Had not the Jews degenerated at the commencement of the reign of Tiberius, so much as to think that sacrifices were alone an atonement for all sins?"

It is well known that the Rabbins, or the Scribes and Pharisees so often mentioned in the gospels, were apparently very pious men, for even the gospels admit this; neither can it be denied that they stood always very high in the estimation of their brethren. Can it be possible, I ask, that they should have obtained and preserved such immense influence from the days of Ezra to the present hour, if their interpretation of the law had been contrary to the generally received opinion? It must, therefore, be admitted, even if there were no positive argument of the fact, that the Jews, in the time of Tiberius, had the same opinion concerning the sacrifices, which they were taught to entertain by Jeremiah and his predecessors; and in consequence, that the Scribes and Pharisees did not believe that wilful sins could be atoned for by offering sacrifices, or by any other means save suffering the punishment decreed for the offences committed.—But that this *was* their opinion we are enabled to prove by positive argument; for we read in *Yomah*, Payreck viii. Mishna 8 : " *A sin-offering and a trespass-offering with repentance* will operate as an atonement."—Mishna 9 : " He who says, ' I will sin and repent, I will sin and repent,' will never have it in his power to repent. He who says, ' I will sin, and the Day of Atonement shall be my expiation,' will not be forgiven on the Day of Atonement. Sins between God and man will be forgiven on the Day of Atonement, but *not* those between man and man, till the offender has made reparation to the other."

This proves most clearly that at no time of our national existence was it considered pardonable to commit sins with a view of obtaining forgiveness by sacrifices or any other method; for it was always well understood, that to obey the word of God is the greatest virtue, and disregarding his law the greatest vice. It must, therefore, be admitted, that *all* the *expiatory* offerings were instituted for sins committed unconsciously or without premeditation—or without having known the action to be sinful. Trespass-offerings, as we have seen, could only then be acceptable when the wronged party had been satisfied; and the other offerings were either brought to return thanks in public, when a man had escaped from danger, or to testify his gratitude for benefits received from the Deity; and the national sacrifices were brought in the name of all Israel, either as atonement for sins or as an acknowledgment of national gratitude.—All this was when our temple yet stood,—the temple called by God's name;—but now our altar lies prostrate, our glorious temple exists no longer—and we wander about without priest, without sacrifice, without incense—and nought is left us but the words of our mouth in our prayers, and the study of the law, as a substitute for the sacrifices once offered up before God's temple. We hope, however, that He will receive our prayers graciously, and look down upon our desolate condition—upon the ruined towers of Jerusalem—upon the walls of the temple blackened by the fire of the enemy—and have mercy upon the dispersed and despised remnant of Israel, who have for so many centuries suffered the just burden of his wrath, and the weight of his chastisement. May He then speedily gather us from all the countries of the earth, reinstate us in our land, restore Zion, and cause again the halls of the temple to re-echo with our songs of thanksgiving to his holy name, and praise to Him, for his unbounded mercy, which endureth for ever. Amen!

CHAPTER XIX.

THE FORBIDDEN MEATS.

If we have heretofore seen our legislator careful for the glory of God and the well-being of society at large, we shall now see him giving and enforcing laws, the observance of which will give every individual of the community bodily health, and greatly tend to his self-preservation; and it is a fact not to be denied, that, in proportion to our numbre, there are more old persons amongst us than amongst any other people.

In whatever light the prohibition of unclean animals, the blood and fat of those even, the meat of which is not forbidden, is considered, it must be evident that the abstaining from these prohibited things will preserve our body free from certain diseases, which are many times engendered by the immoderate, nay often by a very *moderate* use of them. It is on all hands admitted that the eating of swine's flesh will occasion leprosy in the country which our ancestors inhabited; and I am not very sure but that its use, even in colder climates, is any thing but wholesome; but I must leave this point to be settled by physicians, who are, if I mistake not, yet uncertain how to decide.—The eating of blood is *no doubt* very injurious, and one of the eastern emperors, I think one of the Leos, issued a decree prohibiting it in his dominions, and went so far as to endeavour to *prove* its pernicious effect, by writing himself a book

on the subject, or having one written under his own superintendence.—Moses* also prohibited shell-fish, snakes, amphibious animals in general; creeping things of all kinds, and those fishes which
have not fins *and* scales; nay many quadrupeds and all birds of
prey were also interdicted by God through him; and he says:
" That it is God's intention, that we should be a *holy* people, and
that the *eating of forbidden food would make us unclean, and of
course our life would not be holy, if we pollute ourselves by what is
prohibited.*" If it be granted even that the eating of the flesh of
the swine is not unwholesome in countries where the climate is cold,
(which is, however, by no means conceded,) we have no right to
permit ourselves to eat the same; for our law does not lay down its
unwholesomeness as a reason, but gives it as the will of God, that
we should abstain from it; and since no other injurious effect is
mentioned, save that forbidden things will contaminate us, what
right have we to suppose the prohibitions on this subject repealed?
—" because we are no longer in Palestine;"—but, should not the
use of forbidden things make us as much unclean here, as in Palestine or the deserts of Arabia?

But if we even waive altogether the unwholesomeness of forbidden
animals as a reason for their being interdicted, which, as said already, can hardly have been the sole motive for the enactment
under discussion: we can discover a cause perfectly consonant with
the idea we entertain of the goodness of the Deity, *in the object*
which He always had in giving his precepts—which is, the *moral
perfection of ourselves.* He wanted to train us up in obedience and
submission to his will, and gave us therefore various enactments,
which tend to call for a vigilance over our inclinations, and demand
a constant surveillance over our conduct. If, then, some actions
are at times not forbidden, and even praiseworthy, there may be circumstances when they may be pernicious, and to be avoided. In
truth, we will discover, that almost for every act permitted, something else is prohibited, and thus the whole system of clean and
unclean, of permissions and interdictions, may be referred to the

---

* The reader will please to observe that whenever the terms our legislator
enacted, Moses commanded, and others of like tenor are employed, they mean
nothing else than that *God* commanded *through* our legislator or Moses.

grand ulterior reason of the descent on Sinai, to raise up a holy people and a kingdom of priests.—As a further illustration of this
principle, the reader will please to reflect on the following examples.—One of the chief subjects in the law, and concerning which
we have many regulations, is the intercourse between the sexes; it
is sin, a breach of moral duty to seduce any female; but it is *not*
wrong to persuade a woman to marry us, *and thus* this connection,
which in the one instance is *sinful*, becomes in the other *lawful*, nay
even praiseworthy and necessary. But we are not permitted to marry
every female; for by our law (see several passages in Leviticus and
other places) the wife of another man is prohibited, as are also certain other persons who are connected with us either by the ties of
relationship, as sisters, daughters, aunts, and some others; or those
who are connected with us through marriage either to ourselves or
to near relatives, as our wife's mother or sisters, our father's wife,
and others mentioned in Leviticus; nay at certain periods our own
wives are prohibited. And so heinous were such illegal marriages
considered by God, that He in most cases made them punishable
with death, both to the man and the woman! It will readily be confessed, that the permission of such acts would be ruinous to the
peace of families, if not of whole societies, and that they have been
so, even to the latter, can be easily demonstrated by the destruction
of the greater part of the tribe of Benjamin, as related in the book of
Judges, and by the demolition of Troy. It is unnecessary to search for
other examples, for these two are enough already to prove my assertion.—There is yet, however, another restriction laid upon our
inclinations in this respect, namely that we are not to marry an un-
married woman, though unconnected with us, if she *does not belong
to the descendants of Israel*, unless she take *previously*, from *no love
to the man*, but *sincere affection to our religion*, the yoke of this religion *freely* and *voluntarily* upon herself. The same is the case
with a *Jewish female*, for she has no right to marry any man who
is not called by the name of Israel. (See Deut. vii. and Ezra, and
Malachi.)

The drinking of wine, in general, was not interdicted; but the
priests, when they were about to commence the service in the temple, and the judges, before they entered upon the hearing of any

case, were forbidden to taste wine or other spirituous liquors. (See Leviticus x.)

It is not unlawful to wear garments of linen and woollen, when these two materials are unmixed; but it is prohibited to wear any garment made of linen and woollen mixed together.

A murderer after he had been tried and found guilty, was to be executed, or in case he should have made his escape, the nearest relative of the murdered (the avenger of the blood) was permitted to remove the monster out of the world. It was nevertheless strictly forbidden to touch the murderer, although wilful murder was punishable with death only, before he had been tried by his peers,* (see Numbers xxxv. v. 12,) no matter how aggravated or enormous his guilt might have been.

We have thus seen that our religion is intended to bridle our passions and restrain our desires; and we may therefore assign this as a reason, and perhaps as the only probable reason, that certain kinds of animal food were interdicted. God allowed us a great number of birds, an immense number of fishes, four kinds of winged insects, and ten kinds of four-footed animals, besides all wholesome vegetables. He has therefore left us enough for our support, and restricted us at the same time from the other quadrupeds, birds, fishes, and insects, to bridle our desires; and we are therefore to abstain from these things, because it is the will of God. If we then disregard this precept, and transgress, if we say, " what difference can it make to God, if I eat the meat of an ox or a swine," we offend against his will, we pollute ourselves, by what goes into the mouth, and can consequently lay no longer any claim to holiness; for the term " holiness," applied to mortals, means only, a framing of our desires by the will of God, by that rule which He has promulgated as the standard of right; the subduing of our passions, because He desires it; and lastly, by doing as much good to all mankind as lays within our power. Does not then the strict observance of our law demand this small sacrifice at our hands? Have we not enough to eat without

* I have introduced this modern word in this place, because the whole nation of the Israelites were equals, and no one had a superior claim to honour above the other, except in so far only, as he was the better and more useful man; of course there could be no *aristocracy*, as long as the Israelites adhered strictly to the Mosaic code.

touching forbidden things? Let me beseech my fellow-believers, not to deceive themselves by saying, "there is no sin in eating of aught that lives;" on the contrary, there is sin and contamination too.—Thus God tells us—and is his assertion not to be regarded more than the dreams of pretended prophets or the sneers of unbelieving enemies of our faith? Let the Israelites, if they love their religion, not be deterred by the taunts of one sect or the sneers of the other, and let them only persevere and conform in this important particular to our law, and when asked for the reason of their abstinence let them refer to the Pentateuch, and say : "Here is our warrant."

Not alone in regard to unwholesome food, but also in other respects, has our law been careful of our personal ease and safety.— Although no evil can betide us without God's sufferance, we yet find that he commanded us (Deut. chap. xxii.) : "To make a railing round the roof of the house, that no one might fall therefrom." It is no doubt well known, that the houses in Palestine were flat-roofed, and that people frequently went up there, particularly in summer evenings, and they often spread even fruit upon them to dry, nor was it very uncommon for several to meet in the *Aliyah* for discussion or prayer.* To prevent accidents therefore, which might otherwise have easily occurred, the above commandment was given. There are many similar ordinances in the Bible, but it is needless to transcribe them, as one example will suffice to prove the extreme care our law takes of the welfare of every individual of the nation, no matter how humble his station.

————

It is well known, that among many nations it is customary to show the most extravagant signs of grief at the death of any person ; they pull out their hair, tear their bodies in the most shocking manner, and show other fantastical marks of outward grief. The Romans employed gladiators even, (i. e.—men trained to fight for the amusement of this enlightened people,) who fought till one or both were killed, whenever a respectable man died. This fashion was carried to such a cruel extent, that—if I do not altogether err—on more

* See Mishna, Shabbath i. 4, also the excellent descriptive novel, Helon's Pilgrimage to Jerusalem, where the reader can obtain a great deal, and generally *correct* information with regard to the customs and mode of living of the ancient Jews.

16

occasions than one, a hundred of these miserable beings were sacrificed to the manes of the departed. This custom was horrible, yes! horrible beyond conception, and yet the most refined nations of antiquity, the Greeks and Romans, indulged in this and similar practices, and a man like Marcus Tullius Cicero could be deluded enough to defend them. And at the present day, as has been mentioned already in the foregoing chapter, the Indian widows, from some superstitious notion or mistaken principle of affection—it is needless to determine which—burn themselves upon the funeral piles of their husbands. Though they do it, for the most part, very unwillingly, their infatuation is nevertheless so great that they do not even question the authority of their priests for recommending and enforcing such brutal sacrifices. The most horrid scenes are frequently exhibited at these suttees, as they are called, and to the shame of the local government be it spoken,* they seldom, if ever, make any attempt to rescue the poor victims, impelled by foolish enthusiasm, from the ruffian grasp of their immolaters, who, during the lighting and burning of the pile, make a terrible and deafening noise with drums and other discordant instruments, to drown the shrieks of the women as they are gradually consumed, and this very often under the most agonising tortures!

Not so is Jacob's portion; thus are not *we* allowed to act. We read in Deut. chap. xii. " that we are children to our God, and that we are not permitted to pull out our hair, and mar our bodies at the

---

* Since writing the above, the author has understood that hitherto the British government would not interfere, because the Hindoos are so jealous of their ancient customs, that it was feared that the abolition of this practice might perhaps subvert the dominion of the British in India. This may have been in some measure an excuse for the government; the greater cause therefore have the friends of humanity to congratulate themselves, that at last an enlightened and moral ruler, the Lord William Bentick, has interdicted the burning of widows, and he deserves the greater glory, as all his predecessors were too much deterred by real or imaginary fears from engaging in the cause of this useful reform. Be this as it may, the argument in the text is not in the least weakened by the abolition of this custom at this late hour; for what can be advanced in exculpation of the Brahmins, who at all events *did* encourage the ignorant females of their nation, and goad them on by visionary hopes, fears, and affections? What can be said of the *holiness* of any institution, which produces such self-delusions? (May 20th, 1830.)

death of any one," much less to murder others at the funeral of a
friend or relative.—The intention of this commandment is probably
this: Religion, at least such a religion as it is our fortune to possess,
should inspire us with confidence in God, and an acquiescence in his
judgment, and soften our grief so much, that under any affliction, we
should be firm and resigned enough to exclaim with the holy writer :
" Though He slay me, yet will I trust in Him !" The severest blows
are oftentimes the most productive of happiness in their consequences, or at least, that which wears such a formidable aspect, as almost
to cause us to despond altogether at first sight, loses many of its
terrors when nearer viewed, and at moments when we have become
more collected, when the lapse of some little time enables us to take
a calm survey of the event we so much deplore. Often, to the most
forlorn, unexpected help arises, and the gloom of despondency is full
many a time suddenly dissipated by a light from above, as bright as
the instantaneous meteor in a dark night, but as lasting and beneficent as the light of the sun. Many, no doubt, who will read this,
have encountered manifold adversities, some of them have perhaps
seen, in early youth, a near connection consigned to the tomb, others
may have stood weeping at the bier of their parents, others again
may have been left destitute orphans without a protector; and yet,
have they not all of them experienced that there is never a wound
inflicted, without a healing balsam being sent to alleviate the pain of
the sufferer ? Perhaps the orphan, who pronounced at his father's
grave the words of the Psalmist: " My father and mother have left
me," may have also had occasion to express his gratitude to God by
exclaiming : " but the Lord has taken me under his protection."
Why should we then fear, when we are apparently unfortunate ?
why should we destroy our health, or deprive ourselves altogether
of life ? if the very circumstance of our present distress may redound
to our temporal as well as spiritual advantage ; and when besides we
ought always to bear in mind, that there is One above who directs
our destiny. We have a beautiful example of resignation given us
in the Pentateuch : Aaron had lost his two eldest sons on the day
they were installed in the priestly office ; Moses told his brother,
that God had informed him that He would be sanctified through
those who were near Him, (i. e.—the otherwise pious men) ; and
Aaron remained silent, and in obedience to the divine command, he

suppressed the feelings of the father, conscious that the punishment of his sons for their *one* transgression would act as a salutary admonition to the people, who would thus be made more careful in their course of life, seeing that the very pious and most exalted did not escape merited punishment.—Like Aaron's grief, therefore, should our grief always be, silent but sincere; we should feel the weight of God's chastisement, yet know how to bear—how to be resigned to his wise decrees. " You are the children of the Eternal, your God," the father punishes not his son in anger, with unfeelingness—no, he inflicts slight punishment to induce him to mend some evil habit, or corrects him for some transgression against paternal authority. In the same light should we view whatever the Almighty may send to us. If we are thankful for the good which we daily and hourly receive from his bounty, we ought also not to murmur, when evil befals us; have we drunk deep of the cup of happiness, let us not repine, if with the sweets of life the bitterness of wormwood is now and then mixed. We all must die; death will not spare the most exalted, the most beloved objects; it behoves us, therefore, to restrain our grief from becoming too violent; for, in the first place, it would be injurious to our health, and then, it would manifest a dissatisfaction with God's dispensation. But let us not in the hour of joy be too much elated, nor grow careless by uninterrupted success; but we should consider how soon our joy may be turned into sorrow, and how speedily our smiles may be chased by the tears of anguish. Let temporal happiness inspire us with gratitude to God, and compassion for mankind, and let adversity teach us resignation to God's will, and to feel for another's woe. And since we daily see, how brief all joys are, how soon life may terminate, we should live so as always to be prepared for death—so, that no vice may disturb our dying bed, and we be ever ready to return our soul pure and unspotted to the God who gave it—to make it deserving of that happiness in the world to come, of which it is his wish that we all should participate. (Deut. chap. v. v. 26.) May we live to see the day when all mankind have become virtuous and good, and all are willing to acknowledge themselves servants of the Most High, and to worship Him in truth and sincerity. Amen!

CHAPTER XX.

THE GOLDEN CALF.

We have thus endeavoured to give clear and convincing arguments in favour of the beauty and necessity of that part of our law, frequently denounced as superstitious.—With how much *injustice* this charge has been made, I leave every candid man to decide, without even attempting to enlist his *feelings*, being sure, that his *judgment* must be in favour of our laws. If we now seriously reflect upon the nature of our religion, it must be admitted, that this, our religion, must promote devotion to God and peace among men. Can any thing more be asked, that these laws should effect?—That they were often violated by the very persons to whom they were given, we dare not even attempt to deny, for Moses himself has left us undoubted evidence of the fact. We shall therefore be met by the following objection: "If it be true that the Israelites received the law from God, in the manner related by Moses, how did it happen, that they so often transgressed and acted so contrary to that system, which is *in fact* so *very* beautiful?"

It is lamentable, but not the less true, that few men are taught wisdom by experience, and that the number of those is smaller still who are made good by mere precept alone, though their teacher be the wisest and most exalted. Even at the present day we generally find, that many a man, when in trouble, will promise any thing and every thing to be forgiven for the wrong he has done; but no sooner is he out of trouble, no sooner is he pardoned, than he again commences his old career, and commits anew the same follies which have occasioned him so much distress. This is the conduct from one man to the other, whom he, perhaps, may hope to deceive by outward appearances of reformation; yet even towards our Maker do we often act thus. In trouble, at the death of a friend or relative, we suddenly grow wonderfully pious, we seem *strangely* reformed, we view our former course of life with real or affected

horror, as sinful and unbecoming mortals, who receive all they possess from God, and we determine to do better for the future. When
the impression, however, is once weakened by time, when forgetful-
ness has taken off a little from the keen edge of our grief: we are
our former selves again—God is forgotten—his law neglected
—and our calamities are scarcely remembered—we make merry at
what we then call trifles, and often pretend to be surprised at our
own folly, for having been *weak* enough to be affected by occurrences, which were, to make the most of them, but *natural.*

Is not this a true picture of the conduct of most men? Where,
in fact, is that man to be found, who is *always* mindful of passing
events, and regulates his life by them?

Just so were our ancestors. They had been slaves in Egypt,
their redemption was sudden, and we may say would have been unexpected at the moment it took place, if they had not been previously prepared for it by the *plagues* which befel their oppressors.
After their redemption, we have seen that the law was given to
them, and its precepts were contrary to almost every thing they had
been accustomed to in Egypt. There was besides an immense
number of persons in the camp, who were *not Jews*, (Exod. chap. xii.
v. 38,) and whom we afterwards find (Numb. chap. xi. v. 4,) not alone
murmuring themselves, but exciting the Israelites also to rebellion.
After the promulgation of the *ten commandments* Moses re-ascended
the mount, and staid there forty days and nights. The people, particularly the strangers, were not yet used to the rule of the *divine
law :* they could yet hardly understand how God could be worshipped without symbolic idols, altars, sacrifices and priests; for idols
had been interdicted, and they had not yet heard in what manner
the sacrifices were to be offered, what kind of place for the worship
of God they were to have ; and as yet the first-born of the families
were the priests, according to patriarchal custom. All this was
new and strange to them, and when they saw that Moses staid out
longer than they expected, they became restive, and were *probably*
afraid, as we may infer from their address to Aaron, that he had
died upon Sinai ; being therefore now without a leader, they desired
a symbol of God, which might be carried before them as their en-
sign of war, for so it is said : " Rise, make us gods, which shall go
before us." It is said in tradition, that they applied first to *Hur,*

who, together with Aaron, had been left as governors during Moses's absence ; he, however, refused, and was immediately slain by the infuriated mob. They then came to Aaron, who did all in his power to procure delay ; he demanded the ear-rings and other ornaments of the women and children, hoping that they might refuse to part with them. But the men fearing delay, or perhaps discovering Aaron's unwillingness to obey them, immediately gave him *their own* ornaments. Aaron saw now no means but to comply with their demands, and at last a *golden calf* was made under his auspices. The calf, as is well known, was the deity of Egypt, and it is very probable that Aaron chose this image to remind his brethren how *ineffectual the Egyptian gods had been to save their worshippers from destruction.* But as soon as the *strangers,** who were *Egyptians,* saw *their old god,* they exclaimed to the Israelites : " These are thy gods, oh Israel, which have brought thee out from Egypt !" When men are once wavering, it is but a *slight step* to *apostacy ;*

---

* This explanation of the thirty-second chapter of Exodus may seem very strange to those who have never heard it ; but, in the *first* place, let it be considered, that Hur is never mentioned after this event, though he must have been an intimate friend of Moses and Aaron, he being first with Moses and Aaron on the hill during the battle with Amalake ; and next he and Aaron were appointed judges during Moses's absence.—In the *second* place, the address " These are thy gods, &c." can not possibly have originated with the Israelites themselves, which, if it were the case, could not be reconciled to the language of the text ; we must, therefore, conclude that this address was held by the strangers, who had followed our ancestors from Egypt. The probable meaning of these words is this : " You Israelites have, till this moment, thought that it was a new, unheard of God—the Eternal—who had redeemed you from slavery ; but think no longer so—it was *Osiris, Isis, Apis, and the other gods of Egypt,* who were your redeemers. They were incensed at the injustice done to you ; and the punishment inflicted upon the Egyptians was their work ; they gave you food in the wilderness ; and as for the law given from Sinai—that whole affair was a contrivance of Moses himself. But see, here is your god, and is not his image good evidence of the fact, that he has come to resume his rule over you ; you—who have so long lived in the land where he is worshipped ?"—I do not know that this opinion agrees with that of any other commentator ; but I do not wish to force *my opinion* upon any one, I just give it as it occurred to me while writing, and if it be erroneous, let my readers reject it ; only let them not think me presumptuous, nor the explanation absurd, for it is founded upon the plain and literal translation of the Hebrew words.

once dissolve the bond by which we are bound, and we rush head-long forward, without once looking to see in *what direction we proceed.* Just so was it with a part of our ancestors; I say a part, for all did *not* sin: they had begun to doubt the truth of Moses's mission on account of his absence, and no sooner, therefore, had they an excuse for deviating from their duty, than they followed the way of error, and instead of adoring the all-powerful God, they worshipped " the image of a *grass-eating ox.*" Aaron did not long remain unconscious of the fatal error he had committed in not *sacrificing himself* to their resentment, rather than yield to the unreasonable demands of the Israelites and strangers. He therefore built an altar before the calf, and exclaimed aloud before the assembled people: " To-morrow is a feast in honour of the *Eternal.*" The meaning can easily be discovered to be: " Do not, my deluded brethren, imagine that *this* calf is God, or a symbol of God, for He has told you that he is not to be represented by any living thing; by aught either in the heavens, the earth, or the water. Apis, Osiris, and the other idols you saw worshipped in Egypt, are not gods; for, if by them are understood the sun, moon, stars, and the creatures around you, then they are the creatures of *our God,* and ought, for this reason, *not* to be worshipped, for worship is due to the Creator alone. But, if they are supposed to be independent deities, and possessing power of themselves, then they have no existence at all, for nothing exists that is not derived from the God we adore. Wait therefore my brethern, and act not with precipitancy; wait until to-morrow, perhaps our beloved Moses may return, and to-morrow then shall be a day of feasting in honour of the Eternal our God, who is your King, Protector, and Redeemer, and whom alone you ought to worship !"

It often happens that good advice is not listened to, if men are predetermined to do wrong; and the same was the case with the Israelites. For they rose early on the following morning, and performed their unholy rites round the statue of the calf, and showed, by this conduct, how little they had corrected the evil habits they had contracted in Egypt; and gave a warning to all how dangerous bad company and bad example are, particularly to young persons, before their character is well formed.

While they had yet scarcely time to commence their horrid

dance, Moses received the two tables of the covenant from the Most High, who then also told him that the Israelites had so soon departed from the way which He had pointed out to them. Moses, being bidden, descended from the mount, and at its foot he met his trusty servant Joshua, who had remained there ever since he had been upon Sinai. The mount yet blazed (Deut. chap. ix.) when Moses returned to the camp with the tables in his hand, but he threw them down and broke them at the foot of Sinai, as soon as he had arrived at the camp, and had seen " the calf and the dancing." For he argued : the uncircumcised is not even permitted to taste the passover-lamb, and thus he is disabled on account of the *non-fulfilment of one commandment only* from being in every respect a true Israelite ; and can this people, who have in a measure all become idolaters, be worthy of the *whole law* and *those statutes*, more dear than gold, and more costly than pearls ?

But not in vain reproofs did Moses idle away the time which was of necessity to be devoted to action. The man of God stood in the gate of the camp, and exclaimed : " Who is for the Eternal come to me !" and *they* came, who had not forsaken their God, namely, the children of Levi ; and they proved on that day *their adherence* to God at the risk of their lives. The small number of the Levites is well known ; they were, in fact, the smallest tribe of Israel ; yet did they *singly* brave the immense numbers of the other tribes, not to reckon the strange mob mixed with them. But the Levites did not regard numbers—they heeded not the ties of friendship, it was enough for them to know that on *that day*—so was the will of their God—they should strike for the glory of his holy name, and three thousand idolaters fell before the swords, which had never been unsheathed in vain. From *this day*, however, they became consecrated to the service of their God, and war was no longer to be their trade. The sword of *destruction* was henceforward taken out of their hands, and the *book* of the holy and *life-giving law* was put there in its stead : the teaching of this book, the attendance at the sacrifices, and the service at the temple, were entrusted to the Levites, as a reward for the willingness which they showed in the execution of a duty at all times painful to the heart that feels, and to the mind that is conscious of its own imperfections.

" But was not Moses's order to slay the idolaters cruel and unne-

17

cessary?"—That three thousand is a large number we are ready to confess; but we assert that it was not cruel, and that the destruction of this large number was called for by the most imperious necessity. Hitherto, it will be perceived, no punishment had been inflicted upon the Israelites, though they had frequently deserved it; because God had compassion for their weakness, and He pardoned them according to his great mercy. But when they had, at the time we are speaking of, altogether thrown off the yoke which they had voluntarily accepted to bear, it became absolutely necessary to teach them by *acts*, but not *words*, that on no account could the *second commandment* be transgressed with impunity; and they were made to feel that God, who is kind and delays his anger a long while, is sure to punish every disobedience against his will. And since it had thus become necessary to punish, was it not proper that all those who had been equally guilty and active in crime should be equally punished?—They, also, received a practical lesson, that a handful of men, when protected by God, are more powerful than great armies; as the Levites, confiding in God, overcame multitudes, who had but just chosen Apis as their god, who was unable to save them from the sword of the servants of the Eternal.

To prove more fully to the Israelites the utter weakness of their idol, Moses reduced the whole to powder, which he mixed with water, and gave it them to drink.—When idolatry had thus been eradicated in one day, Moses announced that he would go again upon the mount Sinai, to pray to God, and ask forgiveness for their transgression.—He did go, and remained there forty days and forty nights, without food or drink, and lived happy in receiving the word of God, and in obtaining the pardon of the erring Israelites. Though he was told that *their* destruction should be the means of *his* elevation, yet did he not desire greatness for himself which must have been attended by the destruction of others; and he asked *to be blotted out of the book which God had written*, (i. e. Moses offered himself as a sacrifice, even so far that his name might be altogether forgotten,) only that the Israelites might be preserved and forgiven. But God would not accept Moses as a sacrifice, thus teaching the world that *one man can never be sacrificed, that any other man or even a whole community might escape without punishment*, but the sinning person himself, and none other in his stead, is to die. (See

Exod. chap. xxxii.) Although God would not forgive the Israelites, and punish his messenger in place of them, He nevertheless pardoned them upon Moses's intercession; but He also made known to them, that all ornaments must be laid aside, that those things which had induced them to sin should be no longer a temptation in their way to make them swerve from their adherence to God a second time. The people mourned, and obeyed the commandment, and showed us by so doing, that whenever we wish to repent seriously, we must abstract ourselves as much as possible from the affairs of this world and its allurements, and place before ourselves in the strongest light the power of God, his kindness, and his mercy.

Moses was after this ordered to prepare two tables like those he had broken; he therefore descended from Sinai, and made them as he had been commanded. He again ascended, and staid a third time forty days and nights upon the mount; at the expiration of which period he returned to the camp and deposited the tables, which were inscribed with the Decalogue, in a wooden ark. (Deut. x.)

Moses now made known to the Israelites, that he had received the commands of God to build Him a temple, where He should be worshipped, and that the expenses of the building were to be defrayed by voluntary contributions. The people had now an opportunity of showing if they had truly repented of their former folly—and they did prove their sincerity; whatever was wanting, gold, silver, precious stones, in short all which had been demanded was cheerfully given, and even more than was actually needed was brought to the workmen, so that at length Moses was obliged to proclaim: "That no one should bring any more contributions for the service of the holy tabernacle."—The workmen, who were selected from all Israel, and had knowledge to do all kinds of work for the holy service, made all things necessary exactly after the model which God had shown to Moses; and when all was finished they received the blessing of their great teacher, who wished them the grace of God and his future protection! Moses then set up the tabernacle, and the glory of God filled it, and the pillar of light shone upon it brightly every night; and the admiring Israelites were thus convinced that God was amongst them continually, to protect them, and to shield them from all danger.

As the Israelites were drawing near the land of their destination, they desired that spies should be sent, to see which road they ought to take, and what cities they should come to. The spies were sent, but like other travellers, ten out of twelve (the *number* sent) magnified real dangers, and invented others which had no existence. The whole congregation rose in rebellion against the messenger and the anointed of the Lord; and the mob would have attempted to stone them but for the timely interference of Caleb and Joshua, two of the spies.—All lamented the fate that awaited them; they feared to enter the land which had been promised them as an inheritance, and they proposed returning to Egypt, where they had been slaves. This conduct was highly offensive to the Deity, who, in consequence, bid Moses to tell the people, that all over the age of twenty should die in the wilderness, where they should wander for forty years; but that their children, or all those under twenty years old, should enter the land, which had been promised to Abraham, Isaac, and Jacob; and that farther they should not advance against their enemies, but return towards the Red Sea.—O strange inconsistency! as soon as they had heard their doom, and the injunction to return, and after ten of the spies had died, they were all willing to go, and even tumultuously demanded to be led forward. In vain did Moses entreat them to desist, for that they would be surely beaten by their enemies; they, however, did go forward, and suffered what Moses had foretold. They wandered then for forty years, sustained solely by the providence of God; and thus was a people raised up, free from all admixture of evil, for all the bad men died by degrees, as related in the fourth book of Moses; and those whom Joshua led over the Jordan were all worthy of being the people of that God in whose name they went forward against their enemies, and by whose aid they obtained possession of their inheritance.

I have not thought it necessary to explain every one of the rebellious actions of the Israelites in the wilderness; but I just extracted these two to show that the unwillingness of our ancestors to obey the will of their God does not prove that He never revealed himself to them; and I hope that it has been clearly demonstrated, that their rebellious disposition may have been altogether owing to the weakness of human nature; and secondly, to the peculiar circumstances under which they found themselves. Besides, it must be well remembered, that our law was not given to us to *force* our compliance; far from it,—God gave us the laws, known as the Mosaic, as a rule to regulate ourselves by in our intercourse with one another, and for our conduct towards Him; and we have seen that He made his will known to us with a view to teach us how to distinguish between right and wrong, because our reason, unaided, does *not* guide us correctly, But having once pointed out " what is right" and " what is wrong," He gave us the choice, either to obey his will, which is " to do good," or to disobey it, which is " to do evil." (Deut. chap. xxx.) He, however, at the same time tells us the consequences of our choosing the one or the other; namely, that by obedience to his will we shall be made happy—by disobedience unhappy; or rather, in the words of the holy book, we have the choice between *doing good and live*, and *doing evil and die*. God advises us, however, to choose " life," for it is more pleasing to Him to reward the virtuous than punish the wicked. (See above, commentary on the Decal. chap. xiii.) Then, again, it must be borne in mind, that all the laws, as has been already said, were no less new to the Israelites than to any other nation; and it took, therefore, in the natural course of things, some considerable time to make them perfectly acquainted with the divine ordinances. If Moses now *had not* recorded their frequent apostacies, but had only given the history of a people, all the time they were under his guidance, acting obediently to God, and with deference towards himself, we should have been very much inclined to doubt the veracity of the narrative, for then some wiseacre *might* have said with some show of reason : " It is impossible that among three millions of people there should arise no dissatisfaction with a self-constituted ruler, who was one of their number, and had therefore no right to command his equals. He had, besides, promised them to bring them to a land flowing with milk and honey; but, instead of doing this, he keeps them for the space of forty years in a frightful wilderness, where not even fresh water is to be found." Such a nation of *saints indeed* would with justice have been considered an improbability, not to say an impossibility, unless we should believe that their nature had been changed! This, however, would virtually have changed their freedom of action, and of course such a hypothesis is utterly fallacious, it being not only contrary to revelation, but also to common reason.—The Israelites had been so long slaves under idolatrous masters, that they were not altogether free from the influence of the Egyptians amongst them ; and as Moses had been absent a long while, they became alarmed, and they required another leader in the place of Moses, whom they either supposed dead, or what is worse, that having once attained his object by depriving the king of Egypt, who was his personal enemy, of their services, he had left them to their fate, under a pretence of going to receive new laws for their government, finding himself unable to keep the promises he had made them. We have seen with how much cunning the designing strangers took advantage of this feeling among the Israelites, and the consequent apostacy of the latter, the adherence of the tribe of Levi to God, and the subsequent punishment of the idolaters. From this affair, and the other murmurings and backslidings of the Israelites, it will appear that Moses conceals nothing that happened to him and the people under his charge ; he also tells us that his government was not acquiesced in by all, but that he was perpetually assailed by riotous meetings, and grieved very frequently by the obstinacy of a people to whom he was so devoted as to offer his own life a sacrifice for their welfare. We have thus the strongest evidence of the truth of what he says regarding the history of the Israelites, since he is at no pains to conceal any thing which might induce some to believe that this dissatisfaction was deserved by him.—To sum up the whole in a few words : human nature was not changed ; propensities to err were not removed ; and although the Israelites had a rule to go by, yet could they not so soon forget old and deep-rooted habits ; *force*, therefore, *and persuasion*, were both necessary to make them remember the new law ; and thus were we already very early taught by *practical* lessons, " that no good goes unrewarded, and no evil unpunished."

I do not wish to palliate the sins of our forefathers, but only to show that their sinning is *no* evidence that they did not receive the law ; besides, let it be considered, that although they sinned, their transgressions were not more numerous than those of the best men living at any time and in any country, if we take into consideration the length of time of which Moses speaks, and their former state ; and though no such crimes, as they were guilty of, may be *now* committed, let it be observed, that the world has many other failings which our ancestors had not; further, that the sins of the *fathers* tended greatly to confirm the *children* more strongly in the law of God, since they saw how much evil springs from disobedience, and how many blessings flow from a cheerful submission to the will of God!

CHAPTER XXI.

INSPIRATION AND PROPHECY.

If we carefully examine the biblical records, we shall discover that prophets were not alone found amongst the Israelites, but also amongst other nations, previous to 'Móses, and during his lifetime. We find two mentioned, namely, Job* and Balaam, who were sent

---

* It is the generally received opinion among the Rabbins, that Job died during Moses's lifetime; at any rate, it is acknowledged by all, that this patriarch lived in a very remote age, and it is unnecessary for me to make an enquiry in this place, if his death occurred at the time the Rabbins say it did, which is at all events very probable.—Let me here once for all remark, that I am really astonished at the presumption of antiquaries, who, no matter with how little reason, set gravely about to determine the time and mode of every thing in history; they affirm things as true upon the most frivolous data, and upon equally trivial grounds reject all which they do not *wish* to believe, and thus it is not to be wondered at, that they so often arrive at conclusions the very reverse of truth. And no class of writers have been more abused by this class of reasoners, than our sacred writers and Rabbins.—Having said thus much, I shall resume the subject which I intended to explain.—I have said that the opinions of the Rabbins concerning the time of Job's death is very plausible, and as there is certainly no positive proof against this tradition, we Jews will continue to think it true, till we see some more conclusive reasoning against its probability, than the unsupported assertion of any man. If we then assume it as true, that Job died at the time mentioned, it follows : that the light of revelation was not yet extinct, though the patriarchs, to whom this revelation was first given, had long past away. We find Job bringing sacrifices in honour of God, fearing, that his

as *messengers*, at least in so far, as to make the will of God known to those who were immediately about them ; and others, as Abimelech and Laban, who received prophecy for their own guidance. (See Gen. chap. xx. v. 3, and ibid. chap. xxxi. v. 24.)

Not all the prophets received their mission in the same manner, nor had they all an equal degree of knowledge of divine things and of sanctity, if the frequency of inspiration be taken as the test.—We generally find that when the spirit of prophecy came over a man, he could not remain standing, but fell involuntarily down, as Abraham, Ezekiel, and Balaam. Most of the prophets prophesied only once, or when there was any urgent necessity of making something known to the people, leader, judge, or king; of the first, we can cite as a remarkable instance the seventy elders in Numbers, chap. xi., and of the second, the many prophets mentioned in Kings will serve as an illustration.—Moses, Samuel, Isaiah, Jeremiah, and Ezekiel have left us accounts of their first appointment to the dignity of prophets, and from their histories we can learn what kind of men were thus honoured by their Maker ; they were all, namely, men of unimpeachable morality and virtue, and ready to fulfil the object of their mission at whatever personal risk to themselves ; with the exception

children had, in the moment of conviviality, been forgetful of God's mercy and blasphemed Him in their hearts. Job lived in a district of Idumea, and his close contiguity to the Canaanites must lead us to the conclusion, that they were neither ignorant of Job's person nor of his mode of life, and they therefore must have known too, that their abominable conduct was displeasing to the God whom Job worshipped.

I deemed this necessary to defend the Israelites against the charge of having *murdered* the nations of Palestine, who *are said* to have been ignorant of the will of God. It will however not be disputed, that they had some knowledge, not alone of the patriarchal revelation, but also of the Exodus and the promulgation of the law from Sinai ; yet did they persevere in their course of life, and they were for this reason alone doomed to destruction. (See Deut. chap. ix. v. 5.) God sent the Israelites to drive them out and take possession of their land. But our ancestors, after they had subdued or driven out the Canaanites, imitated their example; they too were therefore nearly all destroyed, and the remainder driven into captivity; for, as they did that for which their predecessors had suffered, they were no longer permitted to inhabit the land which had been given them, because of the iniquity of these predecessors; and thus we see that retributive justice will reach nations no less than individuals, and this we are taught throughout all the prophetic books.

of Balaam, who, though probably not virtuous, was yet gifted with prophecy, and this must teach us, as well as many other acts of the Deity, that our reason is not capable of understanding all.

In investigating the prophetic histories, or what is the same, all the books of the Jewish canon, it will be discovered that inspiration was of two different kinds: the one was *inspiration proper*, and the other *prophecy*. The inspired man, or one endowed with the holy spirit רוח הקדש whilst speaking or writing, was he, who wrote or spoke by himself (but not to others) what he felt within himself to be the will and word of God ; or one who wrote down what had happened before him, or was to happen after him, as it was made known to him by a knowledge superior to that with which he was generally endowed. Inspired writers of this kind are David, Solomon, Daniel, Ezra and Nehemiah. All these men, as will be seen, were never sent out to *communicate to others* what had been imparted to them ; but they wrote down or spoke as to themselves what they felt convinced to be *that* wisdom and *that* knowledge, which their God had revealed to them. Thus David said : " The spirit of the Lord spoke *within* me, and his word was upon my tongue." (See 2 Sam. chap. xxiii. v. 2.) If we now wish to determine what is *holy spirit* or *inspiration*, we must say : It is the endowment of superior knowledge proceeding from God as a special gift to the person so gifted, which inspiration compels him to write and speak only what is, was, or will be true, and prevents him from committing any error in the facts he relates as happening, past, or coming, because his knowledge ranges over events and circumstances, and the nature of both, as if they pass in review before him ; or, in other words, a man truly inspired can commit no error, but must speak the truth.

A man endowed with *prophecy*, on the contrary, was a messenger sent to tell to others the will of God ; he was therefore not permitted to keep any thing imparted to him *a secret*, but he was to go forth to the nation and communicate to them either the good or the evil message, which had been entrusted to him. (See also, 1 Sam. chap. iii. v. 17, where we read, that Samuel concealed nothing that God had told him from Eli, who had even required this frankness from the young prophet.) We must, according to this definition, call Moses, Isaiah, Joel and others, *prophets*, since they were messengers sent to speak. The prophet, like the inspired writer, could

18

not err, for it is impossible to think that God, who sent him to *speak* a particular message in his name, should not have imparted to him the truth.

Some of the prophets had power to work miracles, these were chiefly Moses, Elijah, and Elisha, who were the most favoured of mortals, even so far, that Elijah never tasted the cup of death, but was translated by a whirlwind into heaven. (2 Kings, chap. ii.) But let no man think that any undue partiality was shown to these men, for they were the most virtuous that ever lived, and as such they were entitled to, and did receive the highest favours.—The miracles wrought by them demonstrated also, that no matter how great the miracle is, it entitles not the man, through whose agency it is performed, to receive adoration or reverence, other than should be shown to a man noted for his virtue and favour with God. For what could be more extraordinary than Moses drawing water out of a hard rock, or Elijah, Elisha, and Ezekiel reviving the dead? But neither they, nor the people before whom these miracles were exhibited, ever thought that they proceeded from any inherent power in those prophets; and when Elijah had been answered with fire from heaven, (1 Kings chap. xviii. v. 39,) all the people cried out: "The Eternal is the God, the Eternal is the God!" Thus we see, that the miracles of the prophets were only considered as a confirmation of their prophecy, and it was well understood, that the performer of miracles was only the instrument in the hand of God, and therefore the three aforementioned prophets could not claim any merit in bringing the dead to life again, for any other man might have done the same, if he had received the commission to do so.

Properly speaking, we had no *oracles*, but all the predictions amongst us were the word of God, only made known in different ways. The nature of inspiration and prophecy has been already explained, and I shall now give an account of the *Urim* and *Thumim*, which served as a guide to our ancestors. According to the generally received opinion among us, the Urim and Thumim was a *holy name* written by Moses and placed by him between the folds of the breast-plate, one of the robes of the high-priest. All the letters of the Hebrew alphabet were engraved upon the stones of this plate, and when any question was to be answered, (upon the requisition of the chief judge or the leader of the people,) the priest looked upon the breast-plate, and which ever letter he saw shining forth he bore in mind, and did so with every other one as it shone, and when no other reflected light, he was convinced that the answer was complete. To make this obscure description more intelligible, I will introduce an example from the commencement of the book of Judges. It there says, that the Israelites, after the death of Joshua, enquired which of the tribes should go out first to attack the enemy; to which question they received a reply: " Judah shall go," Heb. יהודה יעלה : the priest saw the י shining, then ה, and so on, till he had seen in succession the nine letters composing these two words, which combined in the order they appeared, made out the reply asked for. Though this reply was very brief, it was nevertheless all that was necessary, it being concise and explicit; there was no room left for a doubt or to put a double construction upon this reply, as was invariably the case with *oracles* invented and conducted by men. Let us for instance take the celebrated answer the Athenians received, when they were threatened with an invasion by the Persian Xerxes. They were told to defend themselves behind wooden walls. This oracle, as it stood, had certainly no other meaning, than that the Athenians were lost, as apparently there was no more safety for them, than for a man who would endeavour to shelter himself behind a wooden wall, when attacked by an immense host well provided with instruments of attack. But Themistocles advised his townsmen to seek safety on board of their fleet, and do thus what the oracle demanded of them to do. They did so, and the victory of Salamis was the fruit of this wise counsel.—But can any man imagine, that in case the Athenians had been defeated, the priests of Delphi had no door by which to escape ; or to speak more plainly, that they would not have been able to interpret their prediction so as to suit the event ?

A similar duplicity in oracle-reply we find in the book of Judges. The notorious Micah had made himself an image and oracle, and appointed a young Levite to be his priest. Some men of the tribe of Dan came by accident to the house, and when they asked the priest: " If the oracle could tell them if their journey would be prosperous," he answered them : " Go in peace, the way you go is נכח the Eternal." The word נכח means here ostensibly*—*agreeable to ;*

---

* See the commentary of Rabbi Solomon Yarchi, on this passage.

but it also means *before, known, laid open*, and the phrase therefore, may mean : " Go in peace, the way you go is known to the Lord," and by implication not to this idol ; true, the men were successful, but if they had been otherwise, he could not with propriety have been called *a liar*, since he had said nothing positive, and in fact he could not have chosen any word so well adapted to his purpose of mystifying, as this נכה, he so adroitly used.

This may seem to some an unnecessary digression, but in fact it is not. Attempts have been often made to call the Urim and Thumim *oracles*, and some go even so far as to give this name to the altars or other monuments, on which particular passages of Scripture had been inscribed.—I should have no particular objection to the word *oraculum* itself, which means—first, a place where divine answers were obtained, and secondly, the divine answer itself, though even this would not exactly express the nature of the Urim and Thumim, as we have explained it above. But no Jew, who is alive to his national honour, can suffer an idea to be entertained, that our mode of obtaining the decision and the knowledge of the will of God had any thing in common with the oracles of the Greeks and Romans ; one was by the positive command of God—the others were by the jugglery of priests and madmen ;—one was always clear and decisive, and the event never belied the prediction—the others were always ambiguous and uncertain, and no more dependence could be placed upon them, than upon the divinations of gypsies and fortune-tellers of the present time.

It will be evident from the foregoing definitions, that *inspiration, prophecy*, and decision through the Urim and Thumim, were equally infallible, or whatever was announced in either of the three modes was of necessity true. But if it should have been discovered, that any prediction did not correspond with the event, it must have been clear, that this prediction was not made by inspiration, but was an invention of the pretended prophet.

In Deuteronomy, chap. xviii. will be found a prohibition of all *superstitious* enquiries into futurity ; we should, namely, not consider one time more propitious or lucky than the other ; should not consult the dead ; nor make use of conjuration, or any other species of fraud and deception, which was resorted to in ancient or modern times. If the power of witchcraft be real or pretended is unneces-

sary to be determined here ; for if it be real, its practice is no less
contrary to our law, than if it be but pretended.   It is also quite
immaterial, whether this power was practised, or even possessed only,
at any time since the creation; it is enough for us to know, that it was
prohibited, and the pretender to witchcraft, necromancy, or the like
practices was punishable with death.   The object of our law in in-
terdicting all superstitious customs, which were current amongst *all*
the nations of antiquity, and are yet practised amongst *most* of the
barbarous communities of the present day, was, as Moses says :
" That we should be perfect with the Eternal our God."   The word
rendered " perfect" is in Hebrew תמים, which is used to express
any thing *entire, complete, without blemish, simple* ; its meaning in
this place is therefore : our confidence in God should be entire, we
should simply put our trust in his protection, and always hope, that
as *He directs our destinies as we deserve, that* only will happen
which is good and redounding to our advantage ; we are, for this
reason, forbidden to dive any further in futurity than God himself
chooses to reveal to us.—Moses therefore proceeds in his discourse
(Deut. chap. xviii. v. 14,) :

   " For these nations, which thou shalt drive out, are accustomed
to listen to observers of time and diviners, but thou hast not received
the like for thyself from the Lord thy God.   A prophet, from
amongst thee, from thy brethren, like myself, the Lord thy God will
raise up unto thee, to him you shall hearken." (Pay attention to his
words.)   " Just as thou hast asked of the Lord thy God in Horeb,
on the day of the assembly, when thou spokest, ' I wish not further
to hear the voice of the Lord my God, nor see any more the great
fire, that I may not die ;' and the Lord then said unto me, ' They
have acted properly in what they said ; I will raise up unto them a
prophet from amongst their brethren, like thyself, and I will put my
words in his mouth, and he shall speak to them all which I shall
command him.   And it shall happen, that I will punish every man,
who will not hearken to my words, which he' (the prophet) ' shall
speak in my name.   But that prophet who shall be wicked enough
to speak any thing in my name, which I have not commanded him
to speak, or who shall speak in the name of false gods, shall die.'
And if thou shouldst say in thy heart : ' How can we know the
word, which the Lord has not spoken ?'   That, which the prophet

speaks in the name of the Lord, and it happen not, nor come to
pass, this is what the 'Lord has *not* spoken, wickedly has the prophet spoken it, thou shalt not be afraid of him." (Meaning : do not
think that you will do the least wrong in removing him from amongst
you by killing him, for he richly deserves his fate, for attempting to
deceive his brethren.)

We have here before us the method by which the truth of prophecy
can be tested. As from a negative we generally can infer the positive, we may conclude in what true prophecy consists from the
foregoing extract. It is necessary : *first*, that the prophet announce
his prohecy, or what is the same, his mission, as proceeding from
the Eternal Lord our God, who revealed himself to Moses ; and
secondly, that the event correspond exactly with the prediction. But
if a man pretending to inspiration should presume to speak in the
name of idols, as for instance, he come with a message from Jupiter
or any other personage or thing, existing or not existing, which receives, or is intended to receive, honours due only to God ; or if he
say such a thing shall happen at such a time, and it does not happen
at the time specified ; or if he predict a thing, the contrary of which
should come to pass ; or if he speak against any one commandment
of the Mosaic law, (this being once laid down as the irrevocable will
of God) : such a man must be considered as a *false* prophet ; that,
which he gives out as prophecy, is an invention of his own, and it
is wickedness in him to presume to palm upon the world his own
ideas as the will and word of God.

If we take this passage in connection with what is commanded
concerning any one, who should advise the people or individuals to act
contrary to the law (Deut. chap. xiii. v. 1—12) : it will appear
that no miracle or sign can be taken as evidence of the truth of any
prophecy, which should be contradictory in any one particular to the
laws given us through Moses. For in the *first* verse we are directed
to observe *every* commandment laid down by Moses, and are *forbidden to add or take any away*, and in the fifth verse we read :
" After the Lord your God you shall walk, and Him you shall fear,
and his commandments you shall observe, and to his voice you shall
hearken, and Him you shall serve, and to Him you shall adhere."
These commandments speak too plainly to be misunderstood ; that
every precept of the law is binding and will be ever binding ; and it

must follow of course, that not one of them will be abrogated, nor any other thing substituted, for any, even the smallest, precept contained in the Pentateuch. We are therefore told, that if any man should even perform a miracle, as an evidence of his mission, when this mission contains aught in opposition to the letter and spirit of the law, he must be considered as a false prophet, or in other words, that which he tells us must be looked upon as an invention of his own, and that therefore the miracle performed, or the sign given, is no proof of the truth of his assertion. For if it were possible that any commandment could be abrogated at any time, it must follow, that what is right to-day, can be wrong to-morrow—or, that God did not know, when He gave the first commandments, what was right—or, that He is changeable in his disposition, and alters the law to suit his caprice—all such hypotheses are rank blasphemy, and cannot be entertained by any man, who is duly impressed with the wisdom and grandeur of God ; for, as the Psalmist and Balaam say : " God is not a man, that He should speak falsely !"

Prophecy now, to be true, must be in every respect agreeable to the precepts of the Mosaic law ; if, therefore, a man comes forward and proclaims his mission, produces proof of its truth, and speaks altogether in confirmation of and according to the *Pentateuch*, he must be believed, and to disbelieve him would be sin ; but for which the person refusing to believe is not to be punished, on any account, by an earthly tribunal, being accountable to God alone. And since we are once upon the subject, I will just remark, that no man could be punished by a court of justice for opinions which he held, till he had proved these, his sinful opinions, by an overt act; for instance, the worship of idols, disobedience to the decision of the San- hedrin, or any ony other wilful transgression of the precepts of the law ; and the maxim of our law is : for opinions we are answerable to God alone—for our actions to men *also*. If, however, a man should be convicted of having spoken as a prophet contrary to the law, he has committed a crime against the well-being of society, and he is punishable with death by a court of justice, although he has performed miracles, *for miracles are no evidence whatever of the truth of any man's mission*, if *no other proof* of his being a prophet be produced.

" In what manner is prophecy to be verified, if miracles are no confirmation ?" To answer this question it is only necessary to

consult three out of the many passages on this subject in the Bible :
namely, Numbers, chap. xvi. v. 28 ; 1 Kings, chap. xxii. v. 28, and
Jeremiah, chap. xxviii. v. 16. From these passages it clearly follows, that the accomplishment of the predictions is the only proof
of their truth ; and it matters not if the accomplishment be a miracle
or a mere natural event, provided it take place at the time [and in
the manner specified, and the prophecy be in confirmation (as we
have seen it must be) of the precepts contained in our law.

1. We read in Numbers, chap. xvi. v. 28 : " And Moses said, by
this you shall know that the Eternal has sent me to do all these
things, and that they proceeded not from my own mind. If these
men die a death similar to that of all men, and the fate of all mortals overtake them, *then the Lord has not sent me.* But if the Lord
create a new thing, and the earth open its mouth, and swallow them
up, with all that belongs to them, and they go down alive to their
graves, *then you will know that these men have incensed the Lord.*"
Here Moses proposed *a test* of his mission, by saying, that the
destruction, nay, the *instantaneous destruction* of the rebels should
be a confirmation of his course being dictated by God ; but that
if, on the contrary, they should die a natural death, every one
should judge him to have acted without authority, and that his whole
course had been a series of frauds and deceptions.—Mark the confidence of the prophet ! He could not, in a natural way, have known
that the earth would be rent asunder the moment he left off speaking ; for though such a thing happens now and then during an earthquake, I do not remember to have read any instance, where a
chasm was produced, at a moment's warning, upon the requisition
of any man, and closed again *in a few moments after*, when it had
effected the purpose of its formation.—But no sooner had Moses
proposed the test than the men, whose names are mentioned in the
sixteenth chapter of Numbers, were swallowed up, the chasm closed
over them, and they were lost from *among the midst of the assembly*, and no other man was injured, save those designated by the
prophet. Although Moses himself is the narrator of this event,
there is yet every reason to believe his account ; for just before he
died we find him reminding the people of what had been done to
Dathan and Abiram, and again detailing the event in a few but forcible words. (Deut. chap. xi. v. 6.) Does now any man believe that

Moses could have been *audacious* enough to remind the people of any event said to have occurred before their eyes, if really such an event had never taken place ? Is it reasonable to suppose that all would not have exclaimed : " We know of no such thing" ?—But we have other evidence to prove that this event was believed and generally accredited long after Moses's death ; for we find in the 106th psalm, verse 16th and 17th : " And they envied Moses in the camp, also Aaron, who was consecrated to the Eternal ; the earth opened and swallowed Dathan and covered Abiram's band." The other events enumerated in this psalm were then and are even now too well known to be doubted ; and *could* the Psalmist have inserted a *fabulous* account amongst historical facts ?

2. In the twenty-second chapter of the first book of Kings we find an account of the expedition of the kings of Judah and Israel against Ramoth, then occupied by the Syrians. Previous to their leaving Shomerone (Samaria) we read that many *false* prophets encouraged Ahab to go, promising him success and a prosperous return. Yehoshaphat, however, the king of Judah, although he was found in company with the most inveterate idolater, was sincerely pious ; and hearing four hundred men all using the same language, he could not believe them inspired, for there is no example to be found where two prophets ever used precisely the same words, although they announced the same message ; for inspiration taught them only to speak nothing but what was true, but never compelled them to use language different from what they were accustomed to ; —hence the difference in the style of the prophets. Yehoshaphat for this reason asked : " If there were no *prophet of the Eternal* (in opposition to the four hundred of Baal) of whom they might enquire ?" And there *was one*—one who braved the idolater Ahab, despite of his being king and capable of injuring him ; but he was in prison by the commands of Ahab ; as Yehoshaphat, however, desired to see him, he was brought in the presence of the two kings. It is unnecessary to transcribe the whole account of Micaiah's prophecy, as every one, who may wish to know it, can find it in the chapter referred to.—Ahab was very angry when he heard the prophet predicting his death in battle ; he ordered him, therefore, to be kept in close confinement, and at hard diet, until he should come back in peace ; whereupon the prophet said (v. 28.) : " If thou return at all

19

in peace, the Eternal has not spoken through me ;" and he added :
" Hear it, all nations !" thus calling upon the whole world to bear witness, that in case Ahab should be killed in battle, (which in fact did
happen,) that then, and then only, would he be considered a true
prophet ; but if the king should return unhurt, then would he willingly forfeit all his claim to that name.—Micaiah, in all probability,
was *not* the author of his own *history ;* and of course it must have
been recorded by some other person, that he predicted the death of
Ahab in the manner related above ; and if it had been untrue, it
could never have been admitted into our historical writings, since
such a remarkable event, as the death of a king in battle, must have
been a matter well known to all the Israelites ; the more so, as
chronicles were kept, in which every occurrence of importance was
immediately recorded ; and could any man have palmed upon the
people a fictitious narrative, the falsity of which might have been
proven by a mere reference to the records of state ?

3. In Jeremiah, chap. xxviii. we read, that a man by the name of
Hananiah, pretending to have been inspired, limited the time of
seventy years, foretold by Jeremiah, as the duration of the Babylonian captivity, falsely to two years only.   In an address of Jeremiah to the people and Hananiah he said: " When the word of the
prophet who prophesies peace comes to pass, then it will be known
what prophet the Eternal has sent in truth." (v. 9th.) To prove further the fallacy of Hananiah's prophecy, Jeremiah announced to him :
" That he should die in the course of the year, as a punishment for the
deception he practised by his pretended mission ;" and Hananiah did
die before the expiration of the year. (v. 17.)—It is utterly impossible to suppose that the prophecy of Jeremiah was written after
Hananiah's death, and that in consequence the pretended prophecy
was indited after the event, or what is the same, that the *prophecy*
was never given. Let us but reflect that the whole affair took place
before a large concourse of people, some of whom must have been
alive in Ezra's time, and able to decide if Jeremiah's account was
true or not ; but since his book was universally received as canonical
by those who returned from the Babylonian captivity, we are compelled to come to the conclusion that every thing happened as Jeremiah himself relates it. If any other proof were wanting, it could
be drawn from the duration of the captivity. Jeremiah himself did

not live to see the restoration, for he died in Egypt long before that time. Now it appears clearly from Ezra, that just at the expiration of *the* seventy years Cyrus, king of Persia, granted the Jews permission to return to their own land; and in consequence, what had been *prediction* in the time of Jeremiah, became *certainty* and *fulfilment* in the days of Ezra and Nehemiah; and that further the prophecy of Jeremiah bears the marks of *true* revelation and inspiration, which have been given in this chapter, as the doctrines proclaimed by him are also in conformity with the Pentateuch.

We have thus incontestable proof that miracles were never appealed to by our prophets to attest their divine mission; but reference was always had on this point to the fulfilment of conditions *previously* stated, that is to say, the accomplishment of the predictions. A similar test was proposed by Elijah to the prophets of Baal on mount Carmel, to prove who was God;—if the Eternal Lord whom he adored, or *what* they pretended to call god. He made a condition with those around him, that the God who should send fire to consume the sacrifices should be acknowledged as the true God. The false prophets were obliged to think this test so liberal, that they immediately consented. It need not be told that their efforts were fruitless (see 1 Kings, chap. xviii.), though they dreadfully cut themselves with swords and lances, as was their custom, till the blood ran down. Not so acted the prophet of the Eternal Lord of heaven: calmly but with firmness did he call the people to him, and thereupon repaired the altar of his God, which had been destroyed.* When the altar was finished, and the sacrifice was laid in proper order upon it, Elijah addressed a fervent prayer to God, whose messenger he was: " To prove on that day to the people that the Eternal is God, and that he himself was the prophet chosen to do all he had done !"—And behold—the fire descended from heaven, and consumed the sacrifice, and the wood, and the stones, and the dust, yea even the water in the trench round the altar ! It was then that the

---

* To sacrifice out of the precincts of the temple was, under every other circumstance, contrary to the law ; but as it had become necessary to prove to the deluded people the folly of idolatry, and since the Israelites no longer went to Jerusalem to worship, Elijah was permitted, but for this time only, to bring a sacrifice upon mount Carmel, as the practical lesson of piety could only be taught at the place and in the manner it was done by him.

eyes of the people were opened, and they beheld clearly that the God whom Elijah proclaimed *is* God, and that Elijah was the chosen messenger of this *their* God.—The prophet stood alone, unaided, amid a people addicted to idolatry but a few moments before—but now they were convinced of their error, they fell on their faces and said : " The Eternal is the God ! the Eternal is the God !" The film was removed from their eyes, and but three words were all they were able to utter, and to this day the words ה' הוא האלהים are the motto of our nation ; when the Day of Atonement is closing they announce that a day entirely devoted to our God is past ; when our brother is dying they are repeated, that he may be reminded, at the moment of his departure hence, of the God of nature, and be admonished to dedicate to Him his last thoughts ; for He is kind, merciful, and ever ready to pardon the returning child, though this return has been long deferred. On both occasions, at the close of the Day of Atonement and of our earthly career, we should be free from sin, ready to meet that God who has so kindly sustained, and so mercifully protected us. Has our life been devoted to his service—have not our sins formed a division between Him and us :—then our prayer on the Day of Atonement *cannot* have been in vain, for our sins have been forgiven. If every Kippur-day (Day of Atonement) has been thus through life—if every year has found us better and more perfect : why need we tremble when death comes near ? Can we not say with composure : " The Lord shall reign for ever ?" Yes, for ever shall his kingdom endure,—like ourselves all mankind shall acknowledge Him—shall seek protection under his almighty power ; and when all nations have been united in his service, all will join us in exclaiming : " Hear, O Israel, the Eternal our God is the only Eternal Being !" He alone is everlasting— no other being exists to share his power—to Him, therefore, we will submit our destinies ; and He will surely assist us. Whilst living we will pay adoration to his name ; and when dying let our last thought be : his UNITY ! his power ! his protection ! and his willingness to forgive the crimes of the returning sinner !

149

CHAPTER XXII.

FULFILMENT OF PROPHECY.

Having seen, in the foregoing chapter, what prophecy is, we ought
next to examine : " Can the prophecies of Moses, or at least a part
of them, be verified by the predicted result or not ?"

We have already seen proven (chap. xii.) that one at least of
Moses's predictions has been literally fulfilled, namely, that the belief in his prophecy should exist amongst us for ever ; since from his
time to the present age every generation of Jews were believers in
the truth of his mission. Although at certain periods of our history religion was sadly neglected : yet were there always some men
who firmly adhered to the law, when even the ignorant multitude
had neglected their duty. Another strong confirmation of our law
can be found in the fact, that the more acquainted a man is with it,
the stronger will ever be his confidence in its divine origin, and in the
truth of *him* by whose instrumentality it was first made public. If
we are asked for proof to sustain this assertion, we can exultingly
point to the long succession of the wisest and most pious men, who,
penetrated with real love of God and affection for mankind, laboured all their life, under every disadvantage imaginable, to perpetuate
what they justly conceived to be the word of God amongst their
brethren. And what was their reward ?—Honours conferred by
princes ?—Worldly riches ?—No, no,—imprisonment, the rack, and
even the scaffold ; to be despised by heathens—hated by the Mahomedans—and persecuted, even to death, by the Nazarenes ! And
did they flinch ?—Did they grow slothful in their sacred avocation ?
Far from it. The greater the danger was, the greater and more
persevering became their devotion. The following anecdote is related concerning the great Rabbi Akiba, who at the age of one hundred and twenty years suffered the most cruel death for his attachment to the law :—" The government had prohibited every Jew,
under pain of death, from studying or teaching the law ; but regard-

less of this mandate did this Rabbi continue to teach publicly, as
formerly he was wont to do. A certain Paphos, son of Judah, re-
monstrated with him on the folly of thus exposing himself to certain
destruction; but Rabbi Akiba answered him with the following parable :—A fox was once walking by the margin of a river, and he saw
the fish moving to and fro in the water, as if they were in fear of
something. He asked them the reason of their continual motion,
when they told him, it was on account of the fisherman who incessantly molested them with nets and fishing rods.—' Why do you not
leave the water,' said the fox, ' and come to live with me on shore,
as your and my ancestors used to do?' ' Really,' answered the fish,
' thou fox, who art generally considered the wisest of beasts, art in
fact the most silly ; here in the water, where alone we can live, we
are afraid ; how much greater reason have we to fear the dry land,
where we are sure to die !' Not long after this conversation, Rabbi
Akiba was apprehended and committed to prison, at the same time
that Paphos was sent there, who being asked by the former what
was the cause of his being there, exclaimed: ' Happy art thou,
Akiba, that thou sufferest for the sake of the law, and woe to thee,*
Paphos, that thy sufferings proceed from unworthy actions !' Akiba's
integrity did not save him from death, and they tore the flesh from
his bones with iron combs ; but he suffered with patience, and continued to say : ' Hear, O Israel, the Eternal our God is the only Eternal Being,' till his soul left its mortal habitation, to ascend to heaven, to receive there everlasting light and permanent unalloyed
enjoyment, as the reward for its constancy !"

Need I mention the many precious sons and daughters of Zion
who laid in heaps, blackening under a summer's sun, perforated by
the dagger of the adversary ? Who does not remember the stakes
burning in Spain, Portugal, France, and England, the best of Jacob's
children, because of their belief in ONE GOD ? And they acknowledged the God whom their forefathers had been taught to

---

* It was very common amongst the Jews living about the time of the destruction of the second temple, to speak of themselves in the second or third
person. See several passages in the Talmud, particularly *Baba Metzeengah*,
Payreck, Hapongalim.

worship, and they died in defence of the faith which had been transmitted to the Israelites through Moses!

In Leviticus, chap. xxvi. v. 32—33, God says: " And I will lay waste the land, so that your enemies, who dwell therein, shall be astonished at it.   And yourselves I will scatter among the nations, and will draw the sword after you, and your land shall be desolate, and your cities shall be waste. "   And has not this actually occurred ?   Are not the once fertile fields of Judah a desert ? the splendid cities of Palestine heaps of ruins ? and the beautiful Jerusalem—the joy of all the earth—is scarcely the shadow of its former self; and really our enemies who now inhabit *our* land, and the stranger who comes from a far off country, are astonished, and wonder : " For what reason has the Lord acted so towards this land, why was this great anger kindled?"   But to our shame we must answer : " Because we have forsaken the covenant of the Eternal, the God of our forefathers, which he made with us when He brought us out of Egypt ; and we went, and worshipped other gods, and bowed down to them ; gods which we did not know, and which our God had not assigned to us.   The anger of the Lord was therefore kindled against this land, to bring upon it all the curses which are written in the book of the law. And the Lord has driven us out of our land in anger, and in wrath, and in great indignation, and thrown us into another land, as we see this day."*

In Numbers, chap. xxiv. v. 24, is the following : " And ships of war shall come from the coast of Chittim, and afflict Ashur and afflict Eber, but it (the land of Chittim) shall also be ruined at last." (This translation is according to Mendelsohn's translation of the Pentateuch.)   At the time that Balaam spoke this prophecy, the Roman state was not in existence, and the other nations, by whom Italy was then inhabited, were not in a condition to send out ships of war to afflict Ashur and Eber.   Therefore, at the time the pro-

---

* This answer is found in Deut. chap. xxix., only that I have taken the liberty of using the *first* instead of the *third* person plural.   My intention, however, is not to change the meaning of the passage in the slightest degree ; but since I could not use words more expressive than those of Holy Writ I applied them as above. I deem this explanation necessary, that none may accuse me of perverting the text of Scripture.

phecy was uttered, it could not have been understood, since the na·
tion to which the prophecy referred was not even in being. But
has not this prediction been literally fulfilled? Did not the Romans
overrun Assyria and Judea? And where are these Romans at the
present day? Where is their splendour? Where is their mighty
empire?—Lost, lost, lost!—The ancient Forum is now a cow-mar-
ket; this place, where once the greatest Roman orators contended
for the victory, is buried under rubbish, and the ruins of buildings
which once surrounded it! The Coliseum, built by the commands
of a conquering emperor by conquered captives, remains now a
monument of the awful vengeance which our God has taken against
Rome, through hordes of barbarians sent to subvert the mightiest
empire of antiquity.—And Italy? is at present divided into many
small governments, scarcely one of which can be called independent.—And the *Italians?* the nobility of their character has past
away; and where can you find the representative of Tully—of
Cæsar—of Tiberius Gracchus—of Fabius the Cunctator? The
energy of the Italians is broken; and those, who once kept a world
in subjection by the terror of their arms, are now an easy prey to
every invader!

Near the close of Numbers, chap. xxxiii., we read that the Israelites
were commanded to drive out the Canaanites, and they were foretold
that those Canaanites, not driven out as soon as it could be done,
should be like thorns in their sides, meaning, that they should but
ill requite the debt of gratitude they owed the Israelites for their
forbearance, but would, on the contrary, be their most inveterate enemies. Our ancestors, knew better, *as they thought,* how to deal
with the aborigines than God had commanded, and they left many
of these wicked people amongst them, only exacting a tribute for the
protection afforded to them. But mark the consequences! The Israelites were immediately notified that it should never be in their
power to expel the remaining Canaanites, and that they should be
their constant enemies; and this was literally accomplished, witness
the subjection of the Israelites (previous to Deborah) to the king of
Harosheth, and David's taking Jerusalem, by storm, from the
Jebusites.

In Deut. chap. xxviii. we have a description of the conquest of
Palestine by Vespasian and Titus; and if Moses had been present at-

the siege of Jerusalem, he could never have better and more forcibly described the sufferings of the besieged.—Of the *Romans* themselves he says: " The Lord shall bring over thee a nation from afar, from the end of the earth, like the eagle *flies*; a nation whose language thou shalt not understand." This nation, *fierce* and *steeled against pity*, was to besiege the Israelites in all their cities, till the strongest and highest walls had been broken down ; and all this was to be in consequence of their non-compliance with the will of God, as contained in the Mosaic law.—And did this not take place? Were not the Romans a nation from the verge of the earth, whose conquests were as rapid as the flight of the eagle? Were they not fierce and steeled against pity? What nation did the Romans ever spare? Did they not rather break the power of every people that attempted to resist their gradual but unceasing encroachments? Just so did they also treat us; they drove us from post to post, and from town to town, till all our cities at last became subject to their sway! and thus was this prediction accomplished.

Deut. chap. xxviii. v. 37 : " And thou shalt become an (object of) astonishment, a proverb, and a bye-word amongst all the nations, whither the Eternal thy God shall carry thee."—*So we are!* Every one is astonished how a nation so favoured by God, could be reduced so low ; when any preacher admonishes the people who flock to hear him, he points either the finger of scorn or pity at us, and exclaims : " See what the Jews have come to!" Whatever wrong is done by one of us, though this one be the most insignificant and worthless, the whole nation is, in a measure, burthened with the stigma; if a woman of our society acts contrary to law, it seems to be of weight enough to throw blame upon every one, who was born in the same faith with her ; yea, our very name has been used to express every thing dishonourable and mean—the noble name of Israelite has been applied to designate a usurer, when usury is universally known to be contrary to the law which the Israelite acknowledges. It is thus, that the curse pronounced against us for disobedience, has been, alas ! too literally fulfilled, and we have become an object of astonishment, a proverb, and a bye-word, and the very meanest of human beings thinks himself superior to the best of our nation.

We have here before us some of the most prominent prophecies concerning the punishment, which was predicted and did actually

20

overtake our ancestors and even ourselves to this very day. It may be, that we are yet to suffer many centuries, for as yet our course has not been in the spirit of true repentance, we have not even now thrown aside the sins for which Jerusalem was twice taken, and the temple twice burnt. Not yet have all the Israelites one heart and one mind in the worship of the Eternal their Redeemer; but whenever they "pursue the true path to know the Eternal," they may rest assured, that their captives will be gathered and restored to their former habitations.—Let us consider the following from the Talmud: Rabbi Gamaliel, R. Elazar ben Azariah, R. Yehoshua, and Rabbi Akiba* were one day standing together, when they saw a fox running out from the place, where the holies of holies once stood; the three first began to weep, whilst R. Akiba laughed; in astonishment, they asked of him the cause of his untimely mirth, but he in his turn enquired: "Why do you weep?" "And should we not weep, when we see the curse so clearly verified? for the mountain of Zion, which is desolate, the foxes walked upon it." (Lament. v. 18.) "For this reason do I laugh," answered the wise Rabbi, "whilst the evil prophecies remained unaccomplished, there might have been fears entertained for the verification of the good tidings promised through our prophets; but now, since we see the evil coming to pass, can we possibly doubt the eventual fulfilment of the consolation of Zion—and does not God rather reward than punish?" His friends were satisfied, and answered: "Akiba, thou hast comforted us!"

And not hope alone, but also a *partial* fulfilment attests the truth of the good prophesied to us. We read in Levit. chap. xxvi. v. 44: " And yet for all that, when they be in the land of their enemies, I will not cast them away, nor will I abhor them to destroy them utterly and to break my covenant with them, for I am yet the Eternal their God. But I will remember them (for their benefit) the covenant of their ancestors, whom I have brought out of the land of Egypt in the sight of the heathens, that I might be their God; I am the Eternal."—This prophecy clearly points out the protecting arm ever held out over the Israelites, and never yet did God leave us altogether at the mercy of our adversaries.—Whenever a plot has

* They lived immediately after the destruction of the temple.

been formed for our destruction, we yet escaped, and often our enemies fell in the snares they had laid for our feet; and though hundreds and thousands of us have been killed in battle—in the amphithe-
atre—by the sword—the gibbet—and the stake, we are still as numerous among the nations as the " dew-drops from heaven," and all
the massacres have not caused a sensible diminution of our numbers.

Another prophecy pronounced by Moses in Deut. chap. xxxii., is
even now in a train of accomplishment. The last song of the law-
giver concludes thus: "Praise* as happy, O ye nations, his people,
for He will avenge the blood of his servants, and render vengeance
unto his adversaries, and wash away the sins of his land and of his
people." (v. 43.) And indeed all who have oppressed us in times
gone by, now, at this very hour, feel the weight of the vengeance
threatened against the adversaries of Israel. See what has become
of Spain and Portugal! countries once flourishing and prosperous,
now impoverished—sunk in ignorance, and degraded! The innocent
blood of God's servants does not cry in vain to be avenged; the per-
pretators of the horrid deeds are slaves—and the places where these
barbarous scenes were witnessed are hourly becoming more like a
wilderness, and it is evident to the most *careless* observer, that all
this is owing to the expulsion of our brethren from these countries;
for since the time of Ferdinand and Isabella, Spain has been gradually declining. The same was the case with England before the
time of Cromwell; civil wars and internal commotions were then
very common, and only since the days of the protector, when the
Jews began to re-enter England, has it risen to that eminence it
now holds among European nations. Verily the prophecy of Jeremiah is every day proving its truth: (Jer. chap. ii. v. 1—3.) " And
the word of the Lord came to me as follows: ' Go and cry in the

---

* I have given a different translation of this verse from the one in the English version, having followed R. Moses Mendelsohn (of blessed memory) who
translates הַרְנִינוּ with, preiset glucklich, that is: *declare happy, praise them as
happy.*—Again, וְכִפֶּר is given in the Eng. Vers. *will be merciful*, when in fact,
the true meaning of this word is *wipe off*, as אֲכַפְּרָה פָנָיו (Gen. chap. xxxii. v.
21,): " I will remove his anger;" I have therefore given it: " He will wash
away the sins;" and thus prophesied Jeremiah : " In those days, and at that time,
speaks the Lord, shall the transgression of Israel be sought for, but it shall be
no more, and the sins of Judah, and they shall not be found, for I will pardon
those whom I shall leave."

ears of Jerusalem,' (proclaim that every one may hear) 'and say: Thus saith the Lord, I remember unto thee the kindness of thy youth, the love of thy espousals, when thou didst walk after me in the wilderness, in a land which is not sown. Israel is holy to the Lord' (consecrated to his service) 'and the first of his fruit, all who devour' (injure or molest) 'him shall offend, evil shall befal them,' saith the Lord." Let therefore all nations be cautious how they meddle with us, lest they offend, and incur punishment.— From the whole of the foregoing it will be clearly seen, that *some* of the good prophecies have come to pass, and can we then entertain any doubt about the ultimate restoration of the Israelites and the gathering of the captives? Let us then, my brethren, await with resignation the time when Jerusalem shall be rebuilt, and the Israelites shall again inhabit the land of their ancestors!

CHAPTER XXIII.

THE RELIGION OF THE BIBLE.

If what has been advanced in the preceding chapters is correct, and there is every reason for its being so: it follows, that the Mosaic laws are of divine origin, and are for this reason, and no other, binding upon us. But some doubter may yet question, if the books we now have are the *same* which were given to Moses, or what is the same thing: "Have not at different times different laws been observed by the Jews under the name of the Mosaic code?"

To answer this question we need only refer to the historical books written posterior to Moses's death, and anterior to the return of the Jews from Babylon. It cannot be expected (because it was unnecessary) that *every one* of the commandments contained in the Pentateuch should be found in the histories and the prophets; but if we find some recorded, (when occasion required,) and those in the very

words of the Mosaic law, we must admit that there is good ground
for believing that the other commandments also, though not mentioned, were then known and practised.

Joshua, the immediate successor of Moses, circumcised the
younger part of the Jews, or rather Israelites, immediately after
they had crossed the Jordan. (Josh. v. 4.)—While the Israelites
were crossing the Jordan, they took with them twelve stones, each
as heavy as a strong man could carry, out of the bed of the river,
which they erected in Gilgal, as a monument that they had passed
through the Jordan in the same manner their fathers had passed
through the Arabian Sea.—When afterwards they arrived at mount
Ebal, they built an altar of unhewn stones, and inscribed thereon the
Deuteronomy, and also brought sacrifices of burnt and peace-offerings, (Josh. chap. viii.) as was commanded by Moses. (Deut. chap.
xxvii. v. 1—8.) They also pronounced the blessings towards* those
who stood upon Gerizim, and the curses towards those upon Ebal,
as commanded in the same chapter of Deuteronomy.—In the same
book, chap. xxi., it is forbidden to let a culprit hang over night on
the gallows, and Joshua invariably acted so.—The land, when conquered, was to be divided by lot among the different tribes, but the
tribe of Levi was to have only forty-eight cities, and a mile round
the cities on all the four sides, just so did Joshua do; and he also
confirmed the commands given to Moses, (in Numb. chap. xiv. v. 24
and Deut. chap. i. v. 36,) by giving Hebron to Caleb, and the land
beyond Jordan to the tribes of Reuben and Gad, and the half of Menasseh. (Numb. chap. xxxii. v. 22.)—In several passages of Exodus,
Numb. and Deut., we see positive commands given to provide cities
of refuge for the man who had slain another unintentionally. Now
let any man compare the thirty-fifth of Numbers, with the twentieth
of the book of Joshua, and he must confess that this part of the law
was existing before Joshua.—In Joshua, chap. xxii., is an account
of an altar built by the tribes of Reuben and Gad, and half of Me-

---

* It must not be supposed, that the blessings and curses were pronounced in
favour of one and against the other division of tribes; but that the Levites
turned, whilst pronouncing the blessings, *towards* those upon Gerizim, and,
while pronouncing the curses, towards those upon Ebal; but in point of fact,
the blessings were intended for all the Israelites, in case they acted right, and
the curses, in case they acted wrong.

nasseh, upon their return to their own land. It is well known, that according to Lev. chap. xvii. v. 8, it was unlawful to sacrifice but at the door of the tabernacle, while it served in place of the temple. The Israelites therefore sent a deputation to the two and a half tribes, to remonstrate with them on account of their building an altar in contravention of the command of God ; but the latter informed them in extenuation of the supposed infraction of the law, that it was but a monument commemorative of the history of the time and of their affinity to the other tribes, and on no account to offer upon it any sacrifice whatever.

In the admirably written address of the great republican leader Joshua, we find him admonishing the people whom he had so long and faithfully governed, in nearly the same terms used by Moses. He even so far agrees with his predecessor, in what may appear to some a trifling, but which is to a Jew of necessity a very essential thing, as to prohibit the swearing by or mentioning the names of idols. (Exodus, chap. xxiii. v. 13, and Josh. chap. xxiii. v. 7.) The reason for this interdiction will be easily discovered by every thinking man ; it was, namely, to prevent their taking a *pretended* oath by an idol, with a view perhaps of deceiving either for their own advantage, for instance, to obtain money, *preserve life*, or the like, or for the benefit or tranquillity of others ; such conduct is condemned by our law, no deception must be practised, but our conduct should be open and free from all duplicity and evasion, and if it be necessary for us to take an oath, let it be by the name of the Eternal, to whom alone we owe *allegiance*. In the same chapter, v. 15, Joshua says : " That as the Israelites had received all the good which God had promised them, they might be sure, that in case of deviation, they should suffer every punishment denounced, even the expulsion from that land they had just acquired by conquest."

At the conclusion of his second harangue (chap. xxiv. v. 15—16,) Joshua proposed to the people a choice of worship, either to serve the Eternal, or the idols worshipped by the ancestors of Abraham in Chaldea, or the gods of the Amorites, " but " said he, " I and my family will serve the Eternal."—It was therefore left to the people, for the third time, to accept or reject the books of Moses ; but then no such thing as doubting existed, they were all too much convinced of the truth of what they had seen, and thus they spoke : " Far be it from us to forsake the Eternal, to serve other gods. For it is the Eternal our God, who has brought us and our fathers out of Egypt, from the house of slavery, and who has done before our eyes these great wonders, and preserved us in all the way we travelled, and amongst all the nations we passed through ; and He, the Eternal, has driven out all the nations and the Amorites, the inhabitants of this land, before us : the Eternal then *we also will serve*, for HE IS OUR GOD." Joshua again reminded them, that the worship of God was not so easy a matter, for that He is careful of his honour, and never suffers sins to remain unpunished, because He is holy. They again assented, though they were now, if they were even not so before, fully convinced that they would be certainly punished if they sinned.—Joshua then addressed them : " You are *witnesses* against yourselves, that you have chosen yourselves the Eternal, to serve Him ;" to this they answered : " We are witnesses ;" they presently added : " The Eternal our God we will serve, and his voice we will obey !" Joshua added all the above to the book of the law of God, and erected a stone as a monument, and said : " This stone shall be a witness against us, for it has heard all the words of the Eternal, which He has spoken with us ;—let it be an evidence against you, lest you deny your God !"—This is the substance of the last address of Joshua ; let it not however be supposed, that he meant to assert, that the stone had *actually* heard the words spoken ; but that the expression is employed figuratively, to indicate to posterity, when- ever they should see this stone, that their ancestors willingly entered into the covenant, *because they had seen all before them*, so that there was no room to doubt, and thus the stone would serve in fact every purpose, *as if* it had heard all and communicated its knowledge to those who saw it.

From the above we can draw the following *incontestable* infer- ences : first, that the Mosaic books existed before Joshua obtained his office of judge ; or what is the same, that they were written by Moses himself, for who else could have done it? Secondly, that Joshua added his own book to the first part of our canon, and it is therefore authentic, having been written by an eye-witness of the facts it contains. And lastly, that at the time of Joshua's death the Israelites adhered firmly to the laws derived from Sinai, and that the third generation from the Exodus willingly accepted these

laws as their code, and the Eternal as their God, having been convinced of the truth and correctness of the Pentateuch by the fulfilment of the predictions it contains, relative to the conquests of
Palestine ; and being impressed with a firm conviction of the existence of the Eternal and his almighty power, having so largely par-
taken of his goodness, kindness, and protection, in all the trying
scenes of their history, from the first mission of Moses down to the
time of which we are speaking.

There are, besides those already enumerated, several other coinci-
dences between the book of Joshua and the Pentateuch, of which, however, I shall only mention the observance of the Passover-feast (chap.
v.) whilst the Israelites were at Gilgal.—We must now examine the
book of Judges, in which we find several instances recorded, in which
the Mosaic law was observed.—Immediately in the commencement
we find, that the people asked advice through the Urim and Thumim.—The messenger, who came to Bochim to announce to the
people that their conduct had been displeasing to.God, made use of
language similar to Moses in the thirty-third chapter of Numbers.
Samson was, by a special message, dedicated to God as a Nazarite
נזיר, and he was ordered strictly to observe the regulations laid down
for the conduct of a person thus consecrated, which consecration
was always voluntary on the part of the Nazarite himself, except
in the instances of Samson and Samuel. (Numb. chap. vi.)—Gideon,
when he had been appointed by the messenger of God to effect the
liberation of his fellow-citizens from the yoke of their enemies
(Judges, chap. vi.), was commanded to cut down the trees, and to
break the altar used for the worship of Baal, conformably to the
repeated commandments in relation to idolatry. (Numb. xxxiii. and
other places.)—Adultery was an unheard of thing in the latter times
of the Judges ; and the commitment of such an act was sufficient
cause to induce the whole nation to take up arms against the tribe
of Benjamin, upon their refusal to deliver up to punishment the per-
petrators of this horrible outrage. (Judges, chap. xx.)

Not only are there confirmations to be found in the book of
Judges of the *imperative*, but also of the historical parts of our law.
I allude, in the first place, to the passage in the song of Deborah
(chap. v. v. 4—5,) in which she plainly refers to the promulgation
of the law from Sinai ; and the language employed bears a close re-

semblance to the beautiful passage in the thirty-third chapter of Deuteronomy.—In the second place, I wish to direct the attention of the reader to the letter of Yiphtach (Jephthah) to the king of the Ammonites. (Judg. chap. xi.) Here Yiphtach, who had been chosen commander against the invader, expostulates with the latter about his unjust irruption into Palestine. He recapitulates in a few words the history of the conquest of the country on the east side of the Jordan, as a justification of its being possessed by the Israelites. He further states, that it had remained in their possession for three hundred years, and if the Ammonites had had any right to it, they would surely have claimed it in all this time.—From this letter of the Hebrew general we must infer, that three hundred years after Moses his history was yet believed not alone by the Hebrews, but was even offered in argument to a heathen king; which could not have been done if the matter in debate had not been known to this king from sources other than the Hebrew writings. For, what would the story avail which Yiphtach tells, if the king could have answered : " All these things are new to me, and I do not believe you ?" But since Yiphtach appeals to the facts which he relates in such a confident and triumphant manner, it must be admitted, that the history of the conquest of Palestine, as related by Moses and Joshua, is the authentic account of this event ; and that further it was a matter of general notoriety amongst the nations bordering upon Palestine.

The book of Ruth, the history of which is contemporaneous with that of the Judges, affords other instances of the observance of several other Mosaic precepts ; namely, the redemption of the land of poor relatives, (Lev. chap. xxv. v. 25,) the espousal of the relict of a near connection, (Deut. chap. xxv. v. 5,) and the leaving of things forgotten in the field for the benefit of the poor and the stranger. (Lev. chap. xxiii. v. 22, and Deut. chap. xxiv. v. 19.) Besides the observance of the written precepts, we discover the custom of confirming a sale, bargain, or contract, by one party pulling off his shoe and presenting it to the other, which custom, only in a different manner, is yet observed amongst us ; namely, one party takes hold of the corner of a garment, and presents it to the other to lay hold of in the same manner, and this ceremony concludes the contract. This custom, recorded in Ruth, is the first example on record of

21

traditional or rabbinical law, and deserves for this reason particular attention.

Having thus taken a cursory view of the three oldest books after Moses's, we will next examine the books known as the first and second of Samuel and the two books of Kings. In the very outset of the first of these books we find, that Elkanah, the father of Samuel, made his annual pilgrimages to the *tabernacle of assembly* at Shiloh, in conformity with the injunction three times repeated in the Mosaic law, to sacrifice the offerings of the seasons and those which he voluntarily offered.—We also see in the same chapter exemplified the most approved mode of praying ; and further, that the heartfelt prayer, though scarcely audible, is that most acceptable to the Deity.—In the second chapter we have undoubted proof, that the doctrine of the resurrection of the body was universally known amongst the Israelites, since Hannah employed this assertion in her song of thanksgiving, after she had presented her son to the high-priest. Another interesting subject can be established by this song, that poetry was an accomplishment not unusual amongst our ancestors, since we see *females* inditing songs of praise, (Hannah and Deborah,) and, of course, a nation, where such exalted sentiments as used by these two Hebrew females were common, must have reached a high state of civilisation.—In Numbers, chap. vi. v. 19, we read, that the priest was not entitled to take his share of the sacrifice, till it was boiling in the pot ; and in 1 Samuel, chap. ii. v. 15—17, we find, that the two sons of Eli are censured for infringing this regulation by demanding the priest's portion, while the meat was yet raw.—In the fourth and sixth chapters we have some curious and important facts relative to the truth of the history of Moses, namely, that the *Philistines* were acquainted with the many plagues the Egyptians had suffered on account of the oppression they imposed upon the Hebrews.—In chap. vii. v. 6, is a confirmation of the truth of tradition, with regard to the pouring out of water on the feast of Tabernacles ; for in this verse we read, that they *poured out water* before the Lord ; that they also fasted that day, and said there : " We have sinned against the Lord ;" and that Samuel held judgment over the Israelites. We must infer from this, that the sacrifice of water was a custom sanctioned by the earliest authorities posterior to Moses—that on the days of fasting the people made confession of their sins in addresses to God—and that restitution was made for any wrong done by man to man, for we read that Samuel sat in judgment. Does this not prove the antiquity of the fast-days amongst the Jews, and of the customs observed on such occasions?

After Saul had been chosen by lot as head of the nation, he being the man whom God had chosen, (Deut. chap. xvii. v. 15,) (which was at the same time recorded, 1 Sam. chap. x. v. 25,) he was despised by the worthless part of the people, who said contemptuously : " What good can this one do us ?" they brought him no presents, as is yet customary in the East, but it is recorded to Saul's honour, that he took no notice of this intentional insult. And now mark the simplicity of those days ; the man chosen from amongst all the nation to be their leader and chief, had just returned from his *work in the field,* when he heard the lamentations of the people on account of the irruption of the king of the Ammonites. But the hero was filled with more than natural courage, and he assembled all the people to follow him and Samuel to battle. They conquered under the guidance of Saul ; and when the people threatened with death every one who should refuse to acknowledge him, he forbade the harming of any one on that account, " for the Eternal had given assistance to Israel on that day."—It will appear from this whole account, that the Israelites followed strictly in the choice of their king the rule laid down in Deut. chap. xvii. v. 15.—In the twelfth chapter of first Samuel will be found the address of Samuel to the people after Saul was finally chosen ; here the prophet recapitulates the history of the Jews *according to Moses's* account of them ; and we have thus for the hundredth time *positive* and *incontestable* proof, that the book of Exodus and the history of that and of the subsequent times were known and *recorded* amongst the Jews, and that the prophets frequently referred to these events as undoubted and undeniable. We further learn from the twenty-third verse of the same chapter, that however wrong the people may have acted, the pious man is not authorised to withhold praying for them and teaching them the *way of right,* and in this respect we see that Samuel imitated Moses ; and if we compare the lives of these two men, unsurpassed by any men of any age, we must acknowledge that Samuel must have known the history of Moses, and followed him as a prototype.—In the fourteenth chapter we have an account of the mode of slaughtering cattle for the use of the people (i. e. *not* for sacrifices) ;· and we shall discover, on examination, that the custom amongst us of *cutting the throat* of the beasts is conformable to ancient usage, and according to the allusion contained in Deut. chap. xii. v. 21.

Though it may not be altogether relevant to the subject under consideration, I cannot omit to notice what is said in the twentieth chapter about the days of the new-moon. We find related, that the two first days of the month were celebrated in the palace of Saul, as is done yet at this time, (and of these two days, the first is considered as belonging to the past, and the second to the new month,) which proves that *our* mode of calculating time is of the highest antiquity. From the 26th verse of this chapter it appears that the laws relative to *clean and unclean*, as laid down by Moses in Leviticus and elsewhere, were practised, and therefore must have been known in the days of Samuel and Saul. According to chap. xxi. v. 7, the commandment relative to the *show bread* (Lev. chap. xxiv. v. 8,) was known and practised in those days, and in the twenty-eighth chapter it is recorded that Saul had removed all wizards out of the land, agreeably to Lev. chap. xx. v. 27, and several other passages in the Pentateuch.

As the second book of Samuel contains but few illustrations of the mode of worship amongst our ancestors, and of the manner in which they observed the law, I shall commence at once with the first book of Kings.—In chap. ii. v. 30, we read, that Joab who, though he was the greatest general of that or perhaps any other age, had committed two murders, which he perhaps did not consider in that light, fled to the altar of the Lord as to a place of refuge ; he refused to leave the sanctuary, and was therefore killed where he was, conformably to Exodus, chap. xxi. v. 14.—Chapter vii. v. 50, we read that Solomon made the vessels of the temple in the manner laid down by Moses. (Exo. chap. xxv. v. 38, and ibid. chap. xxvii. v. 3.)—The tables of the covenant were in the ark (1 Kings, chap. viii. v. 9,) as related by Moses. (Exodus chap. xl. v. 20.)—The festivals also were known and observed, as we are told in 1 Kings chap. viii. v. 65, since we are informed there, that Solomon and all Israel with him, observed the feast (of Tabernacles), and further, that instead of *eight* they celebrated *fourteen* days, the additional six no doubt in honour of the consecration of *the house*.—In chap. xi. v. 1, Solomon is censured for marrying females not belonging to his nation. (See Deut. chap. vii. v. 3—4.)—In chap. xiv. v. 15, the wife of Jereboam was notified by the blind prophet of Shiloh that the nation should be driven out of their land and sent beyond the river Euphrates, for their disobedience. (Deut. chap. xi. v. 16—17.) In the same chapter v. 24, is recorded, among other crimes committed by the tribe of Judah, their infraction of the commandment found in Deut. chap. xxiii. v. 18. We read in the first verse of the seventeenth chapter, that Elijah, surnamed Thishby,* swore by the Eternal God, whose servant he was, that there should be neither dew nor rain for three years, as was threatened by Moses. (Deut. chap. xi. v. 17.) Let us pause here a little, and look at the fearless messenger of God, who despising all worldly comforts, and clothed in a garment made of hair, with a thong of leather for a girdle, advanced boldly to carry the message of the Eternal his God to that king, who more than any other of his predecessors despised and persecuted the messengers of the true God.—In the conclusion of the *sixteenth* chapter we are informed that a man by the name of Chiale rebuilt Yericho, but that all his children died, as Joshua the son of Nun had foretold.† We are told in tradition, that Achab, who pretended to disbelieve Moses, said to Elijah : " See here, the curse of the scholar, Joshua, is fulfilled, whilst that of the master, Moses, and his predictions, are not verified by the event ; for did he not say, that when the Israelites should become idolatrous, there should be no rain, and are we not blessed with plenty, though we worship what Moses calls idols ?" It was then that Elijah swore the dreadful oath, and the prediction of Moses was verified to the fullest extent ; for three years no rain fell to enrich the worn-out land, and the parched soil was not refreshed by the gentle dews of heaven.—During all this time the most pious of mankind was obliged to conceal himself, for his exposing himself then would have answered no good purpose, save to irritate the more strongly the hatred of the sinful king of the Israelites ; but when the time of his prediction was drawing to a close, Elijah again appeared before the king, and after having demonstrated the greatness

* The same prophet spoken of above, chap. xxi.
† See Joshua, chap. vi. v. 26.

and the truth of the Eternal, the God of Israel, rain again visited the land which was suffering from severe famine. I have already explained (chap. xxi.) the sacrifice of Elijah upon Carmel, immediately after which he ordered the prophets of Baal to be killed and none escaped. (Deut. chap. xvii. v. 5.) Again was Elijah threatened by Izabel, the wicked wife of the wicked Achab; but he was protected by God and escaped to Horeb, the mount from which the law had been given.—Achab had endeavoured to dispossess Naboth peaceably of his paternal inheritance ; but this noble Israelite refused to act contrary to the law of Moses, (Lev. chap. xxv. v. 23, and Numb. chap. xxxvi. v. 9,) though he must have known, that a man so regardless of all moral and religious duties, who moreover was in a measure governed by a wife even more than himself addicted to all sinful passions and desires, would not stop at any thing to obtain that which he desired.—In short, Naboth *was* killed, as we are informed in 1 Kings, chap. xxi. ; and when Achab went to take possession of the land acquired in so illegal a manner, he was met by *Elijah*, who then communicated to him the downfal and utter destruction of his house.—Let the reader notice that it was Elijah, who carried this message to the king, before whom he was flying, and we thus have the strongest and clearest possible evidence, that Elijah was one of *those prophets like Moses*, whom God had promised to raise up unto Israel, (Deut. chap. xviii. v. 18,) who were to be fearless of consequences and only intent upon executing the will of Heaven ; and this was also clearly exemplified by the perilous reply of the prophet Amos, to the idolatrous priest Amaziah, as he boldly declared his intention of not complying with the command of the latter, although his life was thereby put in jeopardy. (See Amos, chap. vii. v. 16.)

After Elijah had been taken to heaven, his disciple Elisha was the acknowledged prophet, and before him all the worshippers of idols quailed, no less heathens than the sinners of Israel, for all were afraid to injure the exalted man *through whom God spoke.*—A woman in Shunam had been blessed with a son, as Elisha had promised her ; this child died, and the Shunamith, (i. e. a female resident of Shunam,) concealing this mournful occurrence from her husband, prepared to go to the man of God. Her husband, not knowing the cause of her sudden departure, asked her : " Why'she would go that day, since it was neither new-moon nor *Sabbath ?*" I do not think that there is any mention made of the Sabbath in any passage preceding this, and we have here at least satisfactory evidence, that the *Sabbath* was not alone *known* before the Babylonian captivity, but that on this day the people resorted to the prophets, and since the prophets taught the laws of God, we may also add, that in all probability other men were visited, who, though not prophets, taught the life dispensing words of the law.—The Shunamith gave her husband an evasive answer, and sought out the prophet, upon whose intercession the dead child was revived, and restored in this manner by the manifest help of God to its overjoyed mother. (2 Kings, chap. iv.)

In the thirteenth chapter is recorded the death of Elisha, and that the king of Mesopotamia did the Israelites much mischief; but it is said, v. 23 : "That God had compassion on them on account of his covenant with Abraham, Isaac, and Jacob, so that He would not destroy them altogether." Let the reader compare this verse with Moses's prophecy in Leviticus, chap. xxvi. v. 42—45, and then determine whether or not the writer* of the second book of Kings was acquainted with the *present* Pentateuch. 1 am well aware that the

---

* I am unable to determine who is the author of the book, of which we are now treating, though it must be either Jeremiah, Baruch, or some one of their contemporaries and friends ; for this reason : this and the book of the prophecies of Jeremiah both conclude with an account of Jeconiah's being greatly favoured by Eveel Merodoch the successor of Nebuchadnezzar ; no mention whatever is made of Ezra, Daniel, or Zerubabel, nor of the return of the captives, and we must therefore conclude that the writer of this book must have been ignorant of the fulfilment of Jeremiah's prophecy, and of course that it must have been existing in its present state previous to Ezra, who, therefore, could have had no agency whatever in compiling this or any of the preceding books.—It may be, that it was written by different persons, or rather that Jeremiah or Baruch compiled it from authentic sources ; as upon referring to chap. xix. v. 20, will be found a passage purporting to be a prophecy of Isaiah. Now the manner of Isaiah is so very unique and his style so sublime, that no one can mistake its authenticity ; in fact, it is the same, with some few *verbal* differences, with the thirty-seventh chapter of the book of the prophecies of Isaiah.—He was an eye-witness of the events he relates in his book, and it has accordingly the strongest claims to be generally accredited, and we have therefore sufficient reason to believe that the other sources of the second book of Kings are equally authentic with the nineteenth chapter.

passage in Leviticus referred to, seems to hint at a time when the
Israelites should be captives in a foreign land; yet we may reasonably conclude, that the promise held out for preserving the Israelites
in a foreign land, does also include their preservation from annihilation in their own country.

We find in chap. xiv. v. 6, that Amaziah, king of Judah, having
killed the conspirators who slew his father, suffered their children to
live, because it was written in the book of the law of Moses, by the
command of God : " The parents shall not be killed on account of
the children, nor the children on account of the parents, but each
shall die for his own sins." (Compare with Deut. chap. xxiv. v. 16.)
Azariah or Uziah, the son of Amaziah, attempted to usurp the
priestly office by entering the temple with incense ; but he was
punished with leprosy, although he had led a virtuous life previously ; and he experienced thus the punishment denounced (Numb.
chap. xvii. v. 5,) against the violaters of the priestly privileges, (2
Kings, chap. xv. v. 5, and 2 Chron. chap. xxvi. v. 19,) and was kept
apart from the habitations of other men, like any other leper would
have been. (Numb. chap. v. v. 3.)—The history of the carrying
off the Israelites captives, is given in 2 Kings, chap. xvii ; and the
reason for this punishment is there said to be their having acted
contrary to the commandments given them ; and among other sins
enumerated is their having done like the nations around them, contrary to what is commanded in Lev. chap. xviii. v. 3. and Deut.
chap. xii. v. 29.—In chap. xviii. v. 4, we are told, that Hezekiah,
son of Achaz, king of Judah, broke the copper serpent, which Moses
had made by the command of God, (Numb. chap. xxi. v. 8,) because it had become an object of adoration to the people, who, in
the time of Achaz, were mad enough to worship any thing. We
read also, v. 5, that Hezekiah confided entirely in the Eternal, the
God of Israel ; and that he was more pious than any king of Judah
who went before him or came after him, and (v. 6,) that he adhered
to the Eternal, and observed the precepts which God had commanded to Moses.—In chap. xxiii. v. 21—23, we have an account of the
Passover-feast having been celebrated by Josiah, and it is also said
there, that no Passover was ever held in so solemn a manner since
the days of the Judges. Josiah also read the book of the law to

the people, which was also in accordance with the law as it now stands.

We have in the above instances a concurrent mass of evidence to prove beyond all doubt the assertion : that the law *now* acknowledged as the Mosaic is, in every respect, the same as that considered and obeyed as such before the Babylonian captivity ; for it will be discovered, that from Joshua to Jeremiah all the books of the law, to wit: Genesis, Exodus, Leviticus, Numbers, and Deuteronomy, are indiscriminately spoken of as existing, and that the Israelites either obeyed the precepts they contain, or were reproved and punished if they neglected them. '

I shall now subjoin a few extracts from Isaiah and Jeremiah, relative to the observance of the Sabbath, and one from the latter in relation to servants, and then close this subject, which I am afraid has been spun out already to too great a length.

Isaiah, chap. lvi. v. 2 : "Happy is the man who does this, and the son of Adam who remains steady in it ; who observes the *Sabbath,* and does not violate it, and withholds his hand from doing any evil."

Isaiah chap. lviii. v. 13—14 : " If thou restrainest thy foot on the Sabbath, and refrainest from doing what thou desirest on my holy day, and callest the Sabbath a delight, honoured as a holy (day) of the Lord, and thou honourest it (the day) by abstaining from doing thy ways, (usual occupations,) or seeking thy own pleasures, or speaking words (i. e. conversing about business, see above, chap. xiii.) : then shalt thou find delight in the Lord, and I will cause thee to ascend upon the high places of the land, and will let thee enjoy the heritage of thy father Jacob,—for the mouth of the Lord has spoken it."

Jeremiah, chap. xvii. 21—22 : " Thus says the Lord, take heed for yourselves, and bear no burden on the Sabbath-day, nor bring it into the gates of Jerusalem ; neither carry any burden from your houses on the Sabbath-day, nor do any manner of work ; but sanctify it, as I have commanded your fathers." (See also v. 27, of the same chapter.)

Jeremiah, chap. xxxiv. v. 13 : " Thus says the Lord God of Israel, I have made a covenant with your fathers, at the time I brought them out of the land of Egypt from the house of slavery, and said : (v. 14,) At the end of seven years you shall each let go his brother the Hebrew, who has been sold unto thee, and when he has served thee six years

22

thou shalt let him go free from thee." (Exodus, chap. xxi. v. 2, and Deut. chap. xv. v. 12.)

I deem it altogether superfluous to produce any other instances from the many which offer themselves, to establish that which has been so clearly proven already, that, namely, the books we now have are in fact those given to Moses, for every passage found in the histories and the prophets referring to the law can be easily traced back to the books of our Pentateuch. From this striking coincidence it follows, that the Hebrew prophets and historians agreed precisely with one another, and there can for this reason be no discrepancy in their statements. This is a strong evidence in favour of their inspiration, since we never find two profane historians or preachers write or speak, as if they were animated by one mind. To assert that all the books of the Hebrew canon were written by one man is too ridiculous to merit refutation, since the difference in style and dialect is so great, and each prophet and inspired writer is withal in his own way so perfect, that it is absolutely impossible to entertain such an idea. It is true, that some few men have been good prose writers and good poets at the same time; but I venture to assert, though yet inexperienced, that that man never lived who was capable of speaking like Moses, inditing songs like David, moralising like Solomon, rousing the passions like Isaiah, and melting the heart like Jeremiah. If indeed a man uniting such qualifications ever was or ever will be, he *deserves* to be obeyed; and I am sure that all mankind, except perhaps the envious, would willingly become his followers. It is therefore impossible that any one man could have composed the whole Bible; but I may go a step farther, and say: " That these books were not composed or compiled at *one time*, even by different persons;" and this for the following reason. It is well known, that, however different their style, a great resemblance will still be discovered in their manner of writing amongst authors of one age; there is generally, if I may use the expression, a connecting link, which binds the republic of letters together. Now granted even, that Ezra and his great council were men of the greatest talents—and none is more ready to acknowledge this *fact*, than the Jews, and particularly the humble writer of these pages:—yet I am sure, that every reasonable man, who has independence enough to judge for himself, in despite of the little quibbles of those who doubt the truth of our Bible, will acknowledge, that it is highly improbable, not to say impossible, to believe, that at a time when the Hebrew language had ceased to be generally spoken, and when its purity was destroyed by the admixture of foreign words, there should have been men skilful enough to write the books of Job, Jeremiah's Lamentations, Isaiah, David's Psalms, and the Song of Solomon, not to mention the books of Moses, which show, as clearly as any writings can do, the extraordinary and diversified acquirements and talents of the author, or even authors if you will, though neither 1 nor any other Jew will admit the latter. It is almost needless to mention, that a great part of the books of Daniel and Ezra is written in the Chaldean language, and even the Hebrew, which these two writers use, is, though very appropriate and expressive, not at all to be compared to the writings just above enumerated in classical purity of style. Haggai, Zechariah, and Malachi, the three last *prophets*, equally with the *inspired* writers of their age, made use of a language which clearly proves, that it had ceased to be so well cultivated as in the days of Samuel and Hezekiah. This does not at all diminish the *credibility* of these prophets—God forbid! let the reader but bear in mind what has been said above in regard to the nature of prophecy (chap. xxi.) : that the prophets were only instructed *what to say*, but not *how to speak ;* and this was very proper, for, since they were to instruct the people, it was necessary that they should use language which they themselves, and the people to whom they were sent, well understood. From the whole of the above remarks it follows, that the various books composing the canon of what is called the Old Testament were written at different times, and mostly by those persons who were the chief agents themselves. These men were all inspired, and could, therefore, not err. (See above chap. xxi.) Hence it is that they all agree so well, and that one always confirms the assertions of the other. Since now the *Bible* was and is yet the book chiefly studied by the Jews ; and as it contains such a fund of learning and instruction, we must conclude that the Jews were a highly civilised, though simple and unostentatious people, immediately after the conquest of the land ; and it is no wonder, therefore, that, being once acquainted with such a book, they should always hold to it as their principal support and adviser. We *never* can consent to part with it, or receive any thing in addition to or in lieu of it. Many have railed against us for observing that which one party thinks *insufficient*, the other *superfluous;* but as long as they are unable to give us any thing better, or even any thing at all approaching it in value, we must hold that close which we now so happily possess. The world has never seen a series of books so consistent and so full of wholesome advice ; and *can* we be blamed for refusing to cast off that which is so highly serviceable ? Who can call us bigots, but the very *bigoted infidel* himself—and are not most infidels bigots ? Who dares to call us sceptics, but that unlearned and blind zealot, who knows not what he is about ?—Let me then advise you, all who are the enemies of our faith and nation, to beware how you touch the holy ark of our faith—to beware how you harm the Israelites, for he who toucheth them, toucheth the apple of his eye, says the prophet Zechariah, and know also, that God will again assert the dignity of his holy name, and again have compassion on Israel !

CHAPTER XXIV.

THE HEBREW WORSHIP.

The next point of enquiry is : " Have not the Jewish teachers of the law imposed unnecessary burdens upon the people, subsequently to their return from Babylon ?" Every one knows how easy it is to denounce any body of men however exalted, and it is at the same time most curious, that those who denounce others do so, for the most part, without producing any other proof of *their* being in the right, than their own potent *dictum.* This has been done, I may say, by *all those* who have been so bitter against the wise men amongst the Jews, known at different times under the names of Scribes, Pharisees, and lastly, Rabbins. It therefore remains now to be enquired into, if in fact the rabbinical institutions are contrary to the written law, and therefore unlawful and useless, or if they are conformable to the laws and the prophets, and therefore proper and necessary.—But let me premise, that it is an error, though a very common one, that the Rabbins had their origin only in the time immediately preceding the destruction of the second temple : for if we come to investigate the Jewish antiquities and to fix the period of the first rise of these Scribes, we must at least lay it in the days of Ezra, for to him and his council are ascribed the first rabbinical institutions.

A great outcry has of late been raised against the use of the sacred language, the Hebrew, in our worship, because this language is no more universally spoken, and but little understood.   Several attempts have therefore been made to substitute the languages of the countries in which we are dispersed, in lieu of the Hebrew.   Of course the Rabbins have been saddled with all the blame and odium, as having been the first to force this mode of worship in an unknown tongue upon the Jews, and some *good* souls, more afraid of disturbing the conscience of others, than regardful of their own virtue and piety, have even dared to talk of thus restoring the purity of Judaism, as if any *impurity* had ever been added.   But let us investigate this subject without prejudice and partiality, and then determine according to the light which can be thrown upon it in the few following observations.

" Did those men, generally called Rabbins, *force* the Hebrew, contrary to reason, upon the people, and should it therefore be dispensed with ? or is the establishment of that language an ordinance emanating from the prophets, and which consequently ought not to be abolished ?"

We read (Nehemiah, chap. xiii. v. 24,): " And half of their children spoke the language of Ashdod, and did not understand the Jewish."   It will from this single verse be discovered, that the Hebrew had ceased to be universally spoken, as early as the days of Ezra and Nehemiah.   These two men were assisted in their re-organisation of the Hebrew commonwealth by the three last prophets, Haggai, Zechariah, and Malachi.   If then they established the Hebrew to be read in the Synagogues in their time, we must admit, as believers in revelation, that this was necessary for the promotion of the proper worship ; and that they did establish the Hebrew to be read publicly, is clearly deducible from Nehemiah viii. v. 7—8; for according to this passage all that, which Ezra read, was explained to the people by the men named as being near him ; and thus it happened, that though the Hebrew was not understood by a great part of those present, Ezra did nevertheless make use of it, but it was explained to the people in a language and dialect they understood. The expounder of the law was called מתורגמן (Methurgeman) or *translator*, and we find such a personage mentioned after the destruction of the temple. At present however this has become by far less necessary than formerly ; for at that time books were scarce and could be procured by comparatively few, owing to the great difficulty of multiplying copies ; but now the art of printing has reduced the price of books so low, the religious books especially, being printed in such immense quantities, that every individual, however poor, can procure himself the Bible and the prayer-books. Then again all parts of the Bible are carefully translated, as are also the prayers, and it is therefore easy for every person desiring it, and capable of receiving information of any kind, to make himself acquainted with the meaning of the law and of the prayers in general, though he may be altogether ignorant of the holy language.*   Let me not however be misunderstood, as saying that the Rabbins forbade the use of every language other than the Hebrew in public and private worship ; on the contrary, they permitted the use of any language understood by the individual praying, nor is the language of the country prohibited in public worship. (*Orach Hayim*, Laws of Prayer, chap. ci. §. 4.) It will therefore be evident, that the use of foreign tongues *explanatory* of the Hebrew service is permitted, but the recital of the regular prayers, the reading of the law, and the portion from the prophets, must ever be in the holy and original language.

The greater part of the daily and Sabbath prayers were composed before the destruction of the second temple,—some say by Ezra and

---

* In Germany and the adjacent countries the price of Hebrew books in general use is uncommonly low, and every family, without exception, is provided with the necessary prayer-books and at least the Pentateuch. The access to information is so easy to the poor and unlettered, that it is not uncommon to hear a man, who would be supposed to be ignorant, discussing the moral, religious, and ceremonial duties of our law, in a manner which would not disgrace a man of learning and high standing in society.

his associates—as may be easily gathered from several passages in the Talmud, particularly the *Massacheth Berachothe* (Tractate of Prayers) in which are enumerated the *Berachothe* or blessings to be said before and after the Shemang.* To any person acquainted with the Mishnah it would be entirely superfluous to draw his attention to this subject, and to those who are unacquainted with it, I hope it will be satisfactory enough, that the fact is stated in general terms without citing the several passages. Having thus seen that the use of the Hebrew was established as far back as the days of the last prophets, it remains to be enquired: " Would it be expedient, if we had the right to do so, to abolish the use of our holy language, and substitute the languages of the different countries, in whose boundaries the Israelites now *sojourn?*"—Let it be considered, that our abode in the countries, where we now reside, must not be considered as a permanent location ; but God forbid, that I should insinuate, that we are to consider ourselves absolved from allegiance to the governments and obedience to the municipal laws of the countries in which we are protected, for this would be contrary to what we are commanded by God, through his faithful servant Jeremiah (chap. xxix. v. 7,) ; but I would only remind my brethren, that their abode in any country, other than Judea, is *against their will.* I hope that I am understood, but for fear of any misconception, I will explain myself a little more in detail. We were, in the first instance, driven from Palestine by the kings of Assyria, (see several passages in the second book of Kings,) and next the remaining two tribes Judah and Benjamin, together with the Levites who resided amongst them, were carried away captives to Babylon and Egypt† by Nebuchadnez-

---

* The Shemang is the celebrated passage from the sixth chapter of Deuteronomy, commencing with the words " Hear, O Israel," Hebrew : שמע ישראל (*Shemang Yisrahale*) whence its name. It is read morning and evening, that we may, as our Rabbins express themselves, receive the yoke of Heaven, when we lie down and when we rise up. The parallel passage from the eleventh of Deuteronomy, commencing with the words, " And it shall come to pass if you hearken diligently, &c." and the conclusion of Numb. xv. commencing with v. 37, are also read with the Shemang.

† Strictly speaking, the king of Babylon did not carry the Jews to *Egypt,* for they fled of their own accord from Palestine, to escape his vengeance, on account of the death of Gedaliah. (See Jeremiah, chap xliii. v. 7.)

zar king of Babylon. After seventy years spent in captivity the Jews were permitted by Coresh (Cyrus) king of Persia, who had subverted the Babylonian empire, to return to their own land. Those who did return were, with but few exceptions, either Levites or Jews, (Judah and Benjamin); but the other ten tribes did not return, and their existence has been a matter of doubt and speculation ever since; though according to some accounts they have been lately discovered in Bucharia, a country in the very heart of Asia. The Jews, after building the second temple (see Ezra and Nehemiah) lived for rather better than four hundred years in Palestine, though far from peaceably or independently, as they were often agitated by internal disturbance and molested by surrounding nations; but after this time, they were conquered by Vespasian and Titus, Roman emperors, who, though they are celebrated for their clemency and benevolence of disposition, did yet treat our ancestors in a manner too revolting and too horrible for words to describe. The remainder of the Jews not yet carried off by these barbarous emperors, (for such they were to us at least,) were driven out by Trajan and Hadrian, for which I refer to the histories of those days.—It will be discovered from this account of our people, that our abode out of Palestine is any thing but voluntary on our part. Our expulsion from our land was owing to our deviation from that holy law, which God, in his kindness and superabundant mercy, bestowed upon our forefathers. Our continuation in captivity is to be ascribed *solely* to our not yet having reformed our conduct sufficiently to merit the return of the blessings promised in Deut. chap. xxx. (which see). It is well known that we hope to be ultimately restored to our land, and that this hope is well founded has been shown, I trust to every man's satisfaction in chapter xxii.—Our residence in *all countries*, save *one*, must therefore be considered as a sojourning, though this is of necessity for an unlimited time; for, as we understand the prophecies, there is no specific period fixed in the Bible for Israel's restoration, but all depends upon our being worthy of this signal favour. That at all events the restoration will not be delayed for a longer period than God has fixed in his own wisdom, but which He has not imparted to any man, is not to be doubted. In short, if we Israelites are virtuous, our *restoration*, or what is the same thing, the *coming of the Messiah*, will take place immediately; but if, on the contrary, we continue in our wickedness, then at the *appointed* time.—Since then we are strangers, and as the time of our being re-united is of necessity unknown, it behooves us to be always united by a certain bond of union, to keep us one people, though at opposite corners of the globe ; and secondly, to be united in the closest manner, when our captives be again restored and assembled *in a body* on the high-raised mountains of Israel. We have already a law which, if properly observed, will ever be that bond, which must, owing to its great purity, bind together the Israelites though the distance between them be as great as from pole to pole. But what would be the scene, if upon our restoration, we had in the course of time forgotten that very language, in which the law was first given? How could we be considered a re-united people, if different languages were used by the captives returning to Zion in their mode of worshipping God?

But even without going so far into the recesses of futurity, we can find many good reasons for employing the Hebrew in our prayers, and in reading the law and the other parts of Holy Writ, as it is now customary in the Synagogues. Let it be remembered, that we Jews are in fact a wandering people—we have no rest for the *soles of our feet* (Deut. chap. xxviii. v. 65): we are either driven by circumstances or necessity from station to station, and it may truly be said, there is hardly a spot on earth where Jews are not to be found. It is for this reason chiefly that the Hebrew language ought to be retained both in public and private worship. If a Jew come from China even, as our worship is now constituted, he can enter any Synagogue even in America, and worship his God in company and unison with his brethren there assembled. He uses the Hebrew, and so do they. And this is an every day occurrence ; for Jews from every part of the world do meet and worship together, as if they were natives of the same land. And in our small Synagogue at Richmond are frequently assembled natives of America, Germany, England, France, Poland, and Bohemia, some of whom hardly understand English. They can all join in the worship, solely because it is conducted in the Hebrew, when the use either of the English or any other language would evidently destroy the harmony thus existing.—There is, however, another very weighty reason why the Hebrew language should be used, and this is, the *preservation of the purity of the law !* " But is it possible that the purity of

23

the holy law can be destroyed by the discontinuance of the Hebrew ?"
I will not assert precisely that its *intrinsic* purity could be destroyed
by this or any other means; but it may confidently be asserted,
without fear of contradiction, that if the Hebrew were once dispensed with in our Synagogues, the interpretation of the law would
be rendered altogether uncertain, and thus its *extrinsic* purity would
be so much *marred*, that it might be considered *destroyed* without a
great stretch of the imagination. To establish this upon indisput-
able grounds, 1 beg leave to draw the attention of the indulgent
reader to the following exposition.—If the Hebrew language were
by universal consent banished from our worship, it would follow, as
a necessary consequence, that *translations* or *foreign* originals must
be substituted, unless we would consent either not to pray at all, or to
suffer any fanatic or enthusiast to pray for the congregation in the
wild and mad strains which shock us so much in the worship of
some sects.—If now in addition to this we should have a translation of the law read to the people, we would soon find that no man
would care to know Hebrew. For to what purpose should the Jew,
whose intentions are not to become a classical scholar or a divine,
apply himself to the study of a dead language, which would be of
no earthly use to him when attained ? Curiosity would not, I dare say,
impel fifty out of five hundred to engage in its study, particularly
as in the case of which we are speaking, they would have *authorised
translations* of all the sacred books.—It is really deplorable, that
not more are engaged in acquiring a knowledge of the holy language—a language which our ancestors spoke—a language in which
the law was given.—But can this be a reason for banishing it altogether ? And that this banishment of the Hebrew would be extremely injurious is susceptible of the easiest and plainest demon-
stration.—As it is, those who altogether use translations of the
whole or a part of the Scriptures, are frequently caught in making
the most absurd deductions from the Bible, which, upon examination of the Hebrew text, are no where to be met with. Let us take
one example : there is a trite saying, *man is born to sin*, and many
have attempted to fortify this position by reference to Psalm li. and
Genesis vi. ; and, if you come to investigate the meaning of these
two passages, you would be surprised that no such thing is found in
either of them ; and this is not all, for as far as my acquaintance

with the Jewish canon extends, I never could discover a single passage even to prove that man was born *to* sin. In the fifty-first psalm, David says : " Behold *in* iniquity I was conceived," but not *to sin;* in the sixth chapter of Genesis we read, that God determined to destroy mankind, " *because the desire of the thoughts of their heart was the whole day directed to evil ;*" here is only stated the *fact*, that *that* generation had degenerated, and were perpetually intent how they could do *wrong ;* not because they were *obliged* to do so, but only because they *chose* this course of life in preference to doing right.—In the eighth chapter of Genesis we read that God said : " That He would never more destroy all flesh, as He had done, for the desire of the heart of man is evil from his youth." Now this sentence cannot mean that he is born to sin, and cannot of his own free will do right, without intervention of grace ; but its obvious and only true meaning is : that as we have desires and passions, we are, from our earliest infancy, drawn on by these desires, but we are by no means obliged to yield to them, for in the fourth chapter God told Cain, that though he were *inclined* to sin, he had yet the mastery over himself, to *sin* or *not to sin;* of course man has the inherent power to do right, though his inclinations should point the other way. But how is he to know what is right? Simply by *revelation*, and following that course which *God* had marked out for him. (See above, chap. i.) The investigation of this subject would lead me too far, besides I am fearful of engaging at present in the discussion of the *philosophy* of our law, as I do not think myself qualified to discuss the points which it would present to me, as they deserve ; I will therefore rest here, only assuring the reader that this is not the only popular error* which men have attempted to demonstrate as true with arguments drawn from the Bible.

* The subjoined has been transmitted to me by Mr. Jacob Mordecai, the same gentlemen mentioned in a foregoing note. " The translators of the Bible to suit their purpose, have rendered the 8th verse of the 25th chap. of Isaiah : ' He will swallow up death in *victory ;*' if you consult the Hebrew, the error is immediately discovered, for we read : בלע המות לנצח, ' He will swallow up death for ever ;' it is not written בנצחון *in victory*, but לנצח *for ever.* So that no one could have been ' victorious in death in fulfilment of this prophecy.'— Again we read, Deut. chap. xxx. v. 19 : ' Choose life,' Psalm xxxiv. v. 15: 'Shun evil and do good.' How then can a man be born to sin?"

What I intend to prove by the foregoing example is this. We have seen that by justly investigating the Bible we have overthrown a position so *generally* admitted as true, that to some it may appear to be but little better than scepticism even to doubt it.—If the Hebrew language were now altogether neglected, as some desire, we should be unable to make these investigations. Whatever were asserted upon the authority of any translation, would then of course pass for sound truth, and instead of Holy Writ being the light of the world, it would become the cause of contention. Every man would explain every thing as he liked best, and we should have just as many laws as there were Bible readers. But as long as the Hebrew continues to be studied, there is no danger that any thing of this kind will ever occur, I mean amongst ourselves. It is this which makes the Jews so very formidable in argument; we have the *original* records, and if any man comes to argue from his *copy*, we ask him : " Let us see how your copy agrees with our original;" and we have thus maintained the superiority in argument and controversy in every age and in every country, unless our *reasons* were answered by the sword or the faggot.—The Bible must be literally given; and every word, every letter, nay every point, has its meaning, which must not be lost sight of; no passage must be wrenched from its position to mean any thing or nothing; but, as the whole from the first word in Genesis to the last in the Chronicles (which books are the last in order with us) is one revelation, because all emanates from *one* source, the HOLY ONE of Israel (whose name be praised for eternity!) it is but fair that one passage should be used to explain the other. And the Bible may be compared to an arch, where one stone supports the other ; so, generally speaking, will every obscure passage receive elucidation from another part of the Bible.

This is no fanciful defence of the use of the Hebrew, for the experience of every day proves its correctness ; now let me ask my brethren who have not yet resolved to abandon all : Are you prepared to give up the superiority you possess over every other nation and sect upon the face of the earth? Pause before you strike the

Or if the prophet had intended to express the idea conveyed by the English version, he might also have said : והוא מנצח, he being conquering—*in victory*—יבלע מות *will swallow death ;* but are these words found in the text?

fatal blow; the nations are so alive to your strength, that in some countries they will not allow a clergyman to be licensed who has not some knowledge of the Hebrew. In Germany and England they teach the Hebrew at all their universities, and I verily believe their object in so doing is to be the better able to cope with us. Therefore, for the sake of Heaven, for the sake of your own honour and eternal salvation, listen not to what irreligious men wish to instil in you, and consider and know that your ancestors were fully as wise and as well informed of right and propriety as any modern infidel, and, if I err not, even greatly more so!

I do, with every lover of his people, and venerator of the word of God, deeply deplore the condition in which many Jews, particularly in this country, are found.—Many, and I am sorry to confess, most are altogether ignorant of the Hebrew; this is no doubt an evil, which is of sufficient magnitude to alarm any man who seriously reflects. But this evil is not yet great enough to break down on its account the limits which our ancestors have set! No—instead of finding fault, let those who have the abilities set about enlightening and informing those who are less favoured; let them explain the law, the ceremonies, the object and meaning of the prayers, and my life for it, the outcry against the not understanding of our service will cease. It requires a great deal of labour perhaps to remove the great mass of ignorance—to root out prejudices against the ancient system; but is he a brave man, who turns back at the sight of any obstacle opposed to him? Yet would I not recommend to those, who may be disposed to follow up my humble beginning, to lose sight of discretion; far from it, they must use language mild and becoming; they must endeavour to convince the understanding rather than captivate the fancy; they must endeavour to be plain and intelligible at the expense of being tedious—lest by a display of wit and great learning, they might astonish more than improve. We may be met at the very beginning by difficulties not thought of perhaps, for we may by chance rouse those spirits to greater activity, which have been, and are even now at work to destroy all that is venerable for sanctity and antiquity: but let us work unremittingly, and the victory is ours. Let no man, who bears the honourable name of Israelite, and who has the good of his brothers at heart, be caught sleeping at his post, but let us oppose our enemies with per-

-severance, and use our watchfulness against theirs, and our God will bless our endeavour.—We ought not however to be too much elated by success, for our battle is for *truth* and not for *fame*, and if our object is attained—if we once have succeeded—if we have reached the goal of our desire in convincing all of the righteousness of our law : we should lay down the arms of attack, and only continue to improve our advantage—teach the law which wo havo proved true—spread amongst our brethren the knowledge of their God—and by gentle means lead them back to the fold from which they have strayed! And should we fear to encounter ridicule—or hatred—or scorn—or even persecution ? No—we must act and do our duty, regardless of what men may think, say, or do ; and will not God prosper our undertaking? most surely ; success *must* await us, for never was war waged in a cause more holy ; and our enemies need not then be ashamed to confess themselves vanquished, for not by *us* were they conquered, but by our *God*, who influences our minds, and to succumb to Him is honour, for to Him we all must bow in humble adoration !

CHAPTER XXV.

THE FASTS AND CEREMONIES.

I imagine that what has been said above will prove—first, that the public worship in Hebrew was not instituted by the Rabbins, but by Ezra and the prophets after the partial restoration of the Israelites ; and secondly, that its retention is of the greatest advantage to all the Jews, and its abolition would lead to the most dreadful consequences, which ought ever to be deprecated by every real friend of his religion and of his brethren.—Of the propriety of the second days of the festivals I have already treated above (chap xvii. note) ; I shall therefore begin our next enquiry with :

"Have not the Rabbins usurped undue authority in establishing the fast-days?" I must answer at once, that so far from usurping any authority in this respect, the Rabbins had not any agency whatever in establishing the fast-days, for they were instituted in the days of the prophets, and this was with the express approbation of God. The fast-days, independently of the Day of Atonements, are the fast of the seventeenth day of Tamuz (fourth month); the fast of the ninth of 'Ab (fifth month); the fast of the third of Tishry (seventh month); the fast of the tenth of Tebeth (tenth month); and of the thirteenth day of Adar (twelfth month).—On the tenth day of Tebeth the enemy first approached Jerusalem; on the seventeenth of Tamuz the city was taken, and on the ninth* of Ab the temple was burnt. After Nebuchadnezzar had destroyed the temple, he suffered a small number of our brethren to live in Palestine under the government of Gedaliah, who was treacherously slain by Ismael, son of Nethaniah, on the third day of Tishry. The remnant of the Israelites were now afraid to stay any longer in their country, and contrary to the advice of the prophet Jeremiah they went to Egypt, where nearly the whole of their number died, as the prophet had foretold. (Jeremiah chap. xli. and others.)—These days were therefore instituted as fasts, for so long as the Israelites should remain captives in foreign lands.—On these days we ought to assemble in the places of worship, confess our sins, make restitutions, (see chap. xxiii.) ask the protection of God for the remnant of the flock that has escaped, and pray for the restoration of our national glory at the time of the coming of the promised Messiah.—The antiquity of these days can be proven from Zechariah, chap. viii. v. 18—19 : "And the word of the Lord of Hosts came to me as follows: Thus speaketh Adonai Zebahothe, the fast day of the fourth, and the fast of the fifth, and the fast of the.seventh, and the fast of the tenth shall be to the house of Judah (days of) rejoicing and gladness and happy festivals; and love

---

* These are the days of the conquest of Jerusalem in the time of the second temple ; in that of the first, the two last named events happened on other days, in the same months however ; but since the destruction of the second temple is more to be lamented by us, than that of the first, we fast and mourn on those days upon which Jerusalem was taken and the temple destroyed by Titus.— The city was taken by Nebuchadnezzar on the ninth of Tamuz, and the temple burnt on the tenth day of Ab. (See Jeremiah, chap. lii. v. 6—12.)

you truth and peace." We here see the prophet announcing that these four days, which were in his time (and are now) days of mourning and abstinence, shall, at the time of our restoration, be days of festivity, of general joy, and gladness. The fast of Esther, which is on the thirteenth day of the twelfth month, was instituted to commemorate the troubles in which our ancestors found themselves in the time of Achashveroshe through the evil counsels of Haman. The history of this event is so well known, that a synopsis is not necessary here ; suffice it to say, that the thirteenth, fourteenth, and in walled cities the fifteenth (of Adar) also, are annually celebrated, (the thirteenth as a fast, the other two as days of rejoicing,) in commemoration of our escape from the designs of Haman.—It is hardly necessary to say, that our opponents disapprove entirely our celebrating the downfal of our enemy, when this event took place twenty-three hundred years ago. They say : " It argues a spirit of bitterness and unforgiving hostility, which is highly unbecoming."—This objection would be a good one, if our rejoicing were only on account of the execution of Haman; but this is not the fact, we celebrate *our redemption ;* we rejoice, because we were snatched from destruction, when the whetted sword lay already unsheathed upon our necks ; we assemble to return sincere thanks to our God for the goodness He then displayed towards his chosen people, and pray for the continuance of his vigilance and protection over us, who linger so long in captivity.—Is such a celebration proper ?—To argue this point further, I am afraid, would be insulting to the understanding of my readers, who, I hope, will be intelligent and kind enough to supply the defective details, which now and then may be found in my arguments.

The fast-days are, according to the above, proved not to be of rabbinical origin, but that all except the fast of Esther were instituted by God himself through the agency of his prophet. The fast of Esther cannot indeed be traced to any prophet, but it was received by the Jews then living as a day of humiliation on account of the great deliverance they had experienced, as were also the festivities of Purim (the fourteenth and fifteenth of Adar) for the reason just given. Ever since the days of Mordecai and Esther this celebration has been kept up, and it cannot now be abolished ; first, on account of the extraordinary hold it has taken of the mind of all Jews ; and secondly, because it would destroy a feature in our ceremonies resulting from the most amiable trait in human nature—gratitude. For these days are celebrated every year as a tribute from us to our heavenly Protector, and on these days also we read the history of our redemption, and we return our thanks to Him, who was then as ever our Saviour from annihilation.—To the same cause may be ascribed the festival called Hannuckah, commencing on the twenty-fifth day of Kislave, (ninth month,) and continuing eight days. All conversant with history know that the Syrian king Antiochus oppressed the Jews very grievously, and that they regained their liberty under the guidance of Judah Maccabæus, who defeated the Syrians and drove them from Jerusalem. Antiochus had made unclean all the oil set apart for the lighting of the lamps in the temple, and when the Jews reconsecrated the temple they found but one cruet of oil, sealed with the signet of the high-priest, the contents of which were only sufficient for one day's service. The Jews were not able to procure any other oil, which might be used, for some days; but it so happened, that the contents of the small jar lasted for eight days, till fresh oil had been procured. For this reason do we light lamps on the evenings of this festival, commencing with one on the first, and increasing night after night till the eighth, when eight lamps are lighted. These days, like the Purim, were instituted to keep alive the recollection of our deliverance from an enemy who attempted to root out the Israelites; and wherever Jews are found, they are celebrated as days of rejoicing and festivity, but we are not bound to abstain from labour on those days, since they are not commanded in the Pentateuch; on Purim, however, most persons do not work, but give themselves up for that day to religious mirth, as it may properly be called.—All these celebrations and feasts proceeded from the voluntary burst of feeling of the whole people, but they were not imposed upon an unwilling nation by the command of the Rabbins, Scribes, and Pharisees.

The next question for consideration is: "Did, or did not the prophets prohibit meat, other than that of forbidden animals, prepared by a gentile, to be eaten by a Jew? And is wine of the gentiles prohibited by the same authority or not?" It needs hardly to be told that the Rabbins have received a great share of abuse, as being the authors of these interdictions; but who would not be sur-

24

prised to be convinced that these very Rabbins are as innocent of this as any person now alive? To prove this, however, we need only read the first chapter of Daniel; and is it not surprising, that those would-be-wise men, who spend all their lives, and write folio upon folio, in endeavouring to clear up the mysterious prophecies of Daniel concerning the coming of the Messiah, should altogether overlook what he relates concerning his own mode of life, while in the service of the Babylonian king? He tells us that he came to the determination not to defile himself with the meats (or viands) of the king, nor with his wines, and he asked of Melzar the favour to give him and his three associates vegetables (pulse) to eat, and no *wine*, but water, to drink; though Melzar at first refused to comply with this request, thinking himself in danger of losing his head if his charges did not look so well as the other youths in the palace, he at length yielded, and took for himself the rations furnished for their use, and gave them pulse in place of them. (See Daniel, chap. i.) This whole narrative proves, that any meat not prepared by a Jew is forbidden to us.—The killing of animals, as practised by the rabbinical Jews, is also in every respect conformable to the Mosaic law, where we are in several places positively commanded to let the blood run out (see Lev. chap. xvii. v. 13, and Deut. chap. xii. v. 16,); however any one might be disposed to explain these texts to suit his own views, it may well be doubted if he could break the force of Deut. chap. xii. v. 21, where it says: "Thou shalt kill of thy herd and of thy flock, which the Lord has given thee, *as I have commanded thee*;" commanded where? and since we can no where find the mode of killing commanded in express terms, we must come to the conclusion, that it was explained to the Israelites *orally*, and handed down from father to son to the present day. The great care that has ever been bestowed upon this subject, even in the time of Saul, proves, that there is something more in this than mere invention of men, and that therefore the *tradition* of the *fathers* is true, and founded upon, and agreeable to, the *intent* of the Mosaic law.

It cannot be expected, that I should give an analysis even of our ceremonies, but I may say with truth, that they are of great antiquity, and most of them have even an obvious meaning and are beautiful allegories. For instance, a golden ring is used at our marriages, and when the bridegroom puts it upon the finger of the bride, he says: " Thou art wedded to me by this ring according to the law of Moses and Israel."—The ring is a circle, and when well finished, the point where the two extremes join cannot be discovered; if once a breach be made in the ring, or if it be broken, it cannot answer the purpose for which it was intended, and even if it should be mended, a mark will generally remain of the former breach. Just so is it with the married state. The husband and wife should be like the ring of pure metal employed at their marriage, that is, they ought both to be pure, devoted to the practice of virtue and piety. They should be of one mind, so that their being two individuals should be hardly perceptible; the husband should always pay deference to the wishes of his wife, but it is her duty also to endeavour to win his good will by ready compliance and gentle demeanour; and if it unfortunately should become necessary for either of them to chide the other, let it be done in a spirit of conciliation, let it never be more than remonstrance, for faults are much oftener laid by in consequence of mild reproof, than violent altercation. Let the husband think the honour of the wife his own, and let her look up to him as her sole protector (under God) on earth, whose happiness ought ever to be her chief delight, and which she is to promote by all the means in her power. If they live so, in love towards God and friendship towards one another, the married state must be the most blissful on earth. But reverse the picture, let once discontent take root in their minds, let them habitually find fault with one another, let angry disputes become familiar to them, let the fear of God be once removed from before them—and unhappiness is the lot of both man and wife, and what was once the best blessing becomes now the greatest curse. Though they become reconciled afterwards, painful recollections of past follies will nevertheless often occasion them those pangs of conscience, which are the severest torture on earth. After the ring is put upon the bride's finger and the marriage contract read, the bridegroom gives her to drink out of the cup, over which *grace* has been said, which he then throws upon the ground, so that it breaks. This ceremony also is not without its use, and has the following meaning: " Midst the festive joy of the marriage-day man is too apt to think only of pleasure, nothing but joyful anticipations float before his eyes, and he is forgetful of the ills of life and its close. But like the glass, that lays shivered in a thousand pieces before him, will the joys of life pass away into innumerable sorrows, and the body of man now so beautiful, must in a few brief years be dissolved into its natural elements, the flesh will decay from the bones and become a prey to the worms of the earth." Again—we read in the Talmud: "That on the day the son of Rab Hoonah was married, the latter made a feast for all his scholars and companions. They were all, as he thought, too much rejoiced, and he found them forgetful of the state of captivity in which we even yet linger. Seeing this the pious Rabbi threw down an elegant glass ornament, from a stand near which he stood. The scholars were no sooner aware of the destruction of the rare and costly vase, than they all looked sorrowful about the wanton destruction of what was then very scarce and dear, and they enquired of R. Hoonah the cause of his strange conduct, when he told them : 'Remember the destruction of Jerusalem, remember the burning of the temple, and do not forget that we dwell no longer in our land, and you will moderate your joy !' " And it is just and proper that we should always recollect, that we were hurled from our high estate, and that, like the fragments of the glass strewed about the floor, we are scattered all over the world in small numbers. We ought to act and think like the holy Psalmist, who says (Psalm 137):

" By the streams of Babel—there we sat and also wept—when we remembered Zion. Upon its willows did we hang our harps, for there did our captors ask of us the words of song, and those deriding us—joy, ' sing us some of Zion's songs !' How can we sing the song of the Eternal in the land of the stranger? If I forget thee Jerusalem, may my right hand forget—then may my tongue cleave to my palate, if I remember thee not—if I bring not* (thee O) Jerusalem at the head of my joy !"

Though these ideas may appear to some too gloomy, the reflecting mind will not revolt from them. To remember the hour of dissolution has for the good man and true believer no further terror, than deterring him from sin, that he may leave this world unspotted, and return his soul in the same purity to his Maker, as it was when He gave it to him.—The same is the case with remembering our de-

---

* Or, as R. Moses Mendelsohn translates: " If a tear does not flow for thee, whenever I am rejoiced."

graded political state. The recurrence to our former glory must and ever will occasion the severest pain to a Jew; yet is there something very animating in the idea of our future restoration, and it will incite every good man to act so, that the coming of the Messiah may not be retarded on his account.

Our ceremonies on various occasions have been explained already in some parts of the foregoing pages, and since it is not my present purpose te explain the *ceremonies* of the Jews, it would be quite out of place to dilate on this subject; I shall therefore but remark, that our *mourning* is in most respects just the same that was customary in the times of the patriarchs, which can be easily proved if necessary; and to show with what *feelings* we mourn, I beg to call the reader's attention to the following from the funeral service:

" Thou art just, O Lord, and upright are thy judgments! Righteous art Thou, O Lord, and beneficent in all thy works! Thy righteousness is everlasting righteousness, and thy law is true!

" The judgments of the Lord are true and uniformly just. Where the word of the King is, there is power, and who can say to him, ' What doest Thou?' For He is of one mind, and who can alter it? and what his soul desires He doeth. The rock—whose work is perfect, for all his ways are just; the God of truth—and without iniquity—He is just and upright. He is a true Judge, judging with righteousness and truth. Praised be the true Judge, for all his judgments are just and true."

It will be seen, that when our grief is naturally the greatest, we acknowledge the justice of our Supreme Judge, all whose ways are just.—After this prayer we pray for the soul of the departed in a very appropriate manner, and conclude with the prophecy from Isaiah, where he speaks in confident terms of his hope in the resurrection. In short, the ceremonies of the Jews are conformable to the laws they obey; and the life of a good Jew may fairly be set down as a model of perfection, as far as mortals can be perfect!

CHAPTER XXVI.

THE LAW AND THE RABBINS.

Before 1 conclude this part of my subject, that is to say, the proofs of the divine origin of the Mosaic law and the reasons of the continued adherence of the Jews to the same : I must say a few words relative to the veneration we pay to the *book* of the law itself. The great Ezra* (who was next to Moses the principal instrument of God to *perpetuate* the law amongst us), together with the prophets and the wise men of his time, made a regulation, that the law should be read in the Synagogues every Sabbath, Monday, and Thursday, that the Israelites should never be three days without reading the law or hearing it read. This regulation is not an addition to the Mosaic Law, for there we are commanded that the book of the law shall be read at every time, (Deut. chap. xvii. and several other passages,) and once at least every seven years the chief of the nation was obliged to read the law publicly to the whole assembled people, men women and children, nay even the stranger. (Deut. chap. xxxi. v. 12.) In the same chapter we are commanded : " To place the song in the mouth of the Israelites," meaning, to make them perfectly acquainted with it; upon further examination, however, it will be discovered, that not only the last song of Moses, but also the whole law was to be known to every Israelite. (Chap. xxx. v. 14.) It needs not be told, that in the Mosaic law many commandments are given in general terms, without defining their extent or the *mode* how they should be done; and we find, that God empowered the judges to explain any contested matter, according to the *general* rules given through Moses. (Deut. chap.

---

* That this regulation chiefly emanated from Ezra is the general opinion amongst the Jews, and there is no reason to doubt it, if we consider the great veneration he had for the law. It is, however, probable that the same custom, or a similar one, was common as early as the time of Elisha; for some reasons in favour of this hypothesis, see above, chap. xxiii. p. 167.

xvii. v. 11. and ibid. chap. xxi. v. 5.) This being the case it cannot
be doubted that Ezra and the Sanhedrin, at the time being, had the
right to make the above regulation, it being in accordance with
the general law as laid down in the Pentateuch, and well adapted for
the spreading of this law amongst the people.—According to this
regulation the whole five books composing the Pentateuch are
divided into fifty-four portions, namely, Genesis in *twelve*, Exodus
in *eleven*, Leviticus in *ten*, Numbers in *ten*, and Deuteronomy in
eleven; in general one is read every Sabbath in the year, commencing on the first Sabbath after the feast of Tabernacles, and closing
on the last day of this feast; but in the common years of our calendar, which are only three hundred and fifty-five days, there are
read on some Sabbath-days *two* portions, so as to read the whole
law once at least in every twelve months.—On the festivals and
fast-days portions appropriate to the days are read; for instance, on
the first day of the Passover, Exodus, chap. xii. v. 21,—chap. xiii;
on the seventh day, ibid. chap. xiii. v. 17,—chap. xv. v. 26 ; on
the Day of Atonement, Leviticus, chap. xvi. v. 1—34, and in the
same manner on the other days. On Sabbath afternoon, and
Monday and Thursday, the first section of the following Sabbath is
read. The usefulness of this custom will be apparent to any person
endowed with the smallest share of penetration; the law being continually read to the people, and whereas it has been recommended
by the Rabbins, to read, before the reading in the Synagogue, the
Hebrew *twice* and a translation *once*, it must be continually, in the
literal sense of the words, in the mouth and heart of all Israelites ;
and can they fail, if they attend to this strictly, to become intimately acquainted with the whole law ?—Nor can the Rabbins be charged
with a desire of shrouding the law in mystery and withholding ex-
planations from the people; so far from this being true, men capable
of teaching deliver lectures (in every village and town of Europe)
to the congregation before the afternoon service of the Sabbaths
and holydays; and those who are able frequently give sermons and
discourses of their own composition during or immediately after the
morning-service.

After the reading of the law on the mornings of the Sabbaths
and the festivals, and on the afternoons of the fast-days, an appropriate portion is read from some of the historical writings and the

prophets prior to Daniel, (that is in the order in which the prophets are placed in our canon). The origin of this custom is this: when Antiochus had conquered Palestine he forbade the reading of the law by the Jews, hoping that by degrees it might be altogether forgotten. But so convinced were our ancestors of the good to be derived from the institution of Ezra, that they, not being able to read the law itself, substituted portions of the prophets bearing resemblance to those passages of the law which ought to have been read on that Sabbath. It is well known how cruelly Antiochus treated the aged priest Eleazer and the seven sons of Hannah; but his day of destruction soon arrived, and he was driven from our soil with ignominy and shame; but the Israelites to this day retain the custom of reading the passages of the prophets as just mentioned; and thus not only the law, but also the prophets, will be remembered by us, as the frequent perusal of them must fix them indelibly in our minds.

It is also universally known, that all the copies of the law in use amongst us are precisely alike. If we now wish to know how this extraordinary result was brought about, how it could possibly happen, that in the many countries, where our *dispersions* dwell, all our copies of the Pentateuch should agree: we must look to the mode prescribed by our wise men, before and after the destruction of the temple, for the reason of the miraculous preservation of the purity of the Scriptures.—These men have laid down rules for preparing the parchment and the ink, and in what manner the books of the law, the Thephillin and Mezoozothe were to be written. No man, who has not been previously examined as to his competency in writing and knowledge of the rules, and who cannot produce testimonials of an upright and religious conduct, can be admitted to be a writer of the law. The Massorites have carefully noted every word, how it is to be written; and if a man follows the rules they have laid down, it is impossible but he must write correctly. No book, which has an error in it, can be used for public reading in the Synagogue, and if any error be discovered during the reading of the law, another book must be used. Before a book can be considered as fit for public service, it must have been several times carefully revised. It is unlawful to erase any name of the Most High; but in case the error discovered can not be rectified without this being done, the whole sheet, in which the error is, must be taken out, and a correct one substituted.—The law is written upon parchment, and on one side only ; every word must be written upon lines, and the letters must stand so that no one touch the other. The letters, it is almost needless to say, are Hebrew; they are, however, somewhat different from those used in printing, as some of them have certain marks upon the top, called *Taggim*, which any one can discover by just inspecting one of the rolls, which, moreover, are mounted on two rollers, for the purpose of being the more easily conveyed from one place to the other, and of being better adapted for the use of the Synagogues.

Thus we see, that all the rolls existing are written after one rule, by men who are virtuous and competent to the task ; no dishonour can therefore belong to the name of Scribe ; for can it be dishonourable for a man to be chosen to transcribe the law of his God, when this very permission stamps him as a man of virtue and knowledge? I really wonder how any man, who professes to venerate the Bible, should dare to call the body of Scribes hypocrites, when Ezra says of himself, "that he was a ready scribe of the law of God!" Would Ezra have said that of himself, which would class him amongst hypocrites? And is it rational to suppose, that at any time the whole community of the Jews was so depraved, that the persons appointed to write the law were uniformly taken from amongst those who assumed only the cloak of piety to conceal their hideous moral deformity? It is impossible : and from the time of Ezra to the present day the station of a Scribe has been an honourable one, though worldly riches have seldom been the portion of any one of this fraternity.

If we consider the above with due attention, our astonishment will cease at the accuracy of all our copies of the law. But shall those men, the Pharisees and Rabbins, who strove so hard to accomplish this desirable object, be branded with every opprobrious epithet which malice or ignorance can invent? It surpasses my intellectual powers to comprehend the reason they could have had to take so much care to preserve the law free from *additions*, *alterations*, and *forgeries*, if it was their intention to twist and turn the text as they pleased!—And whilst teaching, that this law must be observed according to the letter, without addition or diminution, can it be possible, l ask, that they should have promulgated aught that was not

25

warranted by the law itself, or the tradition they had received from their fathers? However, I need not trouble myself to find arguments for our opponents, who, as they continually make those charges against our wise men, are in reason bound to explain the above mental phenomenon, and to prove the truth of what they otherwise assert.

But I hear asked on every side : " Did not the Rabbins disagree about the meaning and extent of many passages of the law ?" Yes, they did ; but this is no reason for rejecting their enactments. Let us consider a few moments, if it be possible for a whole assembly of delegates from various quarters of a state to agree in every question of importance brought before them. Let it be borne in mind, that they act under a law whose general principles are known, but whose extent in particular cases is unknown. Each of the members of this assembly is called upon to vote, and to state his opinions and the reasons which govern him in so voting. Each member thus called upon ventures to express his opinion, and to give his reasons for his vote, and the view he has of that general law, according to which he is bound to decide. Can any man assert, with a strict regard to truth and justice, that each one of this assembly may not be actuated by the best motives and the highest reverence for this general law ? If I might be permitted to hazard an opinion, I should say, that this very disagreeing, where no party is personally interested, (as was the case with all the Sanhedrin,) and where each man might relinquish his own views without any personal sacrifice—this disagreeing, I say, proves the sincerity of the individuals composing this assembly, for each man contends for right in the abstract, and his maintaining his own opinion with argument against that perhaps of all the other members, shows, that his veneration for the general law is so great that he cannot remain silent, though he is sure of being in a minority, or perhaps alone.

I will relate one instance of a disagreement of the Rabbins from the Talmud, which, I am sure, will be sufficient to exonerate them from the charge of quarrelling, and endeavouring to make the law obscure by their disputes.—During the time that Rabban Gamaliel was Nahssy, or chief of the Sanhedrin, a man, who lived in the country of the Ammonites, wished to join the Israelites. Rabban Gamaliel was of opinion that he could not be received, for it is written in Deut. chap. xxiii. v. 4 : " No Ammonite or Moabite shall come in the congregation of the Eternal." Rabbi Yehoshua, however, thought that he might be received, " For," said he, " it is well known that Sanherib mixt all the nations (those around Palestine); amongst this number were the Ammonites, who, since that time, no longer exist as a separate and distinct people. Now, since the greater number of the nations thus driven from their homes were not of those whose acceptance as proselytes was interdicted by the passage in question, the living in the country of the Ammonites does not constitute any one an Ammonite ; it may be that *he is* a descendant from this people, but the greater probability is, that *he is not*, for it is a rule, *whatever separates, separates from the majority.*" I do not think that this requires any explanation, for both reasons are very plain. No man reading this can doubt but that both Rabban Gamaliel and Rabbi Yehoshua were sincere and pious Israelites, both passionately attached to the law, and each of them ready to sacrifice his life for the sanctification of God and his laws. On the other hand, no man can doubt that there was good reason for either side of the question, and that, though the opinion of Rabban Gamaliel was strictly according to the Mosaic law, yet did Rabbi Yehoshua clearly prove that the passage cited by the Nahssy was inapplicable in the present instance for the reasons given.*—I beg leave to draw the reader's attention to another circumstance attending this difference. Rabban Gamaliel was a descendant of David, and was besides a man of great wealth and influence ; Rabbi Yehoshua, on the contrary, was but a poor man, who maintained himself by his own labour ; but he was a man of great learning, piety, and virtue. He was not deterred by the greatness of the Nahssy from speaking his opinion freely ; and this is not all, for it was afterwards found that it had been the right one, and it was in consequence adopted.

The debates incident to a disagreement of opinion amongst the Rabbins called forth the most acute and close reasoning, and those persons at all acquainted with the Talmud must acknowledge this

---

* Can the generality of the English tell, if they are descended from Romans, Britons, Saxons, Danes, or Normans, though this mixture constitutes the English nation ?

in spite of themselves. But let it not be imagined, that upon every question arising there was necessarily a difference of opinion; far from it, as a reference to any part of the Mishnah and Gemarah (which both together are called Talmud) will amply demonstrate. I will just mention, that this difference amongst the Rabbins produced no angry feelings, and they ever lived together in the greatest harmony, with but very few exceptions. In fact, they did not contend for the mastery in argument, nor the establishment of their own particular views; but only that the truth might be brought out by discussion, and all their differences were for the sake of Heaven, for the ultimate glory of the name of God. Such differences as these must raise the parties in our estimation, and compel us to respect the opinions of those men, who, with an eye solely to the advancement of religion and social virtue, braved persecutions, and poverty, and distress, to accomplish this noble object. There are materials enough to prove this last assertion more fully, but enough has already been said for the conviction of those who are disposed to be convinced.

I will not attempt to deny that the Rabbins were very strict and austere; but is this an objection to them? Can any man be blamed for adhering to his opinion, which he conceives to be right, even in trifles? I imagine not. Besides, the *limit between right and wrong* is so delicate as to be hardly perceptible, and it is always safer to be too *strict,* than too *lax*, as the author of Lacon so elegantly says: "Many persons say, in cases of doubtful morality, what harm can there be in doing it, but he (the author of L.) would be glad to know what harm there could be in letting it alone."—Why not judge the Rabbins by the same rule? Moreover, let it be considered that many little things, of which we are daily guilty, are unlawful, if we will but take the trouble to investigate our conduct a little. But this is a thing which we will but seldom do. We love ourselves so much, and are so tender of the peace of our conscience, that we will never suffer any disagreeable sensation to disturb us, if we possibly can help it. And this want of courage and command over ourselves is no trifling fault, for if we would always be courageous enough to accuse ourselves, and correct trifling faults in the commencement, or when we first discover in us a strong propensity to any vice, we would often be prevented from committing many crimes, or becoming notorious for vice or irreligion. It is a common and a true saying, that no man becomes bad of a sudden. We commence by doing a trifling wrong, next one of greater magnitude, till by degrees we have broken through every law, both human and divine. We, therefore, read in the second Payreck of Abothe: " And be as careful of a trifling good deed as of a weighty one, for thou dost not know the reward for good actions; and always contrast the loss which any good action may occasion with its reward, and the benefit of sin with its ultimate injury."—Payreck iv. : " Ben Azay says : Run to do any good action, though trifling it be, and shun any sin ; for one good deed is the parent of another—and one sin is the parent of another ; for the reward of any virtuous action is another virtuous action, and the punishment of sin is sin." And do we not find daily, that we never stop short upon the road of *virtue* or *vice ?*—In the same spirit the Talmud also says : " That when God will destroy the יצר הרע *Yaytser harang* (figurative for evil inclinations) he will appear to the pious men as a large mountain, who then will say : How were we able to overcome so large a mountain ? to the wicked, however, he will appear as a hair, and they will say: Woe to us, that we had not firmness enough to overcome even a hair." And so it is, if we take a view of all the temptations we had to encounter, we will often be astonished how we escaped them without giving way to our inclinations. On the other hand, if we have been guilty of any crime, religious or moral, and we take a look at our past conduct, we will often shudder at the *trifle* which was the first cause of our present degradation. Shall I search through the annals of crime and infidelity to prove this ? My readers, I think, will gladly dispense with it ; and each will perhaps be able to supply an example of both virtue and vice from his own recollection.

No rabbinical Jew will, therefore, attempt to deny that the Rabbins were, in old times, austere, as regards themselves, and that they are so even yet ; since this is no fault. But let it not be thought that they are gloomy fanatics and bigots : so far from this being the case, I am inclined to think that they are the most cheerful class of men ; but their hilarity is not boisterous, and their mirth is tempered by piety and a knowledge of the uncertainty of life. The shortness of our existence is not with them a goad to hurry them on from pleasure to pleasure (as with the Epicureans of old) ; but it always reminds them that the time must be spent in good actions—in deeds of kindness towards mankind, and in adoration to God.

Having touched in succession upon those points which appeared to me best adapted to demonstrate the divine origin of our law, I think that I cannot close this part of my little book better than by extracting the following from the Proverbs of the Fathers, chap. ii. :

" Rabbi Tarfone said : The day is short, the work is great (multifarious), the workmen are lazy, the reward is ample, and the master of the house is urgent.—He also used to say : It is not incumbent on thee to finish the work, nor art thou at liberty to divest thyself altogether of it ; if thou hast learned much of the law, much reward will be given thee, and the master of thy work is trustworthy (capable) to pay thee the reward for thy labour ; and know thou that the reward of the righteous is in the world to come !"

No man, whatever his religious principles may be, can find fault with the moral contained in this beautiful allegory, and its force and simplicity are perhaps unsurpassed by any saying that flowed from pens not wielded by inspired writers.—And I believe that it may be asserted, that whatever the Rabbins wrote bears the mark of a high elevation of thought, and a grandeur of conception, and although their figures may now and then seem too bold, yet their meaning is always very appropriate when correctly explained.

In fine, the law given by God through Moses is the citadel, in which we must take shelter ; but let that rude hand be *blasted* which should impiously dare to break down the wall, which our good pastors and faithful guardians have with so much care built around it !

———

O GREAT AND ADORABLE BEING, who didst create the heaven and the earth, and the innumerable planetary systems which shine around us, look down with mercy and compassion upon thy servant, who feebly essays to vindicate the glory of THY HOLY

NAME! O may the words of his mouth be acceptable to Thee, and may nought that he says be displeasing to Thee!—Vouchsafe also to look down from thy high abode upon the descendants of Abraham, of Isaac, and of Jacob, thy servants, and remember Thou the covenant which Thou didst make with them, saying, that Thou wouldst never forsake their children! Grant them, therefore, knowledge and wisdom, that they may all understand thy law, and know what is pleasing to Thee!—Deliver them from all affliction, and bring to fulfilment the prophecy spoken through thy prophet, that the earth should be full of thy knowledge, as the waters cover the sea. May this be thy will, and may we speedily behold thy return to ZION. Amen!

APPENDIX

TO CHAPTER II. PAGE 14.

Some *unfortunate* critic (the Archæologist in the Monthly Magazine for August, 1814) has attempted to prove that the book of Exodus and a part of Genesis were composed about the time of Jeremiah, mainly on the following grounds: first, because the book of Exodus, chap. xxv. contains a description of the candelabre to be used in the temple, which was to consist of seven branches, and Solomon (so says the Archæologist) was ignorant of this commandment, because he made eleven *single* candlesticks, each holding one light (1 Kings, chap. vii. v. 49,): secondly, because the motto, HOLINESS TO THE LORD, which is ordered in Exodus to be put *on all the temple-plate!!!* was not upon the utensils of the first temple, but it was in use during the second temple, (by which, I suppose, he wishes to insinuate that the motto was engraved upon the *utensils* of the second temple); for proof we are referred to Zech. chap. xiv. v. 20: and, lastly, as to the book of Genesis, whereas it contains (chap. xxxvi. v. 31) a list of *eight kings* who reigned in Idumea—לפני מלך מלך לבני ישראל which is rendered in the English version, "before there reigned any king over the children of Israel"—from this it follows, that the book was not written till long after Moses, i. e. after the introduction of royalty among the Israelites; and since the *princes of Edom* are mentioned in chap. xv. v. 15, of Exodus, the Archæologist draws another argument against this latter book having been redacted to its present form before Jeremiah. Reader, hast thou ever heard *ignorance* presuming to teach wisdom? If not, please to procure for thy perusal the 38th volume of Sir R. Phillips's Monthly Magazine, and when thou hast read, with the utmost attention what is said there, pp. 34, 35, by the *learned* critic, in relation to the antiquity of the biblical writings, thou wilt agree with me, that hardly a more foolish piece of criticism was ever committed to paper, and that no man could be more ignorant of the subject he presumes to discuss, than our would-be-learned antiquary. Let us see what he says in relation to the first reason he gives for his assertion, that Solomon must have been ignorant of what is contained in the twenty-fifth chapter of Exodus—because he made "eleven single candlesticks." I did consult the passage in the seventh chapter of the first book of Kings; but, unfortunately for the Archæologist's position, the Hebrew word used is המנרות which ought to be translated "the candelabres," but not "the candlesticks;" and, in fact, the verse concludes with—"and the flower-works, and the *lamps*, and the tongues were gold." I will but briefly state that נר (*Nare*) means *a single lamp;* מנרה (Menorah), however, *an assemblage of lamps,* or candelabre, plural, מנרות, *several assemblages of lamps,* or simply *candelabres;* in short, *Nare* and *Menorah* bear the same relation in Hebrew as *mount* and *mountain* do in English. The ה is equivalent to the English definite article *the;* and for these reasons המנרות should be translated as I have done; and this must be apparent to every one, even if he be entirely unacquainted with the Hebrew. If the Archæologist had now but reflected what could be meant by the definite article, he would have come to the conclusion that it alludes evidently to a known form, which form is given, in continuation, to be *flowerwork, lamps,* and tongues: and is this not the same as we find recorded and commanded in Exodus, chap. xxv?

To his second objection I may answer explicitly, that the critic overshot the mark altogether. The inscription he speaks of, which, by the by, ought, properly speaking, to be given in English, HOLY TO THE ETERNAL, was ordered to be engraved on the *golden plate only,* which the high priest wore over the mitre; but I defy the Archæologist, if he yet lives, or any other person who has adopted his opinions, to produce even the shadow of evidence to prove that this inscription was to be upon any other utensil spoken of in Exodus. Was Solomon now to blame for not doing that for which he had not the least warrant in the Pentateuch? But our critic, to show his complete ignorance, concludes—"but (the motto) was in use on the return from captivity;" and refers to Zechariah, chap. xiv. v. 20. This verse, however, speaks not of the utensils in use during the second temple, but relates to the time of the Messiah, for the prophet says: "In that day there shall be upon the bells of the horses, HOLY TO THE ETERNAL;" and if this is taken in connection with the whole of the fourteenth chapter, every intelligent reader will easily discover, without any aid of mine, the *time* of which Zechariah treats.

26

It will thus be seen, that the second objection is too puerile to deserve further refutation. We now come to the reason given to prove that Moses was not the author of Genesis. The whole objection rests upon the words, "before there reigned any king over the children of Israel;" but if we insert a single particle, namely, "yet," and read "before there yet* reigned," &c. all difficulties will be at once removed; and Moses, then, meant to say, that up to his time eight kings had been reigning over Edom, whereas the Israelites had had no king yet. But some one may ask me: "What proof can you produce that your construction is the correct one?" I will then give this as my reason: Saul, the first king of Israel, was chosen about four hundred years after the Exodus; the Israelites resided, at the lowest calculation, two hundred and ten years in Egypt, during all which time there were probably kings in Idumea.† If we now adopt the opinion of *the critic*, the average reign of these *eight* kings will be found to have been *seventy-six* years! But allow that the last of these kings lived in Moses's time: the whole duration of their collective reign may then be put down at *two hundred and fifty*, and the average reign of each at *thirty-one* years. I will not add one word more, but leave it for all judicious men to decide which hypothesis is the most reasonable.

If, then, the thirty-sixth chapter of Genesis be no objection to its being written by Moses, no argument can be drawn from it against the authenticity of chap. xv. v. 15, of Exodus, because allusion is there made to the dukes of Edom. The Archæologist is further mistaken in supposing that the *Jewish archives*, as he is pleased to style our sacred canon, were ever kept *in* the ark; for in this ark were only the

---

* This has been done by Mendelsohn in his translation of the Pentateuch, and his construction is perfectly consonant with the Hebrew idiom, as it is well known that particles are frequently omitted in this language, when the obvious sense of the passage will supply the deficiency, as is the case in the very passage before us.

† But even allow that Idumea was in the first ages of its settlement governed by Sheiks, or, as they are termed in Genesis, *Alluphim*, hereditary independent heads of tribes: it is yet very reasonable to suppose that the whole family of Esau, together with the original inhabitants of the country, "*the children of Sengir the Chory*," were early united under one common head, though each Sheik or Alluph may have possessed even then some authority under the chief, perhaps in the manner of baronial tenure in the middle ages. And though, if this supposition be true, the average reign of the Idumean monarchs may have been rather shorter than we have supposed, yet can this be no objection to invalidate the position assumed in the text.

two tables on which the Decalogue was inscribed by superhuman agency; but the Pentateuch itself was kept *at the side* מצד *of the ark.* (See Deut. chap. xxxi. v. 26.) When, therefore, the critic wishes to draw a distinction between the "canon of the ark" and the "canon of the temple"—a distinction entirely unknown to the He-brews, because in Solomon's time there were *only the two tables,* (but not *nothing,*[*] as A. says,) in the ark, and no other archives (1 Kings, chap. viii. v. 9,)—he comes to an altogether erroneous conclu-sion; for the very assertion of the passage in Kings, "that there was nothing in the ark save the two tables which Moses had placed there in Horeb," proves most incontestably the truth of the opinion I have ventured to advance.

That, during the reigns of Menasseh and his son, who were very wicked, and addicted to idolatry, the study of the law was much ne-glected, and that, in consequence, the copies of it had become scarce, is extremely probable. When, therefore, Josiah had read the contents of the book which was found in the temple, in the twenty-sixth year of his age, and the eighteenth of his reign, he sent to the prophetess *Hulda*, to enquire of her if she had received any revelation concern-ing what God intended to do to the Israelites, because they had trans-gressed the commandments contained in the book which had been found. What evidence can be produced to establish that this book was *not* the same that was delivered to the Levites by Moses? I may answer, none whatever. On the contrary, when a person reads the twenty-second chapter of the 2d Kings, he will, if not predeter-mined not to be convinced, come to the *inevitable* conclusion, that the book was the entire Pentateuch, since Josiah observed precepts scattered indiscriminately through the whole law, (particularly Exo-dus). And if it even will *not* be admitted, (because the supposition be too bold,) that the book was the autograph of Moses, given to the Levites just before his death, to be kept at the side of the ark, that is inside of the temple, in the *holy of holies*, to be there as an evi-dence against the Israelites,—every one must confess that it must have been a similar one.

The Archæologist is further pleased to inform the world, that "the Hebrew was never the vernacular language of Palestine," and that the Hebrew Bible now extant is "a translation from the original lan-guage, made for the use of the Babylonian court, to enable it the better

---

[*] For he says the ark was empty, and did not even contain the two tables of the covenant.

to govern the conquered province." If any man were to come forward and say, that the Declaration of Independence is a translation of a Chinese document, written three thousand years before the creation : he could hardly be more absurd than the Archæologist is in saying, that the Hebrew was not the vernacular tongue of the Jews, but of the Babylonian court. If he had but turned over to the book of Daniel, he would have seen that the language called Hebrew was *not* the one spoken in Nebuchadnezzar's palace, and that there is a *radical* difference between the Hebrew and the Chaldean languages ; and that the latter was the one spoken and understood by the Babylonians. Daniel, therefore, when he speaks of what occurred in the king's palace, uses the last mentioned language ; but when he narrates his visions and prayers, and in the first chapter, he uses his own vernacular tongue, the Hebrew. If, now, the Hebrew was not vernacular in Palestine; how do the Scriptures exist at all in that language ? Could the Babylonians possibly have ordered a translation into this language, when *they* and the *Jews* were ignorant of it ? What should have been the use of it ? Turn the matter as you will, you *must* arrive at the conclusion, that the Hebrew was the language spoken by the Israelites, previous to their abduction to Babylon, and that the Scriptures ever existed in this same language, and in the same style in which we now possess them.

The Archæologist also says, " that the Decalogue must be an interpolated fragment, introduced after the captivity." His reasons are, first, because Joshua did inscribe the Decalogue existing in his time on a single altar ; and, secondly, because the *long fling* against sculpture could not have been inserted till after the destruction of the brazen serpent. (2 Kings, chap. xviii. v. 4.) Let us consider these objections.

1. " Could Joshua inscribe the Decalogue, as *now* existing, in large legible letters on a single altar ?" I answer, yes ; for in Exodus, chap. xxvii. v. 1, we read that the altar made in the wilderness was to be five cubits long, five cubits broad, and three cubits high ; let it also be considered that this altar was carried about from place to place, but that the one built by Joshua upon mount Ebal was a *permanent* structure, built of blocks of entire and unhewn stone, and so large that the whole Deuteronomy את משנה תורת משה was written on it. (Joshua, chap. viii. v. 32.) If we now even admit that only the Decalogue was inscribed on this altar, (which, however, remains to be proven, for not a word is said about the Decalogue,) and that the altar itself was of no larger dimensions than the one made by Moses, it will yet

strike every one, that there was room enough for the Decalogue upon a surface of sixty square cubits, if the letters were of any reasonable size.

2. "Could the inhibition against sculpture have been known before Hezekiah?" Again I must answer in the affirmative. "But did not Moses make the brazen serpent?" Certainly; but this was by the special command of God. The reason for this order may perhaps have been this: the Israelites, discontented with the manna, began to murmur, and to desire something which they thought better. (Numb. chap. xxi. v. 5.) God, to punish them, sent poisonious serpents amongst them, who killed a "large number of Israel." Being now convinced of their sin, and conscious of their ingratitude towards God and Moses, they besought him to pray for them to the Eternal, to remove the reptiles from them. Moses thereupon was ordered to make a serpent, and fix it upon a staff, that every one bitten might see it, and when seeing it remember his sins, ask forgiveness, and thus obtain a prolongation of life. As we also read in Tractate *Roshe Hashanah*, chap. iii. § 8: "And thus it is also said: 'Make thyself a serpent, and place it upon a staff, and it shall be that every one who is bitten, and looks at it, shall live.' But how could the serpent kill or keep alive any man? The serpent itself could not; but when the Israelites looked towards it on high, and subdued their hearts to their Father in heaven, they were cured; and if not, they perished." This, then, was the object of the brazen serpent; but it was done away with as soon as the occasion for which it was made had passed; and we find no mention made of it till Hezekiah, who destroyed it because the idolaters in his father's time had paid it adoration, *contrary to law*. In short, the brazen serpent was but a *temporary suspension* of a negative precept, similar to Elijah's sacrifice on Carmel (see above, page 147); but this precedent was on no account to be imitated; and can any proof be adduced that it ever *was* by those judges and kings who lived according to the precepts of the law? It will therefore be seen from the foregoing, that the length of the Decalogue is no argument against its *identity*, and that the "*long fling*" against sculpture is any thing but interpolated.

The next subject for enquiry is what the Archæologist says in regard to the *feelings* towards the Egyptians displayed in the second book, the Exodus, namely. He has discovered that its intention is to rouse hatred towards the Egyptians in the bosom of the Jews, I suppose he means by the narrative of our long sufferings in Egypt. But the *insinuation* that Jeremiah therefore must have been the author, (so says the Ar-

chæologist,) is as false as the *inference* is unjust. I do not suppose
that any person will doubt, or even can doubt, that the situation of the
Israelites in Egypt was the most abject and miserable. A historian
of our people, intimately acquainted with all that occurred, and confining himself strictly to facts, transmits an account of the hardships
of our ancestors to posterity, that the latest descendants of Jacob may
learn to know the great wonders and the unbounded mercy of God,
in redeeming his people from a state worse than death. How can he
be charged with sinister motives in so doing? Shall history not speak
what is true, because, forsooth, prejudice might be roused against ty-
rants and oppressors? Shall vice be unblushingly practised, and virtue not even dare to raise her voice to denounce the evil? This
ought certainly not to be. And the tyrant will ever be abhorred, and
the wicked be denounced, as long as men 'love freedom, and preserve
a due regard for virtue.

If, then, the book of Exodus were to give an exaggerated account
of our affliction in Egypt, the charge might perhaps be sustained; or
if the Pentateuch would even insinuate that it were lawful to hate the
people of that country, the author might then be accused, with some
show of reason at least, of displaying too much acrimony. But neither is the case : all our sufferings are described in about fifty verses,
and that without comment, which was indeed unnecessary, for the
enormities practised towards us required not many words to make
them odious; and so far from our being ordered to hate the Egyptians,
we are commanded (Deut. chap. xxiii. v. 8,) to receive the grandson
of an Egyptian proselyte into the congregation, " *because we were
strangers in his land ;*" and this surely looks very different from hating our former oppressors. If Jeremiah, now, had altered the Pentateuch, and added just what he pleased, would he have suffered the
last passage adduced to remain as a *damning record* against him?
Surely not. Upon the whole, it will be self-evident that all the outcry of the Archæologist* is mere imagination, and the emanation of a
mind filled with prejudice, and bent upon weakening the authority of

* This is a proper place to warn my readers against taking any thing upon
trust, till they have examined for themselves. Our law, our prophets, and our
Rabbins have been charged by men of learning even with uttering things which
were the farthest from their thoughts. And though these charges are made
with the utmost *assurance*, yet would I remind my *brethren, the Jews*, that this
is the cloak which *ignorance* usually assumes to hide her defects; *wisdom* is always diffident, and rather yields a little, than, by being too positive, injure the
cause of truth and piety.

the Mosaic law; and that the whole is no more founded upon truth, than his concluding assertion, or rather insinuation, that Jeremiah quoted at *Babylon* documents altogether new to him, up to the time of his making the selections for composing the Pentateuch (!); which must be *untrue*, for *Jeremiah never was in Babylon*, since we know from his own account, that *he fled from Palestine into Egypt*. This country he never left afterwards, for he died there; and I defy any person to produce the slightest proof to establish that he *ever was in Babylon*. The charges made by the Archæologist against Jeremiah for want of patriotism require no refutation, as every body will no doubt be gladly inclined to acquit him of a crime—for crime it is—of which Jews are but seldom guilty; for a national feeling, deep-rooted and heartfelt, is their principal characteristic. And do not the Lamentations of Jeremiah of themselves sufficiently prove how deeply he felt and mourned for the downfal of Jerusalem?

Since some of my readers may perhaps think this criticism of mine out of place, I deem it necessary to state the following reason as my justification. Having seen by accident the remarks of *the critic*, I thought to myself, who is this uncircumcised Philistine, that he blasphemes so against our holy law? Again I reflected, and found that his arguments were perhaps as good as can be adduced in favour of his position. I resolved, therefore, to refute them, thinking that, by doing so, I should in the best manner possible establish the assertion at the head of the second chapter; and I hope that I have proved almost beyond a doubt that Moses, and Moses alone, must have been the writer of the books which bear his name.

In conclusion, I would remark, that most objections raised against the authenticity of the Bible are predicated upon the not understanding of our language and our customs; and it therefore happens, that, whether they are urged by a Voltaire, a Payne, a Cooper, or an unlearned man of the lowest degree, they all bear the characteristic of consisting more of assertion without proof than of sound argument. And however formidable they may appear to one who only reads a translated Bible, which naturally must contain more or less inaccuracies, they can weigh but little with one acquainted with the language and habits of the people to whom the Bible was given. Much more might be added; but the length to which the subject has been carried already admonishes me to desist for the present.

THE

JEWS AND THE MOSAIC LAW.

PART THE SECOND:

CONTAINING

FOUR ESSAYS ON THE RELATIVE IMPORTANCE OF
JUDAISM AND CHRISTIANITY.

BY

A NATIVE OF GERMANY,

AND

A PROFESSOR OF CHRISTIANITY.

כל כלי יוצר עליך לא יצלח
וכל לשון תקום אתך למשפט תרשיעי :

"Every weapon forged against thee shall not prosper; and thou shalt condemn
every tongue rising against thee in judgment."—*Isaiah*, liv. 17.

INTRODUCTION.

Perhaps some person may be disposed to think that it displays a considerable degree of rancour to republish the reply to an attack long since forgotten, or at least lost sight of. He may say : " Few ever read the Quarterly Review, and fewer still pay sufficient regard to its allegations to retain them in memory after a lapse of five years." But I must say in answer, that no one actually acquainted with the true state of the question can assert with any regard to truth, that the charges against the Jews have not been repeated since the appearance of that article in the London Quarterly Review, which induced me to contradict the usual and oft-repeated accusations. In the second place, the authority which the said periodical has amongst the literary world makes its opposition worth something more than to treat it with silent contempt. Besides, a procedure of this nature presupposes such a share of greatness and elevation above the power attacking, such as we Jews can, alas! not boast of at the present time. We have, unfortunately, too often felt the talons of the destroying lion riveted in our flesh, not to dread his roar even now ; and though at the present moment his power of harming be considerably diminished, it behooves us yet to be watchful lest he overpower us from our not heeding the covert where he lies in wait, thirsting for our life's blood. With this I do not mean to say, that those who dislike our code of laws would wish to see us led again to slaughter ; but I may assert, without fearing to be called illiberal, that many a good Christian would be glad to convert us, if not by fair, well, then, by foul means ; but at all events the Jews must be converted. No one can deny that this is a leading principle with a large number of persons, who, we hardly doubt, are actuated by real philanthropy, since they imagine that their doctrines are as beneficial as ours are alleged to be pernicious. Hence it originates, that the name of *infidel* is a favourite epithet applied to us, together with *unbelieving Jew, one groping in darkness, persecuting Jew,* and many more; and hence it is that a late writer, I allude to the Rev. H. H. Milman, in his History of the Jews, says: "That the best and wisest of the Jews were not equal to the Christians;" and that Bishop M'Ilvaine, in his Evidences of Christianity, uses the following phrases: " Had the Jews of Jerusalem been able to deny it, would their *persecuting* enmity have permitted them to be silent ?" and " Consider the three thousand, converted from bitter, persecuting Judaism to the faith of Christ, on the eve of the Pentecost." Who, now, reading these extracts, merely taken at random, would think otherwise than that no morality of the purer kind is taught by the Old Testament, and that the spirit of the Jews is persecution ? And do not the reverend and learned authors of these respective works see that they raise, by their ill-chosen phraseology, a spirit of persecution and hatred towards the Jews in the minds of their readers, although they themselves be free therefrom ?   Add to this, that the infidel Jews are prayed for at prayer-meetings and in public worship, and that God is entreated to convert them to the gospel dispensation: and I am confident that no one will sincerely blame me when 1 maintain, that much ill will is constantly raised, though perhaps innocently, against our people.   We suffer doubly, because we have no means of dispelling the prejudice, except by our conduct, and this is, unfortunately for us, not observed with sufficient impartiality to permit people to form a correct judgment.   Since now the charges of the Quarterly Review, or at least similar ones, are constantly repeated and renewed, I trust that no blame will attach to me for republishing a reply to these charges, although they have been made in their peculiar form five years ago.

Another opinion may be maintained about my unimportance, and the little good I can do by appearing voluntarily and uncalled for as the champion of the Jews.   Indeed this objection is much more reasonable than the uselessness of a defence ; but all I can say in reply is, that my intentions are good, and that, if my abilities and standing are not sufficient, let some one more able, and upon a higher station in life, and more known to the public, assume the responsibility, and he may be assured that 1 shall with pleasure yield him the palm of superiority.

Again, some person may fear that the republication of the four essays subjoined may provoke controversy ; but the same may be urged against every publication upon disputed points of morality, politics, science, and religion ; and let it be observed, that controversy, if carried on in a gentlemanly and modest manner, can do no harm ; and if, unfortunately, controversial remarks should be elicited from any one who may think my observations improper, (which, however, I hardly anticipate,) I pledge myself, should I be prevailed upon to give an answer, not to suffer my zeal to run away with my judgment, and that I shall never let opprobrious epithets be the cause of my forfeiting the claims to moderation which is perhaps the *only*, at least the *chief*, merit of my writings.   In conclusion, I must state, that I mean no personal disrespect to any one by the allusions I may have made, as I feel no ill will towards the respective persons whose opinions I have canvassed or alluded to.   And to show that my comments upon the London Quarterly Review are not too harsh, I have extracted some of the passages I have commented on.   I would have republished the whole article ; but this is useless, as any person can get it who feels a great curiosity to read it ; and then I have not replied to half the misstatements and charges made in the article under question; and even these extracts would have been omitted, were it not that it is better to let every person see that nothing more than justice has been done to the Reviewer.

I. L.

September, 1833.

In the beginning of his remarks, the Quarterly Reviewer says (p. 114):

" Is it too much to say, that we have rather left them among ourselves as vermin, which we know not how to get rid of, than regarded and treated them as the children of a common Father ?   We have not even afforded them any portion of that compassion which usage and opinion would require that we should at least appear to feel for fallen greatness."

This sounds liberally enough,—but, now, as to the remedy, which of course is to be the effect of compassion for fallen greatness (p. 130):

" Civil enactments, with reference to this peculiar people, require much deliberation. We may harm both them and ourselves by hasty and injudicious attempts to benefit them."

After saying that oppression would not do, he continues (p. 131):

" On the other hand, to give all the rights and privileges of citizens to them, *whilst holding to Judaism*, [reader, reflect!] would be to bind ourselves wholly to those who cannot so bind themselves to us; to confer on them a strength which might be turned against ourselves; and to compel them of course to contract reciprocal obligations, which their highest duties—in their view—national, political, and religious, must force them to violate at such a call as they shall believe to be that of their promised deliverer." *Ergo* (page 130): " If the discordant and painful position of the Jews amongst us, and the prejudicial effects of the mode of their existence as a crude, unamalgamated, and heterogeneous mass [hard words, truly], arise from their Judaism, and from their refusal to adopt the religion of Christendom,* then every rule of sound policy urges us to promote, by means of persuasion, [or bribes too?] and as far as we can, the reception of the gospel by them."

The Reviewer expresses himself in the following manner when speaking of the Jews (p. 115):

" The greatest accumulation of them on any one point in Europe is in the countries of ancient Poland, now forming Russian, Austrian, and Prussian Poland, and the modern kingdom of Poland under the sceptre of the emperor of Russia. It is stated by Beer, that many centuries ago a considerable body of Jews migrated from France into Germany, whence many of their descendants passed into Poland; but they must have remained long in Germany before this second swarm *hived itself in Poland.*"

And further down he continues:

" There are great numbers of Jews in the parts of Turkey contiguous to Poland; but *there* they literally swarm; they are innkeepers, tradesmen, distillers of brandy, brewers, horse-dealers, money-changers, usurers,† as every where else; some few of them are farmers

---

* Which is that?—the catholic—episcopal—methodist—baptist—Greek—presbyterian? Would it be possible to convert the Jews to the Christian religion without making them sectarians?

† Mind, reader, *usury* is a trade of the Jews: no Christians are ever brokers, stock-jobbers, money-changers, and usurers,—no, not they indeed! This is all left for the hated Jews to do, for the good reason the Germans gave when they

of the soil. Their numbers have increased of late years so rapidly as greatly to alarm and embarrass the governments of countries which afford but slender resources for a population so averse to be engaged in tillage. The evil of this immense accumulation of such a people, having one common interest and feeling, both of which are foreign to the interests and feelings of the citizens of the state, is felt, especially by the Russian government."

"Since the time of Mendelsohn, many of them have studied with much success in its (Germany's) universities; of these Professor Neander, now a Christian, [mark, now a Christian!] may be cited as a very creditable specimen."—p. 116.

"But when these feudal properties, besides many of the finest houses in the German capitals, passed thus into Israelitish hands, it was in the course of things that the people should view with envy and indignation (!) these foreign unbelieving money-changers [why not at once Christ-killers?] climbing up on the pedestals from which the statues of Christian knights and barons of ancient race had been hurled down by the storms which shook their native land to its centre."—p. 117.

"Pharisaism has descended uninterruptedly to the rabbinical Jews; their modern rabbis are the lineal spiritual descendants of the scribes and lawyers of the time of Jesus Christ; and it appears that the whole of the traditionary additions to the law existing then are in vigour now, and that they have been fearfully augmented since then. We spare our readers citations from the blasphemous and horrible absurdities of the Talmud, which professes to have, as its groundwork, an oral revelation made by God to Moses on Mount Sinai, when he delivered the law to him; nor will we add a statement of the superstitions which harass the Jew, or of that demonology which arrays innumerable maleficent invisible agents in arms against his health and happiness, under all and the strangest circumstances. In Russian Poland the Jews bury their dead hastily, judging them to be such when no steam appears on a glass applied to the mouth. If the jolting of the cart recalls life and action, they believe that it is a devil who occupies the body, and deal with it accordingly: thus says a very respectable Jew, an eye-witness [?] born and bred there. He adds, that they are armed against our reasonings on the Old Testament, (of which, however, they know very little,) by the assurances of their rabbis, that the Al-

permitted Jews to buy stolen goods and take interest for money lent—"Their souls are once belonging to the devil, and it can make no difference whether they have these sins in addition to answer for or not!"

mighty has placed many things in the text as stumbling-blocks to the Gentiles, but that the truth is to be found in the marginal notes from the Targum, which are given as infallible guides to the Israelites alone. They are taught that the seven nations of the land of Canaan were Christian, and that Jesus Christ [!] was a magician. How deeply they feel the want of a mediator, is evident from a part of a prayer used by them on the day of atonement, which runs thus : ' Woe unto us, for we have no mediator.' The Jew on the bed of death can see nothing in his God but an inexorable judge, whose wrath he cannot deprecate, and whose justice he cannot satisfy. At all times, but in sickness especially, the thought or mention of death is terrible to him; the evil eye, ever an object of horror, is then peculiarly so ; they then fear their nearest and dearest friends looking at them. We can find no solution of this mental darkness in those who have Moses and the prophets for their guide, and millions of whom have lived for centuries amidst the civilisation and literature of Europe, but in that curse which God pronounces against rebellious Israel, ' that he will smite him with madness, and blindness, and astonishment of heart ;' and declares of him ' that he shall grope at noonday, as the blind gropeth in darkness ?' But there is a dispensation of heavenly justice and mercy respecting Israel, requiring particular attention. An unheard of crime required an unheard of punishment ; and the race were condemned to the dispersion and captivity in which they still languish. But while other races, long trodden under foot, like the Pariahs of India, lose the keen sense of degradation, and of the injustice of men, through a continued habit of humiliation, and with blunted feelings endure them as a matter of course—it is not so with the Jew. He has implanted in his bosom a national and spiritual pride—a fierce constancy and a contempt of his oppressors, which constantly exasperate and keep alive his sense of pain and degradation. This pride and contempt are infused into him by the extravagant, most uncharitable, and often blasphemous [?] assertions of his rabbi. But from this very arrogance which increases his sufferings, springs that principle of resistance and opposition under which the Jews have clung together and struggled incessantly against the storms that have buffetted them for ages ; and it is this loftiness of mind, so ill suited to their present lot, that will the better enable them to seek, contend for, and maintain those higher and nobler destinies which are placed before their sight in a glorious futurity. It is the consciousness of his past and his future fortunes which gives to the Jew a buoyancy and a tendency to rise above the surface of the waves, even when plunged deep below them, unknown to other depressed nations, and which inspires into him the will and the means to seek the level of his promised fortunes; for even the meanest Jew considers himself as personally invested with national and spiritual greatness. Israel has within him another principle of resistance. He was, from the first, reproached with being a 'stiff-necked generation;' and stubborn as he was in the desert, so he is now, whether you find him in the streets of London, or of Cairo, or in a Polish forest. His eye, his nose, and his narrow upper jaw are not more especial marks of his physical conformation, than is his stubbornness a distinguishing feature of his mind. It is this obstinacy which creates one of our greatest difficulties in dealing with him. Proteus could be bound by no knot, because he perpetually changed his shape—the Jew can be bound by none, because he will not change his. In other nations, corruption and abandonment of religion have been a mighty cause of moral and national decadence: but the moral and national wreck of the Jewish people was caused by their stiff-necked adherence, in despite of type and prophecy, to a religion superseded by a purer code of heavenly laws.

"It has been often observed, that, under every religion which was originally false, or has degenerated into falsehood, the weaker sex is not possessed of the advantages it holds under the true. Superstition corrupts the heart while it weakens the understanding; and where that charity, which springs from a pure faith alone, vanishes, the stronger animal lords it over the feebler. We know how honourable was the situation of the women in ancient Israel. We have Miriam, Deborah, and Hannah, as it were, before our eyes—but the Jewess of these days is treated as an inferior being. Neither religious nor moral instruction is vouchsafed to her; and in lieu of it three observances are imposed on her, as comprising her whole duty: one of them doubles a restraint enjoined to her by the law, the two others are purely mechanical. The only book given to the rabbinical Jewesses, and given in childhood to them, is eminently calculated to fill their minds with the most impure ideas, as well as with the falsest notions of the divinity. There have been, however, of late, extracts from the Old Testament published in Germany, expressly for their use and benefit. An equally mischievous effect in polluting the minds of the boys must be produced by an instruction which they are compelled to make themselves acquainted with—and this also in childhood."—p. 119.

"Is it to be wondered at, that, amidst a people under such spiritual misrule and neglect, confined to cities, in general, occupied mainly in the pursuit of petty gains, under the guidance of the foul and uncha-

28

ritable abominations of the Talmud, a great relaxation of moral principles has taken place, and especially at the expense of those whom
they hate as their oppressors, and despise as heathens and unclean ?
Indeed there are many precepts of their rabbis utterly subversive of
honesty in all their dealings with Gentiles. Antonio Margarita, a
converted Jew of the sixteenth century, reproached them with the *Col
Nidre*, an absolution, pronounced at the yearly feast of atonement, to
all present, for all perjuries and breaches of vows and engagements,
committed by them in the preceding year. It is so called, from the
two words with which a prayer used at that feast begins: the night
and day are passed in prayer and fasting, during which the Jew
wears the shroud in which he is to be buried, a present from his
father-in-law, as it is also his wedding garment; and then this absolution is pronounced to him. But Eisenmenger, in his 'Entdecktes
Judenthum' (Judaism Unveiled), published in the seventeenth century, upbraids them with pronouncing that absolution prospectively in
his day, that is, for the coming year. A German government, aware
of this fact, not long since caused the Jews, when sworn in cases in
which Christians were concerned, to make oath that they were not
present at the last yearly promulgation of this absolution: forgetting
that, if they were present, this last perjury was also comprised in this
precautionary whitewashing. It is not long since (we state the fact
on the best authority) that a Polish Jew hired his rabbi to send the
angel of death to destroy a Polish nobleman, as his only means of es-
caping the detection of an heinous fraud: soon after this, the countess
died, but the husband lived. The Jew went to upbraid his rabbi, who
replied, that 'he sent the angel on his errand, who, not finding the
count at home, did his best by slaying the lady ;' and this satisfied the
complainant. [Who believes this story?]

" It is always and especially to be observed, that these and the like
matters are stated exclusively of the rabbinical Jews, those bent down
under the whole weight of their law as now interpreted, and most especially of them as they are found in their northern hive, in Poland.
In other parts of Europe there are great numbers of Jews, who have
profited very considerably of the civilisation which surrounds them,
and of the morality of the gospel, though without recognising its divine origin. Amongst them there are many amiable, charitable, libe-
ral-minded men, of unquestioned probity, to whose virtues we offer a
willing tribute ; and, small as is the number of English Jews, we have
had, and have amongst us, men adorning this country by their talents
and acquirements, as well as virtues, who trace their origin to them.

But it was Mendelsohn, the translator of the Pentateuch, who was in truth an infidel, that gave the first impulse to the Jewish mind in modern days, and the first blow to Rabbinism: he was seconded by able and learned Jews, his associates; a taste for literature and science was excited amongst their nation."—p. 124.

The article in the Review contains also an account of the Caraites, a small sect, and the only dissenting sect of Jews, settled in Poland and the Crimea, and who are praised as being far superior to the rabbinical Jews, and as being more likely to receive the light of the gospel, since we are told they were unable to answer a missionary who was sent to convert them. The words of the Reviewer are as follows:

"A missionary, who, in travelling through Troki, pressed upon their minds the truth of the gospel in the only short conversation he had an opportunity of holding with them, found them candid and well disposed to listen: they were surprised at his arguments, and little able to reply to them, as they know nothing of the quibbles and subtleties which the rabbinical Jews have long resorted to when engaged in controversy with Christians. Who, reflecting on the pure faith of the Caraites, and that integrity, industry, and virtue, by which they have every where impressed sentiments of respect and esteem for them upon the people with whom they dwell, would not fain believe that, though exiles from Palestine, they are exempt from the worst and final curses inflicted by the Almighty upon Israel for the worst and blackest of his crimes? And who will not be delighted to hear that, whilst the rabbinical Jews can give no clue to the history of this remarkable portion of the race, modern discovery seems strongly to confirm the views cherished among the Caraites themselves? Mr. Wolff, the missionary, having learned that a body of Caraites was established in the desert of Hit, at three days' journey from Bagdad, visited them. The account which they gave him was, that their fathers, during the Chaldean captivity, perceiving that their brethren were corrupting the pure faith by amalgamating with it the philosophical doctrines of the country, 'sat down by the waters of Babylon, and wept when they remembered Sion;' that in order to imprint the Scriptures unmixed on their hearts, they read them incessantly, and were thence called Caraites, or *readers;* and that, when the others returned from the captivity, they separated themselves, to escape their offences and punishments, and retired to the very spot where the missionary found them. He there saw these 'children of the Bible,' as they call themselves, living an Arab life in cottages; they are a very fine people, and the women singularly handsome. He was struck with their unvarying truth, of which their neighbours allow the merits, but practise it not; and they are remarkable for their honesty and cleanliness. They said that they had sent colonies to Cairo and to Ispahan, where a synagogue still bears an inscription, which shows that it belonged to them. Benjamin de Tudela, it is said, found the same people living in the same manner at Hit, six hundred years ago. They speak pure Arabic, but all know and read Hebrew; they state the whole number of their sect to be five thousand, and that they are the original stock of it. They call their ministers ' wise men,' and know not the name of rabbis."—p. 127.

I must make here a remark or two, since the extract here given contains two untrue inferences which I have not noticed in my reply. The first is as to the name *Caraites* having been brought into use during the Babylonian captivity, which is the farthest possible from truth, since the name is mentioned nowhere, at least as far as my reading extends, till long after the destruction of the second temple ; and we must therefore disbelieve the statement of the Caraites, even allowing the Rev. Joseph Wolff did not tell a deliberate falsehood to obtain the credit of a great discovery. The second misstatement is, that the Caraites call their ministers " wise men," from which one would infer that the Rabbinists do not do the same, whereas the contrary is the case ; for we always speak of our *wise men*, but never of our Rabbins ; and any one in the least acquainted with rabbinical writings must know that the phrase of " our wise men say," is that generally used when speaking of the Rabbins as a body. Besides this, the Portuguese Jews, also Rabbinists, call their chief Rabbi *Hacham*, or the wise man. The whole matter is but of small importance, but it proves the unfairness of the accusations against us.

" The Jews at Constantinople, forty thousand in number, and in the parts of European Turkey on and near the Mediterranean, speak Spanish, and appear to descend from Israelites driven from Spain by persecution. The Bible Society are now printing at Corfu the New Testament, in Jewish-Spanish, *for their benefit*."—p. 129.

" When we speak of the conversion of the Jews as a thing which is a desideratum for the European governments, nothing can be further from our intentions than to suggest that they should mix in it directly ; we are well aware that it could not be usefully even attempted by them,—for this, among other reasons,—that their so doing would excite extreme mistrust and jealousy: they should, undoubtedly, however, view such attempts, if prudently made, with favour and good will, and endeavour to lead to them by advice and encouragement. But if political wisdom urges us to encourage, by all prudent and charitable means, the promotion of Christianity amongst the Jews, our religion summons us to the same duty with a far more powerful voice. What can show more strongly that inveteracy of uncharitableness towards the Jews, which has grown out of long indulgence in the feeling, than the disfavour accompanying the attempt to convert them ? There are even many who will contribute to the support of missions to distant nations, to which we owe no atonement, and yet withhold their aid from those whose aim it is to give the gospel to the Israelites who dwell in our cities, and who have so long been trodden down under our feet. That very degraded moral state, which gives the Jew his strongest claim to our assistance, is urged as a reason why it should be withheld from him as one past help and amendment! He is vilified for blindness, perverseness, obstinacy, if he adheres to the faith of his fathers; and he is vituperated as insincere and interested, if he abandons it to profess our own !"—p. 131.

" In this state of things, the question may naturally be addressed to the European Christians : what endeavours they have made to convey the gospel to the ancient people of God.

" We may dispense with any allusion to the Sunday exposition of the errors of Judaism, which the Jews at Rome are compelled to hear, or to the flames of the Spanish *auto da fè*. The Jew has peculiar feelings, which will ever cause him to repel the hand of the church of Rome, even were it tendered in kindness."—p. 132. [But are the Jews more inclined to the Protestant sects ?]

" The next attempt made by any body of men to communicate the knowledge of the gospel to the Hebrews was that of the ' London Society for promoting Christianity amongst the Jews.' It was formed in 1809, and its founders appear not to have known that the Callenberg Institution had existed. It has been for many years a religious society of the church of England exclusively. Its revenues arise from voluntary contributions, and were last year between fourteen and fifteen thousand pounds. It has translated the New Testament into Hebrew, and employs various missionaries abroad, particularly in Poland, where they enjoy especial protection from the government. Other societies have been formed subsequently in Great Britain and Ireland, with the same object, either in connection with that society, or acting independently of it; and the continent is beginning to follow this example."—p. 133.

" The difficulties, however, are great, and must not be disguised. The Jews resisted the preaching of Jesus Christ himself, and of his inspired apostles : the traditions, which so materially aided in causing that resistance, have multiplied an hundred fold since then ; and there arose subsequently amongst them a new and deadly repugnance to the gospel, as being the law of their own persecutors. At the commencement of our Lord's mission, the Jews attempted his life, because he signified to them the call of the Gentiles to the gospel; trodden under foot for ages, on account of their rejection of it, by those Gentiles who accepted it, they traced their calamities up to Christ, with a blindness like that of their fathers, and heaped upon the name of the Son of God a horrible and vindictive hatred, of which the Talmud, in its text and commentary, the Mischna and Gemara, bears dreadful and multiplied evidence. [Where ?]   The rabbis, their spiritual guides and rulers, have moreover most powerful worldly motives for endeavouring to check the progress of the gospel, which they do, by burning tracts and the New Testament, [who informed the Quarterly Review of this ?] whenever they get them into their hands, with unrelenting activity, and by harassing the Jews who are inclined to turn their attention to Christianity, *inter alia*, by curses and imprecations, of which they have long possessed a fearful store, and for adding to which they possess a facility that attests the effects of uninterrupted practice and Asiatic imagination.   Their priestcraft, pre-eminence, power, and worldly wealth are all at stake.   The Jews, moreover, are scandalised, especially on the continent, by our profanation of our own Sabbath, and other prevalent impieties."—p. 134.

" The missionaries in Poland, on visiting places for the first time, have frequently found in the hands of Jews, and conveyed to them by other Jews, New Testaments and tracts originally distributed by themselves: and in one case, a Jew was converted thus by a tract given to him by one of his brethren, who retained his Judaism. Mr. Wolff found at Ispahan and Cashan Hebrew New Testaments, which he had given away at Jerusalem and Aleppo, and had marked; and there were notes subsequently inserted, recommending them to the perusal of the Persian Jews; and there are accounts of New Testaments given to Jews at Ispahan, having been sent to their brethren in Balk, Bokhara, and Afghanistan.   The Jews of one of their colleges at Mosul, near the site of Nineveh, showed to Mr. Wolff a manuscript of the New Testament in Arabic, but written in Jewish characters;

the translator was a rabbi, now dead, but whose son still lives there. Mr. Wolff found it to be a good translation. They refused to part with it. The rabbi had written in it a recommendation to peruse it, addressed to the members of the colleges, and to his descendants. Mr. Wolff found also, in the library of the Spanish Jews at Jerusalem, a Syriac translation of the New Testament written in Hebrew characters. This is the less surprising, as Schultze, in 1754, found the eastern Jews less disputatious than the European, and especially than the German; and they heard him willingly. He tells us, moreover, that they do not talk during worship, as those of Europe do." —p. 136. [What does all this amount to?]

" There is strong evidence that Christianity is making extensive, though secret progress amongst the Jews at Constantinople. Indeed, we think there is every reason to believe that the general extent of avowed Christianity amongst the Jews is very greatly less than that which is concealed from motives of fear, from aversion to, or mistrust of the Christians, and from, in very many cases, the dread of forfeiture of the means of existence, in nearly all, of breaking the bonds of consanguinity and affection. Three such cases of old Jews came lately within the knowledge of one individual of our own acquaintance, within a short space of time; two of them had been converted by the perusal of tracts circulated amongst their brethren, without their having ever conversed with a missionary; yet these men were known to be regularly performing the rites of their apparent religion in the synagogue. [Who believes this?]

" To say the truth, it is not on the number of conversions actual, visible, and averred, effected amongst a people so circumstanced as the Jews now are, that we dwell as the matter of the most importance. The great object is not at present to pursue and hunt down, as it were, single Jews to conversion, but to remove the prejudices, and soften the hearts, and dispose *towards* Christianity the minds of hundreds." * * * * * " In general it may be affirmed, on the best and latest testimonies from the north and east of Europe, and from the Persian and Ottoman empires,—testimonies which coincide completely, and in a way that is most striking,—that very many of the Jews, now bearing far less *hostile* feelings towards Christianity than they used to do, on account of its being professed by Gentiles, have so strong a conviction of the beauty of the morality of the gospel, that they do justice to it in despite of our imperfect practice of it, and say that the fault is in us and not in our law."—p. 138.

" In the German universities, whither the most gifted and ardent of their youth resort, the risk of their falling into scepticism, neologism, the mad metaphysics of the day, or pantheism, is infinitely greater than the chance, in the present state of things, of their enrolling themselves under the comparatively small number of those who, in these institutions, profess genuine Christianity ; and this experience has but too well proved. But further—the Jew, though he may have thrown off rabbinism, can no where have found or undergone a discipline calculated to chasten or subdue that extreme pride which characterises his race ; and, contemplating the doctrine of the cross with a proud and inflated heart, if he views it as a Jew, he will see in it a ' stumbling-block,' and if as a Greek, that is, as a philosopher, ' foolishness.' Then, as for a pure worship, such as the so called reformed Jews profess to seek to restore, we must observe, that no Israelitish Luther or Calvin has as yet arisen to divest Judaism of the rubbish which so miserably encumbers it."—p. 140.

But we must have done with the Review ; and I trust that the extracts furnished prove enough that the scope of the whole article is to excite hostility towards the Jews, and that I have not said a tenth of what could have been urged in contradiction to the slanders heaped upon our poor exposed heads by the learned critic and his hopeful coadjutors, such as unbelieving Jews—heartless apostates— and credulous missionaries.

THE

JEWS AND THE MOSAIC LAW.

PART II.

ESSAY I.

REMARKS UPON THE "PRESENT STATE OF THE JEWS," IN THE
QUARTERLY REVIEW, NO. 75.

Almost every writer upon the condition of the Jews has indulged
himself in showering plentiful abuse upon their moral and religious
character, vilifying their institutions, and denouncing their teachers
and Rabbins. The Jews themselves have commonly been stigma-
tised as dishonest in their dealings, and only desirous of engaging in
small-trade *out of aversion to agriculture, manual labour, and the
sciences.* It is unfortunately true, that most of my brethren in
faith are thus engaged, but let us enquire if the fault be theirs. Let
us for one moment recur to our history since the destruction of the
second temple, and we shall find reasons enough to account for the
present state of the Jews. That part of our nation settled in Syria
were agriculturists and mechanics, as long as they lived unmolested;
they were respected and enlightened, and not alone made the *Talmud* their study, but made also great progress in the other sciences,
particularly astronomy, of which the Jewish Calendar bears honourable testimony, which even the Christians must confess has been
very ingeniously constructed; and several schools, particularly the
one in Suria, were long and justly celebrated. But a barbarous

29

people now occupies this fair land, and the Israelites groan under the heavy oppression which the eastern rulers impose upon them.

The Jews settled amongst the Christians were uniformly hated and detested; every oppressor considered them as lawful prey, and both king and beggar trod them under foot. No Jew was allowed to enter a university; no Jew could be member of a guild, without being which he could exercise none of the mechanic arts; what then was left him but to turn his attention to trade? Could every one be a wholesale dealer? Surely not. Is it therefore wonderful, that by degrees the greater part of our nation became small-traders, shop-keepers, and pedlars? Some in this way amassed considerable fortunes, and, in consequence, turned their attention to increase their wealth, without the trouble and vexation accompanying the afore-mentioned occupations; and thus they became money-changers, and because they loaned money on interest, were directly called usurers. The Christian nobility, nay even kings, became indebted to them, and they acquired in this manner an ascendancy, which was other-wise denied them. I will not dwell upon the many hardships we had to endure; how many persecutions we had to suffer, particularly in England, France, and Spain; how we were driven from town to town, and from country to country; it was then that flocks of Jews, or "swarms," as the Quarterly so elegantly styles them, fled from these countries into Germany and Poland, where, though oppressed, they could at least hope to obtain a resting place for their wearied limbs, where they might dwell to acquire fresh strength to be able to endure new sufferings. It was then that the emperor of Germany took the Jews under his own protection; it was then that the king Casimir of Poland granted unto the people of God those privileges which they yet enjoy there. But even in Germany and Poland we were obliged to suffer much, and many of us were slaughtered, and as the Hebrew elegy expresses it: "The blood of parents was mingled with that of the children; that of the teachers with the blood of the scholars; and the blood of the bridegroom with the blood of the bride."—We were considered as an inferior race, every one spit at us, and no one felt pity for the miserable remnant of a great people. It is true we cheerfully went to meet our death by fire, by water, by the sword and the gallows, nay many suffered themselves to be buried alive, rather than forsake their faith. Our

enemies would compel us to acknowledge a god unknown to our ancestors; but we gave up our lives, exclaiming: " Hear, O Israel,
the Eternal our God is the only Eternal Being," rather than by
changing our belief, live highly honoured and respected by the
world, but despised by ourselves. In all these great sufferings the voice
of the Rabbins was heard encouraging their flock to submit cheerfully to the decrees of Heaven; and they suffered every thing rather
than cease admonishing and teaching the common people. And
could *they acquire glory by martyrdom?* Had they any principles
of their own to establish by their death?—No, so far from either
of these two usual incentives to martyrdom having had any influence
with them, their individual names are almost forgotten, except by a
few of their brethren; besides no history of martyrs ever existed
amongst us: where then was the glory they could hope to acquire?—And they died for the faith of their ancestors—that faith
acknowledged even by the lowest of the house of Israel; where then
were the doctrines of their own, the Rabbins could expect to establish? Who, now, can say that aught but the best motives prompted
them to sacrifice their lives? Who can say that their object was
not solely to sanctify the holy law, by the willingness they showed
to lay down their lives when they were no longer permitted to observe its precepts?—The lives of the Rabbins have been uniformly
moral and pious; and it may puzzle even the learned writer in the
Quarterly Review to find the Hebrew Rabbins act like some of the
many Christian bishops and pontiffs have done. No Rabbin, I venture to assert, ever went forth to battle, to fight in the train of a
conquering prince; no Rabbin ever ordered the eyes of an opponent
to be put out, as one of the early popes is said to have done. Upon
the whole, the lives of the Rabbins may, without danger to their reputation, be compared with those of the best of the Christian divines,
and I even dare say, that in most cases the Jewish Rabbins will be
found to have been the best men.—It is not my object to throw
odium upon the teachers of Christianity, far from it, for there are
many good and valuable men amongst them, many both in ancient
and modern times, who wished and did well to Israel; but only to
rescue the memory of our own pastors from the reproach and contempt which the Reviewer and many kindred spirits would so gladly
bring them into. If what I have said of the Rabbins be true (and I

challenge the world to deny it,) all astonishment will vanish, why the Jewish theologians exercise such a powerful influence over all their brethren ; why their opinions are listened to with such profound deference, and why every Jew should aim that his son should be-come one of the sacred fraternity.

Every person, who dispassionately reads the article alluded to in the Quarterly Review, must be convinced that the writer of it was actuated by, I may say, a deadly hatred to the Rabbins; for what other motives could he have for calling the great Moses Men-delsohn, of blessed memory, an infidel? Has the Reviewer ever read his letters to Professor Kœlbele, in which he defends himself against the charge of being a deist? True, he left Kœlbele in pos-session of the field ; but was that because he could not answer him? Certainly not; it was what Mr. Mendelsohn publicly announced, that, should Mr. Kœlbele think proper to answer him, he (Mendel-sohn) would not think him worthy of a reply, as the letter he was then writing must of necessity be a sufficient answer to all the other could say. I only quote from memory, not having the book at pre-sent ; but I am sure that I have stated the substance correctly. Let any man read the works of Mendelsohn, and let him then pronounce judgment, and I do not fear that he will find him guilty of the *foul* charge of the Quarterly Review.—Mr. Mendelsohn's memory did not need a defence from so obscure an individual as I am ; but I could not suffer his calumniator's assertion to pass unnoticed. For Moses Mendelsohn has done more than any other individual who has lived since the days of Maimonides and Yarchi, for the improve-ment of his fellow-believers.—May he rest in peace, and may all be confounded who speak evil against the righteous.

I will not enter into a systematic defence of the Mishna and Gemara, as I may leave them to defend themselves ; the most pro-found wisdom is discovered in these books, which have always been cried down by infidels amongst ourselves and Christian writers. But though it has often been asserted that the Talmud is a blasphemous work, I utterly and boldly deny it. How often must it be said, how often shall it be repeated, that the Talmud contains allegorical sayings, parables, or fables if you please? Have not the Jews and even the enlightened and liberal amongst the Christians often said so? And the Count Stolberg acknowledges, that the Talmud contains some of the wisest sentiments found in any book whatsoever; and surely he could not be supposed to be in any degree biassed in favour of our Rabbins, as he had forsaken the protestant and joined the Roman catholic church, and I suppose it is well known, that the Romans are no very particular friends to the Jewish doctrines; nor can the count be accused of any attachment to them, although he was compelled to make the above admission; and of this all his numerous writings, after he had become a catholic, will bear ample testimony.—But I leave my subject: what I mean to assert is this, that the allegorical sayings of the Talmud must not be considered as if the Rabbins believed that such things had actually happened, but only as fables, which, under the appearance of marvellous stories, conceal good and wholesome truth; and they adopted this allegorical and hyperbolical mode of conveying their sentiments, as in many instances it might have been dangerous for them to speak plainly.

That the doctrines of the Rabbins enjoin implicit resignation to the divine will, every one will acknowledge who has the least acquaintance with them. The Rabbins also taught the immortality of the soul, before the Christian religion was yet in existence; the doctrine of reward and punishment after death was promulgated by them, as was also that of the resurrection of the dead. They did not, however, teach these glorious truths as inventions of their own; but they brought arguments from the law and the prophets in support of their assertions, and proved, at the same time, that the doctrines of immortality, reward and punishment after death, the resurrection of the *body*, and the subsequent beatitude of the righteous, were taught to the children of Israel by *our teacher Moses* (of blessed memory) himself. Would any man then in his sober senses call such men blasphemers?—men who taught the law without receiving any emolument for so doing, and who literally fulfilled the commandment which God gave to Joshua: " And thou shalt meditate therein, day and night."

Oh, shame! shame! that there should be found in England one man capable of harbouring such a thought. Could the following from the Proverbs of the Fathers, have been written by blasphemers?

" Rabbi (Yehudah) said: Consider three things and thou wilt not sin; know that there are above thee an all-seeing eye, an all-hearing ear, and that all thy actions are written down in a book," (namely, that no action of man will be forgotten.) Abothe, chap. ii. § 1.

" Akabia, the son of Mahallalel, said : Consider three things and thou wilt never come in the way of sin ; whence thou camest, whither thou art going, and before whom thou art destined to render an account of thyself, and appear to be judged. Thy origin was impure ; thou art going to a place where thou wilt be devoured by moths and worms ; and thou must lastly render an account of thy actions before the King of kings, the Holy One, to whom be praise, by whom thou wilt be judged." Ibidem, chap. iii. § 1.

I could select many other passages from the Mishna and Gemara fully as beautiful as the foregoing ; but I deem it useless, as the candid mind must be convinced by what I have said already ; and the prejudiced man *will not be convinced*, though I should write volumes.

I hope that I have thus proved that the Rabbins taught only the ways of piety ; and that, so far from their deserving abuse, they merit praise and commendation for their perseverance in perpetuating the doctrines of our holy faith amidst the thousands of difficulties they had to encounter, and the almost insurmountable obstacles they had to overcome. When they found that all the avenues of learning were closed against the Jews—when they saw that their brethren were driven to occupations which were hateful to them whilst the Israelites yet lived in their own land : they endeavoured to perpetuate the knowledge of our holy law amongst them—and they succeeded. And though many were engaged in useless disputes and too minute researches, particularly in Poland, yet do we find many a great man, even during the times of persecution and trouble : for instance, Abarbanel, Orobio, Solomon Hanau, Menasseh ben Israel, and at last Mendelsohn, and a number of others, whom I could easily enumerate, but I only choose the most prominent out of the many who present themselves. Owing to the exertions of the wise men amongst us, who were the instruments in the hand of God to effect his great and unsearchable purpose, and to the natural firmness and strength of the Jewish character, we preserved our independence of mind and our bond of union, amidst all the persecutions and calamities we had to suffer by the divine dispensation. But was it pride which upheld us? Or was the finger of God visible in our preservation? Evidently the last; for how should pride be powerful enough to effect that in us which it has failed to do in any other nation of antiquity? Was the Roman less fierce than the Jew? But what is the Roman of the present day compared to him who checked the successful Hannibal after the battle of Cannæ? And though we also have lost our national independent government, yet there is that within us which will make us reject with scorn all the alluring invitations, held out by the nations of the earth to join them—although they live in palaces, and stride triumphantly over the fallen sanctuary of Jerusalem, the residence of the Holy One of Israel; for we are upheld by the promise of Him who spoke and the world was called into existence, that He will have compassion on us, and restore the remnant of his people to the land which their fore-fathers inhabited. We have the promise of God that He will never forsake us, for it is written: " If the heavens can be measured above, and the earth beneath, then can I forsake Israel." And is it then pride alone that keeps us united? Contempt for our oppressors? No, it is the confidence in revelation, the certainty *that our day too will come.*

The pressure has already been removed in part, and in many countries do the Israelites now dwell in peace, secure, for the present, under the protection of the governments in whose dominions they live. The age of darkness and oppression, I hope, has passed away; and already we begin to show that we are capable of excelling in the arts and in nobler professions than small-dealing. We formerly were only the most successful merchants; but already there are in Germany men who have distinguished themselves as philosophers, mathematicians, poets, historians, lawyers, and physicians. The Bible has also been translated by Jews, natives of Germany and Poland, in a manner never before equalled; and the names of Friedlander, Ottensosser, Heidenheim, Meier Hirsch, Eichel, Frankel, Steinheim, and many others, are advantageously known in the literary circles of the continent of Europe.—In England, Hurwitz (at present the professor of the Hebrew language in the London university) and Samuels (the biographer of Mendelsohn) have produced books, which are read and admired; and though I am not acquainted in France, Italy,* and Holland, I doubt not but

* It is perhaps known to most of my readers, that the celebrated Tyrolese chief Andreas Hofer was made prisoner by Napoleon some time in 1809, or the

that the Jews in these countries have not remained behind their brethren in Germany, England, and Poland. Though the Reviewer mentions the revival of science among the Jews, he only names Professor Neander, one who has left the faith of his fathers and embraced Christianity. Is this fair dealing? Are there no more men of fame amongst the German Jews than this apostate? It is about as fair as if a future historian should mention Benedict Arnold and William Hull as the most distinguished American generals and patriots, or praise Richard the Third and James the Second as the best of English kings. I only remark this to show with how much candour the Reviewer treats us.

Many Jews, particularly the younger part, have given up trade as their sole occupation, and turned their attention (particularly in Bavaria) to the learned professions and the mechanic arts. But in the latter they have, for the present, many difficulties to encounter, as the Christians are for the most part unwilling to take apprentices or journeymen who will not work on the Sabbath (Saturday). Yet, under all disadvantages, the Jews are doing tolerably well; thus clearly establishing that it was not their fault that they were engaged in small-trade for so many centuries.

The Reviewer says, that the females were kept in profound ignorance, and treated as an inferior race, and that, moreover, the only

---

commencement of 1810. He was carried to Mantua in Italy, and tried, as if he had been a French subject. He was very ably defended by his counsel, a young *Jew*, by the name of Basseva (if I recollect right); and this defence was so able that the biographer of Hofer regretted very much that he could not succeed in obtaining a copy of the speech of Mr. Basseva. I do not suppose that it will be objected to the ability of Mr. B. that he did not succeed in clearing his client; for every one knows the clemency of Napoleon's court martials, and Hofer shared but the same fate with the ill-fated Duke of Enghien. But I am not going to turn politician, and to discuss the measures of Napoleon's government; I introduced this subject only to show in what estimation Jewish talent is held by the German writers.—It is probably known to all reading men, that whenever one of our society commits a crime, the public is informed " that Jacob Moses, *a Jew*, broke into the house of, &c.;" whereas our virtues are passed over in silence. But to the honour of the biographer of A. H. (whose name I do not know, as the book was anonymous) be it spoken, he states explicitly : " Mr. Basseva, a young Israelite," thus giving us credit where credit was due.

book they were permitted to read filled their heads with impure ideas. Since I have already shown how accurate the information of the Quarterly Review is, it will easily be believed that this assertion concerning the Hebrew females is equally true with that concerning the Jewish Rabbins. In the first place, it is untrue that the females amongst us are, generally speaking, worse educated than the Christian females. They are early taught reading and writing, as far at least as my information extends; many religious works written in Jewish German, for the most part expressly for them, were formerly read by them with the greatest attention ; and, as far as I have read them myself, they are not only calculated to give them instruction in the ceremonial part of their religion, but also to convey to them their moral duties in a language at the same time easy and familiar among them. At present these books are gradually giving way to others written in pure German : and I have no doubt that in a few years these alone will be in use amongst the female part of our nation. The Reviewer next speaks of extracts from the Old Testament, which, he says, they have commenced putting in their hands ; but I am happy to be able to inform him, that this would hardly be necessary, as the Bible, the entire twenty-four books of the Old Testament, has long ago been translated in German, and printed chiefly for the use of females ; and we had in our family a folio Bible of this kind, printed in the year 5439 of the Jewish era, and consequently is now (5589) one hundred and fifty years old. The chastity of the Jewish females is well known ; and hardly ever does any one hear of a Jewish lady violating her marriage-vow.—The Jewish female is considered inferior to the man only in so far as she is exempted, by the nature of her sex, from the greater part of the affirmative commandments of our law ; and three commandments are exclusively incumbent upon her, which it would be needless to mention, as they are well known to all those who are in the least acquainted with the Jewish ritual. The female, in fine, is treated by the Jews with respect in countries where the female is respected by the other inhabitants, though I can not tell how they are treated in the Barbary states, Turkey, and other parts of Asia and Africa ; although I can freely say, that it would be contrary to the principles of the rabbinical Jews to treat their wives and daughters ill under any circumstances whatever ; which

30

can be proved in the most positive manner from many passages in their writings.

To what the Reviewer alludes, in speaking of the education of boys, as tending to corrupt their morals, I cannot tell; however, I can assert with the strictest regard to truth, that all I have learned at a rabbinical school (and I went to no other until I was thirteen years old,) only tended to teach me how to govern my desires, and curb my passions; and I may say that I know of no Jewish school in which the strictest moral doctrines are not daily and hourly inculcated, fully as well as in any Christian school; and I may be allowed to judge, having been in them both in Germany and America.

I am glad to see that the learned Quarterly Reviewer has so well studied the works of the famous Eisenmenger, and the very acute Antonio Margarita. For the benefit of those who may not know it, I have to state, that both were, as is generally believed, what are commonly called *converted* Jews; the first was a German, and died about the commencement of the eighteenth century, or may be a little later; the second was, I suppose, an Italian, but I have not the pleasure of an acquaintance with him, though that is no great pity, since the Reviewer is kind enough to inform us that this luminary lived in the sixteenth century. It is, indeed, a pity that these learned men no more exist; but we have yet the consolation to know, that they have so worthy an imitator as the London Quarterly Review. To be serious, however, the charge that *perjury is* permitted to the Jews, and that they annually, on the Day of Atonement, have a formula in their prayers absolving them from the keeping of any oaths they may make during the year, is one on a par with the other charges already noticed, and I hope that, from the little knowledge I have of the writings of the Rabbins, I shall be able to refute it, and prove its falsehood.—In the first place then let me premise what the Rabbins think of the Day of Atonement; this opinion is found in the last chapter of *Yoma :* "The Day of Atonement can only be an expiation for sins between God and man; but for sins between man and man the Day of Atonement cannot be an expiation till the offender has pacified the offended :" (that is, has made complete restitution if the offence was a fraud or the like, or retracted slander, or made other atonement, according as the nature of the case might require). Can it now be supposed, that the Rabbins, who taught such doctrines as the foregoing, should for the same day institute a prayer, by which *perjury* was allowed to the Jews? Can it be possible, that any set of men can say that you must satisfy your neighbour before you can be forgiven, and at the same time permit you to swear falsely against him in a court of justice, and thus do him perhaps the greatest possible mischief? But no, the Rabbins never intended that one man should wrong the other, much less was perjury considered by them as permitted, as will be evident by just referring to their writings on this subject.

The prayer of " *Col Nidre*," to which the Reviewer alludes, is in the following words (as translated by David Levi):

" In the celestial tribunal, and in the terrestrial tribunal: by the divine permission of the ever blessed God, and by the permission of this holy congregation, we hold it lawful to pray with those who have transgressed."

" All vows, obligations, oaths, anathemas, excommunications, execrations, expiations, and fines, which we have vowed, sworn, devoted, excommunicated, or bound ourselves by, from the past Day of Atonement unto this present Day of Atonement, which is now come in peace. Our vows are no more vows ; our oaths cease to be oaths ; our anathemas are no more anathemas, and our obligations are no longer binding."

" They all shall be null and void, without power or confirmation. And it shall be forgiven to the whole congregation of Israel, and to the stranger who sojourneth among them ; for all the people did it ignorantly."

In a note to the foregoing, the learned David Levi says:

" That the reader may not be led to misconstrue this form, I think it necessary to observe that the *vows, obligations, oaths, &c.* here mentioned, are such only as apply to a man in his economical state, as mentioned in Numbers, xxx. 2, 3, 4, 5, &c. &c.; but have not the most distant relation to his social character, and the transactions between man and man. No : God forbid ! for all transactions between man and man are sacred, and cannot be dissolved but by the mutual consent of the parties. And so zealous are our Rabbins in inculcating this doctrine, that they firmly believe that there can be no hope of pardon on the Day of Atonement for such as have injured their neighbours, unless they make full restitution to the party wronged, and crave his pardon. From all which it is manifest, that we abhor the idea of any man's freeing himself, by means of this form, from any *oath* or *covenant* which he has entered into with another, as some have ignorantly thought, and thereby brought unmerited reproach on the nation."

If any man considers the above formula with attention, he will easily discover that it relates solely to the vows, &c. made without due consideration, made, for instance, in the moment of excitement, and perhaps forgotten as soon as made. Though such conduct is abhorrent to the spirit of our law; yet we must consider, that " not to angels the law was given;" we are human beings, and thus liable to sin, and in consequence of the frailty of our disposition we frequently make promises and vows, the execution of which we defer from time to time, or it may be, neglect altogether. For this reason did our Rabbins institute the prayer of *Col Nidre*, in which we pray the Pardoner of the iniquities of his people, to forgive us for vows, promises, oaths, &c. which we have unwittingly made, and the fulfilment of which we have forgotten, (or may forget,) either because they had escaped our memory, or because to act as we had sworn would have occasioned us to commit a sinful action.—I hope that I am understood, as what I have advanced is plain and self-evident. Before, however, I dismiss this subject altogether, let me inform my readers, that the foregoing formula is that used by the Portuguese Jews; but the German Jews say instead of " From the past Day of Atonement, &c." the following; " *From the present Day of Atonement until the next Day of Atonement, which may come to us in peace.*" This difference between the Portuguese and the German Jews only varies the form, but not the intention of the prayer, as the one pray forgiveness for the unnecessary vows they have made during the past year, the others for those vows which they may make unintentionally during the following year. Had the Reviewer now only consulted the rabbinical writings themselves, instead of Eisenmenger and similar authors whose interest it evidently was to abuse the religion they had forsaken: he could never have been guilty of thus slandering the Jews, and he would have acknowledged, that the *Col Nidre* has been introduced amongst the prayers for the Day of Atonement with the greatest propriety, and that it must have a beneficial tendency, instead of the pernicious one which he (the Reviewer) and other Christian writers *seem to dread.* I have noticed this charge of the Quarterly Review more at large, as the general belief of it might do us incalculable mischief, and might easily tend to augment the fearful catalogue of prejudices already existing against us.

I should be very glad to stop here, having, I think, sufficiently cleared our Rabbins and brethren in general from the imputations which the Quarterly Review has cast upon their moral character ; but if I should now suffer his assertions concerning our *religious feelings* to pass unnoticed, it might be supposed that *there* at least the assertions (for arguments I cannot call them) of the Reviewer are well-founded, and that in consequence we Jews are in fact a blind flock led by blind shepherds. I must, therefore, endeavour to set him right, but I shall say as little about Christianity as possible, since I do not wish to grow abusive in my turn, and I beg therefore, that whatever I may say should be considered as extorted from me in defence of my faith.

It is well known to those who believe in a revealed religion, that the code of laws by which we Israelites endeavour to direct our course of life has been handed down to us from amidst thunder and lightning on mount Sinai, when all Israel heard the voice of the Almighty proclaim : " I am the Eternal thy God, who have conducted thee out of the land of Egypt, from the house of slavery." Moses, the son of Amram, was chosen by God to be the mediator who should teach the children of Israel " just statutes and commandments," which should endure for ever ; for in many places of the five books of Moses do we find, that *these* were to be *the laws* which the latest posterity of Jacob should obey. How can any man then have the audacity to style our religion a false one, without at the same time admitting that he does not believe in the sacred truths of the Bible ? Shall any man say we are wrong, are infidels, because we will not forsake our religion ? Because we will not consent to change our Sabbath for the Sunday, when God instituted the seventh day as a perpetual covenant between Him and the children of Israel ? —Because we will not mingle with the nations of the earth, to *marry their daughters,* and eat of the flesh of the swine ?—Because under every vicissitude we have firmly maintained our national character ?—But we care not what the world may think of us, as long

as we are convinced of the rectitude and the permanency of our religion, which God has inscribed on the tablets of our hearts, and
established so firmly in our minds that all the powers of hell are
unable to remove it ; for the prophet, in the name of God, tells us :
" And my words, which I have put in thy mouth, shall not depart
out of thy mouth, the mouth of thy children, nor the mouth of thy
children's children, from now and for ever."—Whatever of moral
beauties the Christian religion may have, ours is no less beautiful,
no less effective in raising our ideas from nature to nature's Lord.
To love Him, to confide in his goodness and special protection, is
commanded to us in almost every page of the Mosaic writings.   To
love our neighbour like ourselves is no new doctrine of the gospel,
for this obligation was known already ever since the promulgation
of the law, which commands : " And thou shalt love thy neighbour
like thyself." Isaiah, Daniel, and Ezekiel, spoke of the resurrection and the life everlasting, and reward for the righteous, and punishment for the wicked.   What are then the glorious truths which
the Christian religion, for the *first time*, made known to a world
sunk in darkness?   I am absolutely unable to discover which and
where they are, and 1 should, therefore, be much indebted to any
professor of Christianity who could point out any moral doctrine
which was not long previously taught by our prophets and Rabbins.

We do not believe in the necessity of a mediator between God
and man, in so far as relates to the sacrifice of the Messiah ; for it
is a settled opinion amongst the Jews, that the Messiah need not
die in expiation of their sins, as a strict observance of the divine
law and a confidence in God's protection will lead a man to everlasting happiness, according to their belief.   But we find in the first
chapter of Job that Satan is the accuser of man, and that he recapitulates the sins committed on earth in the heavenly tribunal ; and in
Daniel we find mention made of *protecting angels,* and of Michael
particularly, as the protector of Israel.   Now it is the general opinion of the Jews that the protecting angels will defend man when
Satan accuses.   Having premised this much, I am confident that
the following will be understood, which is an extract from a prayer
read in the German Synagogues on the New-year's-days and the
Day of Atonement :

     " May He, our Lord, yet remember to us the love of Ethan

(Abraham), and for the sake of the son who was bound upon the altar, command our *accuser* to be silent; and for the sake of the piety of the righteous (Jacob), may He to-day pronounce favourable judgment upon us, for this day is holy to our Lord. Though there be *no one to speak in our favour against him who relates our transgressions*, mayest thou yet tell to Jacob the words of law and judgment, and justify us when Thou judgest us, O King of justice !"

The meaning of this is, that although our sins be so great that they can admit of no justification, we yet throw ourselves upon the mercy of God to forgive us, though we be not worthy of this great goodness.

This is the prayer, as I suppose, alluded to by the Quarterly Review; but how different a meaning it has from that the Reviewer gives it, I leave every person to judge for himself. The Jew sees in his God a just judge, who will punish all transgressions; but whose wrath he *can* deprecate by sincere repentance, and amelioration of his course of life. And our Rabbins teach us that repentance, accompanied by contrition of heart, is available on the death-bed of the dying sinner, and that "many a man," as they say, " has bought his world in one hour," meaning, that many have gained happiness in the world to come by repentance on their death-bed. Is it, then, true, that to the Jew the future is shrouded in impenetrable gloom—that he has no means, according to his belief, of satisfying his Creator? No; he has hopes equally well founded, *at least*, with those of the Christian; and he may, like him, look upon a bright and glorious futurity. Since, however, the Christians seem to think our end so miserable, I hope that I may not be considered presumptuous in describing the death-scene of my nearest relative, namely, my father. He had been suffering at intervals, for nineteen years, the most excruciating pains, when the end of his days came near. He had been confined to his bed for three weeks previous; and I had left him to go to the house of one of my uncles, who did not live far off. About nightfall my father felt all at once his strength failing fast, and he therefore sent for me to give me his last blessing and his last injunctions, as it is customary amongst us. I cannot describe my feelings, which were very acute, though I was but fourteen years old, when I approached his bed. He laid his hands upon my head, and pronounced the blessing with which the dying patriarch Jacob has prophesied the Israelites should always bless their children, and the blessings with which, by the ordinance of God, the family of Aaron are commanded to bless the congregation. (See Numb. vi.)   My father saw how much I felt, and how deeply I was affected ; and he therefore said to me in the most collected and calm manner : "Weep not for me ; for my being longer in this world would be but painful to me, and of no use to you, being no longer able to do any thing for you, though I should recover.   As for yourself, be an honest man and a good Jew, and God will never forsake you. Now go, my son ; for your remaining any longer with me might disturb me, and distress you too much."   I then left his presence, as it is considered improper amongst us for the near relations of a dying person to remain in his presence, that his devotion may not be distracted in his last moments, if he sees before him those who are dearest to him on earth, and whom he is so soon to leave behind him, to combat for an uncertain period with the ills and temptations of life.   Soon after I was gone, the members of the Jewish congregation began to assemble to pray at the couch of their dying brother. He prayed with them as long as he was able, then laid himself composedly down, and departed this life without a struggle.   Those who saw his death, and those who heard of it, said : " May my end be like his."   Thus died my father, and though poor, he left a reputation unsullied, and a memory respected by Jews and Christians.   I could bring other proofs of the truth of my assertion, that the Jews can die calmly, and look with composure upon futurity ; but enough has been said already to disprove what the Reviewer has said on this subject also.

I shall not notice what other things the Quarterly Review says about the rabbinical Jews, or about the Caraites, as I know but very little or nothing concerning the latter ; but I cannot pass over in silence what he says in his concluding paragraphs about the mode of treating the Jews in the countries where they are settled.   He says there are but two alternatives : either to drive them out altogether, or to convert them by degrees to Christianity ; as he thinks it unsafe and unwise to grant them civil liberty as long as they remain Jews. He does not seem to be inclined to drive us altogether out of Europe, as that would, by the way, be hardly possible at the present day ; since, in consequence of most of the governments being largely indebted to the Jews, they would be obliged either to pay them immediately what they owe them in money, which they cannot do, or not to pay them at all, or to kill them, which they will hardly dare to do. But he believes that it ought to be tried to convert them by gentle means—to educate them so, that the affection they feel for their ancient religion and customs might be weakened, with a view to induce them to embrace Christianity. But to do this, the *ameliorating societies* must obtain the consent of the parents to educate the children in the manner proposed; for *I do not believe* that any man would advise to inveigle the children away from their parents— or to steal them—or to compel them—or to seduce them clandestinely to enter a missionary-school, although these methods have been partly resorted to. No honourable man can dream of proposing such diabolical plans, and to obtain the consent of the parents themselves to make their *children* apostates is impracticable, as long as the adults are Jews. The only chance, therefore, for bringing about the conversion of the Jews, is to *draw the adults* within the pale of the church. 1 cannot, however, conceive how the Reviewer means to effect this; for compulsion he himself will not listen to; persuasion will not do; abuse will not convert us, as the Q. R. may have experienced himself; to reason us out of our opinions has been tried with little success, as all the arguments brought against us have been again and again overthrown. What then remains to be done? *To bribe us!!* This seems to have been the darling plan of *ameliorating societies* and piously inclined governments of late years. This is to be done in two different ways, either to pay a bounty for apostacy, say two thousand dollars a head, or to give offices to such men of talents as choose to become (outwardly) Christians. The first plan has been tried without success; the American* and

* As the reader may perhaps have some curiosity to know the names of some of those worthies who attempted to save our souls from perdition, by an appeal to our pockets, I have thought proper to transcribe a few from a long list of presidents, managers, &c., which I lately saw (since the publication of this essay) in a little work called " Israel Vindicated," printed in New York, in 1820. This little book is a series of letters, supposed to be addressed by a resident in New York to his friend in Philadelphia, and contains, among other things, some account of the American Society for Ameliorating the Condition of the Jews.—In letter second the writer says, that " although from the arti-

31

London Societies A. C. J. have spent immense sums of money, and
obtained a few vagabondish fellows and some few designing men as
recruits ; but as we have heard so little lately about the proceedings
of these *societies*, we are forced to believe that they have either
contracted their sphere of operations, and work more in silence than
they used to do,—or that they have even dissolved and adjourned
their meetings " *sine die*," for *want of encouragement from the
Jews.*—To bribe through means of office has also been tried; and I
am glad to have it in my power to inform the Reviewer, that it has
succeeded hardly any better than direct bribery. A little while
before I left Germany (1824) I was told, that a young gentleman,
after he had finished his studies, applied to the Prussian government for employment. He was answered, that if he would turn
Christian he might be appointed to the office he solicited ; to which
he is said to have indignantly replied: " I have learned enough to
be able to teach boys, and I need not your offices, if I must forsake
my faith to obtain them."—And so it has always been. Though
Maria Theresa and other European sovereigns tried, by the most
alluring offers, to gain the Jews over, they have never been able to
succeed even partially. This is no idle declamation, but positive
fact, as all those must know who are in any degree acquainted with
the internal history of Germany. The governments of Europe,
therefore, having tried the plan which the Quarterly Review recom-

cles of their constitution it appears, that they propose to establish ' a settlement' for, and to give ' employment' to such of our nation as may apply for
it, yet is it laid down as a proviso, that none shall be invited and received but
such Jews as do already profess the Christian religion, or are desirous to receive
Christian instruction."—The writer next gives a long list of officers—*fifty-three*
in all ; but I must content myself with naming the following : " Hon. Elias
Boudinot, *President ;* Hon. John Q. Adams; Rev. Dr. J. Day, Pres. Yale Col-
lege ; His Ex. William Findlay ; Rev. Dr. A. Green, Pres. Princeton College ;
Herman Le Roy, Esq. ; Rev. Dr. J. H. Livingston, S. T. P. ; Rev. Dr. Philip
Milledoler ; Rev. Dr. James Milnor ; Hon. William Phillips ; Col. John Troup ;
Gen. Stephen Van Rensellaer ; James Wadsworth, Esq., *Vice Presidents ;* Hon.
Peter A. Jay, *Treasurer,* &c."—I do not accuse these honourable and reverend
gentlemen of any other evil intention than *officiousness*, since not one of us
Jews ever desired them to ameliorate our condition; which we do not think as yet
desperate enough to require the interference of the honourables and reverends
just enumerated.

mends, and deeming it impolitic to oppress us any longer, knowing at the same time, that, if emancipated and left to ourselves, we are *able* and *willing* to render the state some service, have in many instances commenced putting us on a level with the Christian population, and this has been already effected in Holland, Bavaria, Saxen-Weimar, and some of the other German states; not to mention the republic of the United States, where we enjoy equal rights and privileges, without any injury to the Christians.

I have lately received a letter from an old and intelligent gentleman in Germany, which states, that King Lewis of Bavaria gave not long since 20,000 flrs., equal to 8,000 dollars, towards the establishment of a Jewish seminary of learning; and that about two years ago a college was established in Münster, the capital of the Prussian province of Westphalia, for the education of young schoolmasters and mechanics among the Israelites. In this institution are taught the Hebrew, German, Latin, and French languages; the Bible with commentaries, the Talmud, mathematics, history, natural history, logic, geography, &c., besides the ornamental branches, as singing, music, and painting. This school is in a flourishing condition, though so short a time only has elapsed since its establishment; and the teachers are both of the Jewish and Christian persuasions, thus proving that we can live in peace with Christians, without *amalgamating* with them. The school is patronised by the Prussian government, which has lately shown itself very desirous of advancing education amongst us, without tacking any degrading conditions to its benevolence. What is most remarkable with the above college, is, that it is established in a town where, no more than twenty years ago, no Jew was allowed to locate himself permanently; and before its establishment the Jewish young men were permitted to study in the gymnasium of that place, where they were just as much honoured as any of the Christian students, of which fact I can speak with the utmost confidence, having been myself a scholar there for two years and a quarter.—In short, in spite of the efforts of our enemies we have continued to flourish and to acquire greater respectability for the last thirty years, and we shall continue to advance as long as we deserve the blessing of Heaven!

I could add a great deal more, but I am afraid that I have said too much already; but I beg every one who reads the foregoing, to pardon my loquacity, since I hardly could say less against the many allegations of the Review than I have done, without being obscure or altogether unintelligible. I dare not even hope that I have succeeded in convincing the Christians of the truth of what I have said ; for it would certainly be very strange if a young man, who, moreover, had not the best opportunities of acquiring knowledge, should be able to overthrow a writer in the London Quarterly Review, who, for aught 1 know, may be a professor in the Oxford university.— But if I have succeeded in allaying a little of the prejudice existing against us, it will be ample compensation for

A Native of Germany.

Richmond, Va., January 6th.

ESSAY II.

I have read with much interest the manly and temperate remarks of a " Native of Germany," published in the Whig, in vindication of the Jews from the calumnies of the Quarterly Review. So far from feeling any desire to perpetuate the prejudice which has so long existed against that unfortunate people, I would on the contrary do all in my power to remove it ; for I entertain no doubt that many of them are as exemplary in their moral habits, as good citizens and as kind neighbours; and therefore equally entitled to the favour of God as those who profess to be Christians. Neither am I disposed to find the least fault with them for continuing in the belief and practice of that religion which was delivered in fire and tempest on mount Sinai, so long as they believe their present happiness and everlasting salvation to depend upon it. I conceive it would be depriving God of the essential attributes of mercy and justice, by rendering Him incapable of saving his rational offspring from perdition, whether they be Jew or gentile, heathen or Christian. They are all equally the objects of his love, whatever may be their faith or condition in life ; even though the force of external circumstances brought about by the pride and injustice of man, may seem to render Him partial in the distribution of his favours. It is declared, on what Christians believe unquestionable authority, that God is no respecter of persons, but *in every nation* those who fear him and work righteousness shall be accepted of Him. It is in the contrite heart that He manifests himself, amongst every people and every colour ; and not to any privileged few, who claim to be the favourites of Heaven. It has always been the custom of particular sects and particular nations, to appropriate to themselves the especial grace of God. But, according to this assumption, all those who believe differently are in danger of the divine displeasure. How partial, how unjust, is such a belief calculated to render a Being who is emphatically pronounced to be Love !

It cannot be expected, under the present condition of the human mind, that all the nations of the earth will ever arrive at that state in which there will be a uniformity of belief in what all may deem essential. The same causes which actuate them to think differently now, will continue to produce the same effect, until mankind shall be released from the fetters of prejudice ; and from the influence of education, example, and authority. But amidst the endless variety of nations that people the earth, I have never heard of any that did not acknowledge the existence of certain obligations to a superior Being, and have recourse to some plan to testify their duty and allegiance. Whence could such impressions have been derived but from the fountains of truth, how much soever they may have been subsequently obscured by the inventions of men ? The scriptural writers abundantly declare that God has written his law upon the hearts of *all men ;* and by consulting that law, that still small voice which saith to us, " this is the way, walk ye in it," we have every assurance of pleasing Him whom we serve.

So far, therefore, from excluding the Jews, and I may add, every other nation, from the benefits of salvation, I am free to acknowledge them equally the heirs of a glorious immortality with the Christians ; and equally acceptable in the eyes of a just and merciful God, in so far as they respectively strive to perform his will. To every man is given a certain duty to discharge, a certain talent to improve ; and it is doubtless the same with nations : and as all are faithful and obedient in the performance of this duty, would it not be derogatory to the divine goodness to presume that they will be debarred from the enjoyments of a future state ?   In accordance with this view of the subject, I think a greater responsibility rests upon Christendom than any other division of mankind, in proportion to the superiority of that system of morality which they profess to venerate : and this brings me to notice (which, indeed, was a principal object in taking up my pen) some remarks which " A Native of Germany" has used in reference to the duties imposed by the Jewish and Christian laws. He says, if I understand him, that no glorious truth, no moral doctrine, is brought to light by the gospel, which was not equally inculcated by the Old Testament or the Talmud.   The moral duties taught by the gospel, according to the light in which I view them, are of a far higher order, and of more universal application, than those enjoined by the Mosaic law.   It is true that one of the commands of the latter is : " Thou shalt love thy neighbour like thyself;" but viewed in connection with other parts of that law, the meaning of the term *neighbour* is by no means so comprehensive as it is under the Christian dispensation.   It only extended to those of their own tribe or nation under the Mosaic system ; whereas under the gospel, it is made to embrace *all* who may be placed in a situation calculated to excite our sympathy and demand our assistance.   See the parable of the Samaritan.   That the Jewish precept did not extend to other nations is evident from the fact, that the Jews were commanded, or believed they were commanded, to wage war against the neighbouring countries, to slay their inhabitants and dispossess them of their inheritances.   This is so common a feature in the Jewish history, that it is unnecessary to specify any particular passages.   But what was the command of the blessed Author of the Christian religion ?   " Ye have heard it hath been said, an eye for an eye, and a tooth for a tooth ; but I say unto you, resist not evil."   " Ye have heard it said, thou shalt love thy neighbour and hate thine enemy ; but I say unto you, love them that hate you, bless them that curse you, and pray for them that despitefully use you and persecute you." And the most conclusive reason is given to sustain the force of this divine injunction ; namely, that our heavenly Father makes his sun to shine, and his rain to descend, upon the just and the unjust. Is there not far more sublimity in these high commands of universal applica-

tion, than in the Mosaic precept of so limited operation? Again:
" Whatsoever ye would that men should do unto you, do ye even so
unto them." These exalted precepts were intended to be our rule
of action in our intercourse with all men ; the polar star by which
to regulate our course whilst travelling the journey of life. I am
here speaking of genuine Christianity, such as we sometimes see
exemplified in the world ; not of that mongrel and monstrous species
which too often usurps its place. And it is with sorrow that I am
here compelled to ask " A Native of Germany" to extend that favour to us which he solicits for the Jews ; and not to judge all of
us and our religion by the practices of some. I confess there is,
too generally speaking, such a lamentable diversity between our
profession and practice, that they are the direct antipodes to each
other.

Let it not be said that these heavenly injunctions cannot be fulfilled. Surely they never would have been promulgated, on what
Christians must deem such high authority, if they had been beyond
our attainment. It has often been urged that if any nation were to
comply literally with the commandment, *to love our enemies,* and on
no occasion to resist them by force, it would soon be overrun and
plundered by warlike and avaricious neighbours. But, fortunately,
there is a living fact to the contrary ; a fact which merits one of the
brightest pages of history. I allude to the settlement of Pennsylva-
nia by the illustrious Penn, whose colony flourished amidst tribes of
fierce barbarians, while other settlements on this continent, supported by the force of arms, were with difficulty effected. Here is a
splendid illustration of the effect produced by the practice of the
Christian virtues, against which there never was any legal enactment by any people : and I am informed that to this day the Indians
cherish a lasting friendship for that society of which Penn was the
ornament and the founder. In like manner, if we were to do as we
would be done by, what changes would it produce in the world ! No
longer would be exhibited the singular anomaly which our country
presents, of being the freest nation on the globe, and of holding at
the same time, in corporeal and mental subjection, a million and a
half of our fellow-beings. Such a state of things could not exist.
But yet we are a people making the most exalted profession of righteousness, holding in pious contempt the Jew and the heathen, and

handing them over to reprobation without the least mercy or remorse. Is not, then, the language of inspiration as applicable now
as it was when it was uttered? "This people draweth nigh unto
me with their lips, and honoureth me with their mouth, but their
heart is far from me."

A PROFESSOR OF CHRISTIANITY.*

ESSAY III.

TO " A PROFESSOR OF CHRISTIANITY."

You will easily believe me, that I received much real satisfaction
from reading your reply to that part of my " remarks" in which I
asserted, that *not one single moral doctrine* was for the first time
taught in the gospels; as you have so well preserved that gentle

* The writer of this and the fourth essay is a member of the " Society of
Friends," who resides about twenty-five miles from Richmond. It happened,
strange enough, that a note to which my name had been signed was inserted,
much to my chagrin, along with the first essay, which, as the reader will see,
was intended to remain anonymous; but my name having once been made public as the writer of these unpretending essays, I became indebted to this circumstance for the pleasure of a correspondence, which was carried on for some
months, with the Professor of Christianity, as he wrote to me a few days after
the publication of his last essay, disclosing to me his name and profession. I
have endeavoured to prevail upon him to give me permission to make his name
public; but in vain, as his modesty will not permit him to appear publicly as an
author. I regret this determination, but since it seemed to be particularly disagreeable to him to be known, I would consider myself guilty of a breach of
confidence were I to disobey his injunction.—All that I have heard of him has
impressed me with the belief that he is a man of a finely cultivated mind, and,
what is more, one whose principles are followed up in his conduct; I, therefore,
am happy to repeat the favourable opinion I had conceived of him from reading
his reply to my first communication, and which I accordingly expressed in the
following essay. It has been my fortune but once to meet with him; but
he may be assured that I shall ever be ready to redeem the pledge I made
when he was yet unknown to me, and always be prepared to extend to him
the right hand of fellowship, though we differ in opinion.   I. L.

spirit of forbearance, which should characterise generous opponents, who are both aiming for the attainment of truth. If your conduct in life corresponds with your sentiments as avowed in your reply, (of which, however, I have no doubt,) I shall be very glad to hail you as a friend, and extend to you the right hand of fellowship, though we differ in our *religious opinions.*—You shall, therefore, receive that courtesy from me which you have displayed; and I beg of you to consider none of my strictures as personal; for although you are altogether unknown to me, since I never have heard your name even, I yet feel a high regard for a man so generous and mild. These being my sentiments, you may ask, why I should *reply to you* then? But please to consider, that thinking you had erred, I deem it necessary to remove the impression which you may have left upon the minds of the public concerning our religion, which is the more expedient at the present moment, as I understand that the subject under consideration has lately excited deep and universal interest throughout this city among the thinking and intelligent citizens.

In the first place then, you do us no more than justice to believe, that we can be good citizens and kind neighbours, no less so than the followers of the gospel, for this has been proved by the experience of ages; and I can assert, without the least fear of contradiction, that, wherever the Jew was kindly treated, whenever he received any benefit from a gentile, he was always ready to acknowledge the kindness of his benefactor; as ingratitude towards man is not a trait in our character, though we have frequently acted ungratefully towards the Deity, for which we even now suffer our punishment, in the dismemberment of our nation, and the loss of our land. But notwithstanding we have been gradually dispersed over the whole face of the earth after our expulsion from Palestine, we are nevertheless, emphatically speaking, *Israelites,* the same now, which we ever were; we possess the same laws, the same customs, nay, retain the same features even, which we had in our own land, and through all the revolutions and changes of time we have preserved our national identity. All the celebrated nations of antiquity have, I may say, mouldered away, for there was no *living* principle in their constitutions; and in vain does the astonished traveller look for the people which built the Egyptian pyramids and temples; Greece and its ruins remind us that a wise and powerful nation *once*

32

existed there; and Italy presents to the searching eye of the anti-quary only the remains of a nation which once dictated laws to the whole civilised world. But though Palestine is no longer the land possessed by the people of God, yet can the true representatives of its ancient possessors be met with in every country, who are essentially *one* people, though scattered throughout all the countries of the earth; and their preservation as one nation is owing to the living principle of their constitution, a constitution given them as a special gift from their Maker.—All nations have ever admired this close bond of union existing amongst us, and the unanimity with which we have always, under every vicissitude, resisted any interference with our moral and religious duties; for on no account did we, or can we, suffer any stranger to advise us in any matter of conscience, if we deem his advice contrary to the standard of the Mosaic law.

For this our constancy we have been abundantly vilified, have been called obdurate Jews who wilfully resist the light of the gospel; and we have even been *considered as inimical to the Christians,* because *we would not, could not, embrace Christianity.*—I must confess, we are determined never to change our faith, and of course we must be considered by Christians enemies of their belief; but though I admit this, I utterly deny that we do think ourselves permitted by our religion to hate the Christians themselves; on the contrary, we believe ourselves bound to live in good fellowship with all men, no matter what their belief may be.

You seem to think, my dear friend, that the gospel has the superiority over the Mosaic law, in so far as the former commands universal love, while the latter prescribes love for the children of Israel alone. But is your position correct? Or is what you say true, that the *Jews so understood* the commandment: " And thou shalt love thy neighbour like thyself?" You say, the Jews must have *interpreted the law so,* as they had frequent wars with the surrounding nations, and they thought themselves obliged to slay the inhabitants and to plunder their property.—But pardon me, my friend, you have misunderstood the Jewish law, or you have forgotten the precepts of the Old Testament. The law relative to war is found in Deut. chap. xx. v. 10—19 inclusive, and is in the following words:

" If thou comest nigh unto a city to make war against it, thou

shalt proclaim peace unto it.   And it shall happen, if it answer thee
peace, and open unto thee, then all the people found therein shall be
tributaries unto thee and serve thee.   But if it will not make peace
with thee, but will wage war against thee, then thou shalt besiege it ; and when the Eternal thy God has delivered it into thy
hands, thou *mayest* smite every male thereof with the edge of the
sword ; but the women, and children, and the cattle, and all that is
in the city, namely, all the spoil thereof, thou shalt take unto thyself, and eat the spoil of thine enemies, which the Eternal thy God
has given thee, &c. &c."

I am well aware that my translation differs from the English version, as the English Bible says : " Thou *shalt* smite, &c." which I
have rendered " *mayest ;*" but I have preferred to adopt the interpretation of some of the Rabbins ; and the passage thus rendered
gives only a permission to slay the garrison, those capable of bearing arms, but forbids, on any account, to injure the women and
children, who cannot participate in the war, from the nature of their
weakness and dependence.   I do not believe that any man can make
any objection to the interpretation I have just given ; and every
one I trust will then acknowledge, that so far from our law allowing
the massacre of the inhabitants of the countries at war with the Jews,
it tended greatly to soften the rigours of war, as carried on in ancient times, since it prohibited the *molestation* of the *women* and children, when even in Christian countries the former are not always
exempt from violence ; and surely I *need not* bring examples from
history to *prove this*, as, alas ! examples are *too often met with*, and
many scenes of violence have been enacted by warriors calling themselves *Christians*, which present instances of atrocity *too horrible*
to be related.

A second enquiry presents itself : " Did the Jews think themselves
bound to go to war with their neighbours, or was it only in cases of
necessity that they were embroiled with other nations ?"   Without
hesitation I answer: That war was considered amongst us as the
greatest evil, and was only resorted to to repel invasion, and to
secure the peace of our boundaries. (For proof read the books of
Samuel and Kings.)   " But was not David a conqueror ?"   True
he was ; but was he the aggressor ? or rather, was he not forced to
war by the Philistines, Edumeans, Syrians, and other nations ?   Did

they not invade his country, and insult the ambassadors whom he had sent with a letter of condolence to the king of the children of Ammon? Was he to stand by and see Israel slaughtered, whom he was appointed to govern like *the shepherd governs his flock?* Was he permitted, I ask you, to see the wolves come amongst the flock and bear some of the unoffending sheep away? Was he, again, permitted to see the ambassadors of the people of God ill-treated by a barbarian king and his barbarian people?—And, to conclude my queries, did not the almighty Protector of Israel sanction those enter-prises by giving David success in all his undertakings? Can any human being believe, that God would be so partial, so unjust, as to give the Jews success when they went out beyond the borders of their land to pillage and slaughter their unoffending neighbours?—No! no! the divine Judge would not encourage such deeds even amongst his people, for all the world is his, and the life of one man is as dear to Him as the life of the other, and He is no respecter of persons, no favourer of the oppressor ; but He is ever ready to save the weaker from the hands of him who is more powerful.

But you will say : " Were not the Jews a warlike people, lovers of strife and fight ?" *Again I answer, no ;* for we read in Levit. chap. xxvi. v. 6 : " And I will give peace in the land, and you shall lie down, and none shall make you afraid ; and I will remove the evil beasts out of the land, and the sword shall not pass through your land."—And in the sixth chapter of Judges we find Deborah alluding to the great want of warlike instruments among the Israelites ; and if a person reads the book of Judges, which comprises a history of three hundred years, he will discover, that war was a more un-common occurrence among our ancestors than among any nation of antiquity, or even modern times !—But what I intend to prove is, that peace was considered by the Jews as the greatest blessing which the Almighty in his kindness could bestow upon them. This doctrine was taught them by the Mosaic law, since God promised them peace as a reward for their obedience to the divine will ; and in the book of Judges we find, that whenever the Israelites were doing the will of Heaven, they had security and peace ; but whenever they deviated, they were punished with war and desolation : and it is recorded, that *God sent the surrounding nations* to oppress them, as a punishment for their disobedience ; and the Philistines, in particular, were for many years the oppressors of the Israelites, and were not subdued till the reign of David.

I hope, my dear friend, that I have proved to your and every candid man's conviction, that we abhorred war, and thought it always a curse, and never considered it a pastime or an employment worthy of the generous and brave youths of Israel; whereas you no doubt know that, in the middle ages, Christians of every rank and age studied war as a science, and practised it as a game for their daily diversion; and I suspect that the horrors of the tilt-yard occupy yet their due share in the history of chivalry.

But you may say: " That the Jews kept at peace with their neighbours from policy, from fear of consequences arising out of a state of war; that, however, towards *individuals* of the gentiles they were illiberal, thinking themselves *not bound* to love them." But if you will only examine the sacred books of the Mosaic law, I do not doubt but that you will confess your error. We read in Exodus, chap. xxii. v. 21: " Thou shalt neither vex a stranger nor oppress him; for you were strangers in the land of Egypt."

Ibidem, chap. xxiii. v. 9: " And thou shalt not oppress the stranger; and you *well* know how a stranger feels, for you have yourselves been strangers in the land of Egypt."

In Leviticus, chap. xix. we find the following:

v. 33. " And if a stranger sojourn in your land with you, ye shall not vex him"—(*neither vex him with words, nor do him actual wrong*).

v. 34. " But the stranger who dwelleth with you shall be unto you as one born amongst you, and *thou shalt love him as thyself;* for you were strangers in the land of Egypt : I am the Eternal your God."

Here, then, my dear friend, you have a complete refutation of your opinion, that the Mosaic law did not enjoin universal love. Now do tell me, do you find any passage equally decisive with the foregoing, in any of the gospels? Can it now be said that the gospels have any superiority over the five books of Moses in this respect? But I will not rest here, and will go a little further, and tell you, that the Mosaic law looks even farther than your gospels in the protection of the oppressed part of mankind, namely the *slave;* for it is written, Deut. chap. xxiii. v. 15 and 16 : " Thou shalt not deliver unto his master the servant who may escape unto thee from his master. He shall dwell with thee in the midst of thee, in any place which he may choose, in any one of thy gates, where it pleases him best; thou shalt not oppress him."

You may perhaps be disposed to confess that the Old Testament *does* contain the doctrines which I have advanced; but you will say that the Jews did not understand them so—in fact, you have partly said so already—you have asserted it, without proving it further than by referring to the general history of the Jews. You know, however, that it is very easy to make assertions; but they cannot stand unless supported by substantial proof. I will therefore first deny your assertion, and then bring proof of the truth of what I advance.

We all know that the temple which Solomon built was finished in the four hundred and eighty-seventh year after the promulgation of the law on mount Sinai; and of course *we all must* admit that the opinion at that time prevailing, concerning the meaning of *any part of the law*, must be considered as a pretty correct standard by which to ascertain the meaning the Israelites attached to the law, which was then, as it is now, our guide through life. It is a lamentable fact, that the Old Testament, particularly the historical part, is but little read by the Christians; and therefore do we find men of learning, nay, preachers, having an inadequate acquaintance with the sacred books of the Israelites. I will therefore transcribe a portion of Solomon's prayer in the temple at its dedication, as contained in the eighth chapter of the first book of Kings, v. 37—43.

"If there be in the land famine, if there be pestilence, blasting, mildew, locust, or if there be caterpillar; if their enemy besiege them in the land of their cities; whatsoever plague, whatsoever sickness *there be*; what prayer and supplication soever be *made* by any man, *or* by all thy people Israel, which shall know every man the plague of his own heart, and spread forth his hands toward this house: then hear thou in heaven thy dwelling-place, and forgive, and do, and give to every man according to his ways, whose heart thou knowest; (for thou, *even* thou only, knowest the hearts of all the children of men;) that they may fear thee all the days that they live in the land which thou gavest unto our fathers.

"Moreover, concerning a stranger, that is not of thy people Israel, but cometh out of a far country for thy name's sake, (for they shall hear of thy great name, and of thy strong hand, and of thy stretched-out arm,) when he shall come and pray toward this house: hear thou in heaven thy dwelling-place, and do according to all that the stranger calleth to thee for; that all people of the earth may know thy name, to fear thee, as *do* thy people Israel; and that they may know that this house which I have builded is called by thy name."—(*English version.*)

I know very well that the last part would have been enough for my purpose; but I extracted the first one also, to show to those *who may not be so well acquainted with the Bible*, in what manner the wisest of men prayed for the nations who *do not belong to Israel:* he first prays that the Supreme Ruler may listen to the supplication of the *penitent* Israelite; and then, that when he who is no son of Jacob comes to pray in the sincerity of his heart, because he has heard of the glory of God, he also may be graciously received, and have that granted unto him for which he has petitioned the throne of grace.

We find, in the second book of Kings, that Elisha healed the leper Naaman, though it is well known that the nation to which he belonged was frequently at war with the Israelites; thus we find him assisting not alone a gentile, but even an enemy. What, then, becomes of your assertion, that the Jews did not practise acts of universal benevolence? Let me advise you, my dear friend, to read the books of the Old Testament well before you venture on such dangerous ground again, as asserting things about us Jews which you might not be able to sustain with incontestable proof when called upon.

In support of your assertion concerning the beauty of the gospel, you introduce a few verses from the *sermon on the mount*, in the fifth chapter of Matthew. By so doing you have imposed upon me an invidious task, that of attacking in some manner the Christian religion, when I should have been very glad to have let the gospels rest. But I am now called upon to defend the tenets of my faith, and I dare not, therefore, shrink from the responsibility thus thrown upon me, although this happens without my desiring it.

Let me premise, that the religion we profess is divided into three parts; first, duties towards God; secondly, duties towards our fellow-men ; and lastly, duties towards ourselves. The duties towards God require of us the belief in the Creator, confidence in his protection, hope in his salvation, and the observance of those statutes which He has made known to us as his law. The duties towards our fellow-men consist in acts of charity and benevolence, and in abstaining from injuring them in their persons, property, and honour. Duties towards ourselves are : self-preservation and self-defence ; by which I mean, that first, we ought not to depend upon others for our support, if we are ourselves capable of earning a living ; as it is beautifully said in the Proverbs of the Fathers : " Sweet is the learning of the law combined with labour, for to be engaged in both makes us abstain from sin ;" and secondly, that we ought to be careful of preserving our health, and therefore any unnecessary exposure of ourselves is unlawful. Self-defence also demands of us to conduct ourselves so that we shall not be exposed to the hatred and violence of others ; but if in spite of all our endeavours, we are molested and violently attacked, it is lawful to prevent our adversary from injuring us, (or even others,) and if he attempts to kill us, it is even permitted to slay him if we can prevent him in no other manner : in support of this position I refer you to Exod. chap. xxii. v. 2.

Again, it is a settled point with us, that not one commandment, or part of a commandment, of the Mosaic law, was ever repealed, or can be repealed, except in the same manner as it was promulgated ; that is, before the whole nation of Israel, in the same manner as the law was given on Sinai. These preliminaries are a *sine qua non*, without which no argument, however ingenious, can stand the test of Jewish criticism. Let us now apply this rule to the chapter of Matthew in question, to test its correctness. In the outset, he, whom the Christians call the Messiah (Christ), says himself : " Think not that I am come to destroy the law or the prophets : I am not come to destroy, but to fulfil, &c. &c." Here, my dear Professor of Christianity, you have it *from what you must think the highest authority*, that the *gospels* must, in *every* particular, conform to the *Mosaic* writings, which, let me repeat, were given by the Author of all for the government of Israel ; and as you believe in revelation, you must acknowledge that these writings contain the best code of laws that can be devised. Well, then, when Matthew says : " Swear not at all," the Christian writers are puzzled how to explain it so as to reconcile it to the Mosaic law, which permits oaths under certain circumstances (" And by his name shalt thou swear"); the learned Doctor James Beattie, therefore, explains it, as if its meaning were " any unnecessary oath," which, however, can hardly be the intent of this passage.—What Matthew says in the same chapter from verse 38 to 41, I am bold to assert, has not been fulfilled by fifty men from all Christendom ever since Christianity was established ; and if these doctrines were adopted as the general rule of society, every wicked person could *with impunity despoil his unoffending neigh-bour ;* and let me ask you, can this be the will of God ? For what purpose did He command the election of judges, if it were not to see the innocent righted ? And have the Society of Friends,* who, more than any other Christian sect, endeavour to obey the commandments under consideration, ever acted up to the latter of them ?

In the forty-third verse of the same chapter Matthew says : " Ye have heard it has been said, thou shalt love thy neighbour and *hate* thine enemy, &c." Now pardon me, my friend, when I beg of you to tell me in what part of the Old Testament, or any other Jewish writing, this sentiment is to be found ? Hate our enemies ?—Heavenly Father has it come to this, that thy children, who have suffered for ages persecutions without number for the SANCTIFICATION OF THY HOLY NAME—who have been slaughtered like the sheep that are dumb before their shearers, without murmuring, without repining—shall thy children, O our Father above, be accused of hating their enemies ? Do they not pray to Thee daily : " To prepare the world for thy kingdom, Almighty God ! to cause all flesh to call thy name, and to bring to Thee all sinners of the earth—that all may receive the yoke of thy kingdom, and that Thou mayest speedily reign over all for ever, for thine is the government, and for ever and ever Thou wilt reign in glory ?"—Again, we are commanded in Levit. chap. xix. v. 18, that we shall not avenge

---

* When this was written, I was not aware that the Professsor of Christianity was a member of this sect, as I rather supposed him to be a baptist minister by the name of Henry Keeling, who at that time edited a paper at Richmond, called the " Religious Herald" : but I was only induced to mention the Friends, as the Professor of Christianity had brought them forward to prove that the gospel doctrine, " resist ye not evil," could be fulfilled ; it will, however, be seen, that it can only be *in part*, since the *literal* obedience to it is *impossible.*

33

ourselves, nor even, as we rabbinical Jews understand the word תטור *Thittore* (translated in the English version "nor bear any grudge") to tell those who have offended us : " Look here, though you would not do me the favour I asked of you, yet will I not do like you did to me,—here is what you asked for."—In Exod. chap. xxiii. v. 4—5, we are positively enjoined to *assist our enemy*, when we see him in need of our assistance.—In chap. xxiv. v. 17, and chap. xxv. v. 21, of the Proverbs of Solomon, he tells us : " Rejoice not when thy enemy falleth, and when he stumbleth let not thy heart be glad ; lest the Eternal see it, and it displease Him, and He turn his wrath from him."—" If thine enemy be hungry, give him bread to eat ; and if he be thirsty, give him water to drink, &c." Thus we see clearly, that the Old Testament enjoins those *exalted doctrines*, for which you give the gospel the sole credit.

But you will say, Christ lived in the time of the Scribes and Pharisees, who did not act so ; who were hypocrites, and deviated from the letter of the law ! Indeed ! but even here you would be mistaken ; for we find the following in the Talmud : " A stranger came to Shamai, and told him, " Rabbi, I wish to become a proselyte ; but you must teach me the law while I can stand on one leg ;" but Shamai turned him off, not thinking it possible to teach him the law in so short a time. The stranger went next to *Hillel*, surnamed the elder, and repeated the same request ; " My son," answered the Rabbi, " what is disagreeable to thee do not to thy neighbour, (or companion,) for thus it is written : ' Thou shalt love thy neighbour like thyself ;' this is the principal commandment, and if thou observest this strictly, thou wilt easily observe the other precepts of the law.' "—What the Talmud says concerning the punishment of him who makes his antagonist ashamed in public is also found in the Proverbs of the Fathers, where we read : " He who makes the face of his neighbour turn pale in public though he has knowledge of the law, and has otherwise acted well, will not share in the happiness of the future life." What new doctrine then, I ask you again, has the gospel taught to the Jews ? since the Old Testament contains all the *practicable* moral doctrines, and the Rabbins (Scribes and Pharisees) of the time of the reputed Christ, did invariably preach in the temple and the synagogues doctrines conformable to their text-book, the twenty-four books of the Jewish canon.

I have thus, I hope, made my assertion good, that our law is a perfect model of a moral, religious, and civil code, that there is nothing too much, and nothing too little in it ; and in fact, if any man will but examine the wonderful effect it has had of keeping a *dispersed nation united, in every sense of the word,* he must acknowledge : " That no nation, though ever so great, has such just statutes and commandments as those which the Eternal our God has given to us."

You, my friend, call upon me to do the Christians that justice which I demand at their hands ; I am willing to concede all that Christians deserve, and I have already acknowledged, and shall always do so, that I have been very kindly treated by them, and shall always, till my dying hour, remember the benefits conferred on me by some of them.—But while I do this, I must repeat and re-assert, that the prejudice existing against us is highly unjust, and even condemned by that law which you as Christians are bound to respect. This was the reason why I undertook, in the first instance, the defence of our people from the vile and insidious attacks of the Quarterly Review ; and the same reason impels me now to answer you, though even here I am very willing to admit the difference which exists between your mode of warfare and that of the above mentioned magazine.—Pardon me one more remark before I dismiss you altogether. Do you know that what you profess about universal salvation is no Christian doctrine ? Do you know that it was first taught, and I may say, taught only, by the Jewish Rabbins ?—And do you know that if you believe in the gospels, you must renounce this doctrine as *not orthodox ?* How this may be I leave you to settle with the Christian divines ; but I must enter my protest against what you say about the voice of conscience ; for revelation was given to assist us in *forming a correct* course of life, and if conscience could of itself effect this, to what purpose was the law then given ? —But our opinion is, that our law was given as the standard, to which all nations were ultimately to resort as to a rallying point, till which time every man, *who is no Israelite,* was to be saved, if he acted according to the *light given him,* and only observed the precepts of general revelation given to Noah, which are to be found in the ninth chapter of Genesis ; and it was therefore the practice of the Jews, whenever they conquered, to make the subdued nation conform to the "seven commandments of the children of Noah," as they are called in the Talmud.—Each son of Israel, on the contrary, is bound to observe all that lies in his power to do, as otherwise he will be punished for good deeds omitted and sins committed.

It would be a great satisfaction to me to be assured that I had effectually removed the ill-will so many feel towards us—that I had contributed a little to make the Israelites more respected in this country, and especially in this city. Let me, however, at the same time call upon my brethren, those who with me believe in the same *immortal, unchangeable God;* who with me are bound by the same faith ; who with me live in the land of the stranger—far, far from the sweet hills of Israel—far, far from the sacred banks of the Jordan—far, far from the holy Jerusalem, the city where God's glory used to dwell ; who with me hope to reach a glorious immortality, when God will open the graves of his people, as promised by Ezekiel ; —let me call upon them to arouse from their lethargy, to break the chains of listlessness, by which they are bound. Let them draw the bond of union closer—let each man forget the injuries done by his neighbour—and then show the world what Israel can be even in captivity. Let them show their attachment to that beautiful religion which has ever been the admiration of the world, and prove themselves, by conforming strictly to the spirit and letter of the divine law, worthy of that glorious futurity, for which they are destined by the God of nature, by the ever kind Father of Israel !

In conclusion, I think it necessary to make an apology, why I, a young man, who have hardly reached the age of manhood—who, moreover, am a foreigner, should step forward to do that which older and wiser men than myself have omitted to do. But I hope that my justification is contained in the following from the thirty-second chapter of Job, which, with little alteration, is well applicable to the present case :

" And Elihu, the son of Barachel the Buzite, answered and said, I am young and ye are very old ; wherefore I was afraid, and durst not show you my opinion. I said, Days shall speak, and multitude of days should teach wisdom. But there is a spirit in man : and the inspiration of the Almighty gives them understanding. Great men are not always wise ; neither do the aged understand judgment. Therefore I said, Hearken unto me ; I will also show mine opinion.

Behold, I awaited for your words; I gave ear to your reasons, while ye searched out what to say. Yea, I attended unto you; and behold, there was none of you that convinced Job, or that answered his words: lest ye should say, We have found out wisdom: God thrusteth him down, not man. Now he has not directed his words against me; neither will I answer him with your speeches. They were amazed; they answered no more; they left off speaking. When I had waited, (for they spake not, but stood still and answered no more;) I said, I will answer also my part; I also will show my opinion. For I am full of matter; the spirit within me constraineth me."

Like Elihu I have considered it my duty to speak, because older men did not speak; and I was thus in a manner compelled to assume the fearful responsibility of accepting the challenge, which others neglected to do. I have, like the holy writer, endeavoured to abuse no man, nor to flatter any one; but have given, as far as 1 believe, things their proper names, without intending to give offence to any one; I have tried—

" Nothing to extenuate, nor set down ought in malice."

How far I have succeeded I leave others to judge; and I only beg of all to listen to my defence with patience, and to read my remarks to the end.   I dare not hope that which I have written will stand the test of severe criticism; but I request that every fault may be ascribed *to the head, but not the heart of*

A NATIVE OF GERMANY.

Richmond, Va.,
    Sunday morning, January 25th, 1829.

ESSAY IV.

TO " A NATIVE OF GERMANY."

There would have been less occasion to offer myself again to your notice, if the language I used in my late very imperfect essay had not been misconceived. The limits I had prescribed myself did not allow me sufficient room to express my meaning with all the clearness I could have desired; and I am therefore under the necessity of explaining my views more fully. Before I do this, however, permit me, my dear friend, (and I reciprocate the term with the utmost cordiality,) to express the gratification I feel that you were so well pleased with the spirit of my remarks. In return, I beg leave to offer my acknowledgments for the courtesy and kindness you have shown in replying to me. I am happy in having so generous and temperate an opponent. Indeed it was the presence of those estimable qualities in your vindication of the Jews from opprobrious and unmanly attacks, and not any predilection for controversy, that made me consent to claim your attention at all. I wish you every success in your attempts to allay the prejudice that exists against your nation; and I trust your appeal to the liberality of an enlightened people will not be in vain, so far, at least, as it may be enforced by the virtue and integrity of your lives. To this test I doubt not you will be perfectly willing to submit yourselves.

In the application I intended to make of the passage from Matthew, chap'v. v. 43, " Ye have heard it said, thou shalt love thy neighbour and hate thine enemy," you have entirely misapprehended my object; and I am the more grieved at it, as you have manifested so much generous sensibility on the occasion. I cheerfully acknowledge that, if war is admissible, the provisions of your law tended very much to mitigate its rigours, considering the principles on which it was waged by cotemporary nations. When I quoted the precept— " But I say unto you, love your enemies," I did it for the purpose of showing, that not only war and every species of violence, but every thing like *hatred*, is opposed to the benign spirit of the gospel. To say the least, you cannot deny that war was tolerated under certain circumstances by the Mosaic law—indeed, you have defended it to a particular extent. But the gospel injunction, if I understand it, strikes at the very root of all discord and dissention, by inculcating brotherly love and peace ; for if the passions and feelings which lead to strife are subdued, all contention must cease to exist (a). And in this view, the injunction is in perfect harmony with the angelic anthem chanted on the birth of Christ : " Glory to God in the highest, on earth peace, good will towards men." In these few words the character and object of his mission are beautifully declared ; and the whole course of his ministry, the whole tenor of his spotless life, go conclusively to show that it was for the attainment of this end that he laboured and that he died. Our religion in its purity is emphatically a religion of charity and peace. This feature so strikingly pervades the whole series of the writings of the New Testament, that I believe (b) nothing can be found in them which will bear an opposite construction, when taken in connection with the whole. " My kingdom is not of this world ; if my kingdom were of this world, then would my servants fight." John xviii. 36. This language was uttered at a time when Christians must all believe that it was in the power of Jesus to call down assistance even from heaven, to (c) protect himself from the violence of man. We can imagine no situation when the desire to avail ourselves of relief can be greater, than when we are in the act of being dragged to a cruel and ignominious death. And the apostle James asks, " Whence came wars and fightings among you ? Come they not hence, even from the lusts that war in your members ?" iv. 1. Now, my dear friend, though you say the Mosaic law is a superstructure of perfect symmetry, in which there is not the least disproportion, " nothing too much, and nothing too little,"—you must either prove the advantages of a state of war, however modified, in favour of the happiness of mankind, (d) over the contrary state of peace and good will, to enable you to establish the superiority of that law,—or you must acknowledge its inferiority to the gospel. And I will endeavour to deprive you, from your own showing, of any argument you might advance in support of a justifiable resort to war. You say that the Jews considered peace as the greatest blessing, and that this doctrine was taught by the Mosaic law, inasmuch as God promised peace as a reward for their obedience to the divine will. You more-over state that, whenever the Jews were doing the will of heaven, they lived in perfect security; but when they were disobedient, God sent the surrounding nations to oppress them. Now, if peace is a blessing, and obedience to the divine will is a sure means of meriting and enjoying tranquillity, my position is established, that war is not only no part of the divine economy in the government of mankind, but that it is in every aspect offensive in the sight of heaven. Is it not, moreover, a rational conclusion, that when the children of Israel had been guilty of a defection from the law of God, so as to call down his displeasure upon them, he would, even if they had not re-sisted the scourge sent to chastise them, have interposed his power-ful arm in favour of his chosen people, as soon as their transgressions had been atoned for by suffering or repentance? (e)

I am sensible, my friend, and I shall not affect to conceal it, that you may retort with far more severity than you have indulged, and demand, in a voice of thunder, if universal love be so strongly incul-cated by the gospel, why do not its followers practise it? It can only be accounted for on the supposition that they had fallen short of a complete and unreserved submission to the will of God. And wherever this disobedience exists, in every age and nation, the result is invariably the same, namely, aggression, insult, and injury, and a consequent substraction from the sum of human enjoyment. Jews and Christians have alike been guilty of a departure from the spirit of the religion they have respectively professed; and if a comparison were instituted, it would be found that there is hardly any thing in the Jewish wars, down to the destruction of the holy city, to which a parallel might not be furnished in the butcheries which have been practised at various times by the nations of Christendom. If Christ had commanded his followers to hate, not only their enemies, (for that, comparatively speaking, would have been mercy, if they had proceeded no farther,) but all mankind, and one another, they could scarcely in some instances have resigned themselves more complete-ly to his will. Not only can the golden regions of Mexico and Peru attest the tender mercies of Christian warfare, but history records many a bloody conflict waged by one Christian power against another, in the holy cause of religion; and individuals have been subjected to martyrdom, and communities to massacre, for the ostensible purpose of promoting the glory of the God of love! Indeed, a faithful ecclesiastical history would, 1 fear, embrace one half the crimes and enormities of Christendom. But though this may be an awful truth, still it does not impair the intrinsic excellence of the gospel, any more than the iniquities of the Jews detracted from the purity of the law of Moses. No abuse of any blessing can constitute a valid objection against the use for which it was designed. (*f*)

But you may say all this is a Eutopian scheme, incapable of being realised. In reply, my friend, 1 would again refer you to the pages of history, where, in " words that burn," you may discover that it has been triumphantly reduced to practice, under the auspices of the wise and benevolent Penn, who has been eulogised by the philosophic Jefferson as one of the greatest lawgivers of any age. One clear (*g*) and incontestable fact cannot be overturned by all the wit and ingenuity of man.

After this exposition of the peaceful character of the gospel, it may not be necessary for me to notice particularly your evidence to show that the oppressed part of mankind, namely, the slave, was more humanely provided for by the Mosaic law. If I have succeeded in convincing you that violence and injustice form no part of the gospel, it must follow that slavery, which is one of the most odious species of violence, inasmuch as its effect is to bind the free spirit of man, which should be left as uncontrolled in the exercise of its legitimate powers as the air we breathe, is at war with the whole genius of the gospel. If, after all, however, and contrary to my most sanguine expectations, it can be established that war and slavery are not incompatible with genuine Christianity, I should then enter upon a vindication of its excellence with extreme diffidence.

In enumerating the duties which the Mosaic law imposes, you divide them into three classes, namely, our duties to God, to our fellow-men, and to ourselves. That the gospel imposes solemn duties of the same character, cannot, I presume, be denied by its most inveterate enemies. Now, admitting the Jewish religion to be founded on the power of God, which I firmly believe, (though adapted in some of its details to the particular state of the children of Israel,) I may reasonably ask you to make the same concession in regard to our religion, in so far as it enjoins the same duties with yours. The same truths cannot be derived from sources contradictory in their

34

nature. If any great moral duty is founded on the power of God in
one instance, it must be equally so wherever it is known and acknowledged. If this concession is granted, I presume you will not
withhold your assent to the following propositions : 1. That the
object of true religion is to reform the heart, and cleanse it from all
impurity. 2. That consequently no religion of which this is not the
legitimate effect can be of any value. If, therefore, this be, in any
degree, the effect of Christianity, which I have feebly endeavoured to
show, just so far is it entitled to respect, and no farther. (*h*) It is
far from my intention, however, to be understood as confining the
exercise of these redeeming virtues to those who profess the Christian
name.

In every important discussion, it is proper that a definite meaning
should be attached to particular terms. This is the more indispens-
able on the present occasion, as you seem to have taken a very
limited view of the *gospel*. The New Testament is not the gospel
of Christ, but a written testimony in support of it. " *The gospel is
the power of God unto salvation*." Romans i. 16. Wherever, therefore, the power of God is manifested to salvation, there is the gospel
known. The apostle Paul says, moreover, that " it is preached to
every creature under heaven." Col. i. 2, 3. It follows of course
that the law of Christ cannot be any external written law ; and
though many of my fellow-professors believe it to be essentially
such, yet there is no evidence in the New Testament at all conclusive in support of such an opinion. We are never referred to it as
containing *in itself* any redeeming power ; but Christ and his apostles unceasingly directed the attention of the people to the *spirituality* of religion. " And I will pray the Father, and he will give you
another comforter, and he shall *abide with you for ever*, even the
spirit of truth, whom the world cannot receive, because it seeth
him not, neither knoweth him ; but you know him, because he
dwelleth with you and shall be in you." John xiv. 16, 17. (*i*) This
spirit of truth was to teach his followers *all things*. v. 26. " For
the wrath of God is revealed from heaven against all ungodliness
and unrighteousness of men, who hold the truth in unrighteousness ;
because that which is to be known of God is manifest in them, for
God hath shown it unto them." Rom. i. 18, 19. And the same
apostle goes on to say in the same epistle : " The word is nigh thee,

even in thy mouth, and in thy heart; that is, the word of faith which we preach." x. 8. "The grace of God that brings *salvation* has appeared to *all men*, teaching us that by denying ungodliness and worldly lusts, we should live soberly, righteously, and godly in this present world," &c. Titus, ii. 11, 12. "We have also a more sure word of prophecy (than the outward knowledge of Christ); whereunto ye do well to take heed, as to a light that shineth in a dark place." 2 Peter, i. 19. These are a very few of the passages that might be cited from the New Testament to prove the entire spirituality of the gospel. And this gospel-state is so clearly foretold by the sacred writers, that it will be unnecessary for me to refer to more than one or two passages in the Old Testament in evidence of it. "But this shall be the covenant that I will make with the house of Israel: after those days, saith the Lord, I will put my law in their hearts, and write it in their inward parts; and they shall teach no more every man his neighbour, and every man his brother, saying, Know the Lord; for they shall all know me from the least of them to the greatest of them." Jer. xxxi. 33—34. "And it shall come to pass afterwards, that I will pour out my spirit on all flesh." Joel ii. 28. And Moses expressly speaks of this same spiritual guide and teacher, when in his last and solemn advice to the children of Israel he says : " This commandment, which I command thee this day, is *not hidden from thee ;* neither is it far off: but the word is nigh thee, (*k*) in thy heart, and in thy mouth, that thou mayst do it." Deut. xxx. 11—14. These passages are also referred to by the apostles, in proof of the religion of Jesus Christ. It is in this comprehensive law, that the beauty, the simplicity, and the efficacy of the Christian religion consist. It is this word of God " which is quick and powerful, even to the dividing asunder of soul and spirit," that may be said to be the flaming sword which guards the entrance into the paradise of God, through which none can pass without having every thing slain that is opposed to the divine nature.

Such a religion as this cannot be extended nor limited by the notions or opinions of mankind, concerning outward or temporal circumstances. This view is predicated on the fact, which is alike obvious both to Jew and gentile, that goodness or righteousness is the same thing in all ; and is the effect of a power which proceeds from the same universal and blessed fountain, and produces the same

fruits in every individual of the human family who submits himself
to its influence.   Doubtless it was by this efficient power that Abel
offered an acceptable sacrifice ; that Enoch walked with God ; that
Noah preached and practised righteousness ; with all the other illustrious examples which are recorded in the Old and New Testaments.
The histories of nations or individuals are religiously available to
the rest of mankind, only because of the developement of the principles by which they were actuated in what they did : and it would be
as rational to deny, that the principle of honesty or piety would
make men honest or pious in the present day, (and without distinction as to nation or profession,) as that the sun shines with the same
light, and produces the same effects upon the earth and all its inhabitants now that it did five thousand years ago.   Permit me, my
friend, to call your attention to the universality ascribed to this
power in Isaiah, chap. xlix. v. 6. " It is a light thing that thou
shouldst be my servant, to raise up the tribes of Jacob, and to restore the preserved of Israel : I will also give thee for a light to the
gentiles, that thou mayst be my salvation to the ends of the earth."
I believe it is a pretty generally received opinion, both with Jews
and Christians, that those passages which relate to God's saving
power, both in the Old and New Testaments, should be interpreted
as referring to a *person*.   It is true that it is personified ; but so is
wisdom, so is *death*, and so is *Jerusalem*, and many other things
that all men know are not persons.   The words of the prophet,
therefore, as I conceive, are only truly and adequately interpreted,
when applied to the universal power and wisdom of God, (*l*) which
indeed did raise up the tribes of Jacob and restore the preserved
of Israel ; and has been, is now, and always will be, the only saving power to the end of the earth.   No matter in what person, or in
what period of time it may be manifested, whether in Enoch, or
Joseph, or Daniel, or Paul, or Peter ; or in the supremely holy and
blessed Jesus ; it is still the " only thing under heaven, given
among men, by which we can be saved."   It is the " fountain of
living waters" streaming through all generations, applied to all conditions, and perpetually performing the same glorious work of
cleansing the defilements of the human mind ; and producing a change
in all its propensities and faculties : so that in the beautiful, figurative
language of the prophet, " the wilderness" of human nature is

changed into an " Eden," and the " desert" of human thought and affection " into the garden of the Lord," where " joy and goodness" spring up in the place of " weeping and wailing ;" and " thanksgiving and the voice of melody" supplant the doleful *Chorazins* of " mourning and lamentation." As this great and momentous change is accomplished, the prophecies are found to be actually fulfilled in the experience of every individual who submits to the divine government. The mind is then no longer under the necessity of looking outward, or backward, or to futurity, for the coming or appearance of God's Messiah ; but he is found to be present to rebuke all fierceness and contention : and by the introduction of peace and love, to cause them to " beat their swords into ploughshares, and their spears into pruning hooks." For every impure, dishonest, proud, or revengeful temper becomes the object of his judgment ; and as the creature submits to his blessed operation, he changes these dispositions into concord and harmony ; so that those which were as ravenous as the " wolf, the leopard, and the young lion," become as innocent " as the lamb, the kid, or the fatling, and so gentle that a little child can lead them." And I appeal to the experience of all, if we have not witnessed the presence of this holy and heavenly being, conversing in secret, by means of thought and affection, with the heart ; and producing all the righteousness we ever knew, and all the happiness we ever felt. In the operations of this living reality does the Christian religion consist, according to my belief, and not in the dogmas of men, nor in their conjectures concerning external historical events. He who becomes a subject of the government of the spiritual Messiah, is introduced by him into holiness and purity, whether he call him by one name or another. For it is the *thing* that produces the *effect ;* and not the *name by which it is called.* All the prophetic declarations of the reign of the Messiah, are predicated upon such a change in the human mind, as is above referred to ; for it is impossible, in the nature of things, that righteousness should cover the earth as the waters do the sea, by any other means than the suppression of all unrighteousness. But the power which is alone able to perform these miracles of love and goodness, must be omnipresent ; and, therefore, as Moses testified, it is not far from us : " it is very nigh thee, in thy heart and in thy mouth, that thou mayst do it." (*m*)

In conclusion, my friend, though these are my views, I always hope to be able to extend to others who see through a different medium, that charity which I am well aware I shall need on account of my own imperfections. You say you are determined never to change your faith. It is far from my desire to make proselytes, for the *name* is perhaps no essential part of Christianity. It is by " doing justly, loving mercy, and walking humbly ;" doing to others as we would they should do us ; loving God above all things, and our neighbour as ourselves ; that we fulfil the end for which we were created, at least during our present state of existence : and whoever does this I hope to regard him as a brother, let his name be what it may.   A Professor of Christianity.

_____

NOTES BY I. L.

Although it was my first intention to let my friend have the last word, yet upon re-perusing his production, I think it necessary to comment on several passages, where I believe he has fallen into unintentional errors, which are owing altogether to his not having been taught to view things with the eye of an Israelite, or, in other words, that he, like most Christians, has thought proper to spiritualise the Scriptures, and to invest prophecies with meanings which are not warranted by a literal interpretation of them.

(*a*)—" All contention must cease to exist." This is no doubt true, for the absence of evil inclination is of itself a sufficient guarantee, that its fruit—evil deeds—will not exist : but the precepts of the Mosaic law, " if I understand *them* right," forbid hatred altogether, for we read in chap. xix. v. 17 of Leviticus : " Thou shalt not hate thy brother in thy heart ;" and it follows from this, that, if hatred and manevolence are banished, strife and war cannot take place, especially as we are forbidden to take vengeance upon one another. But it is not the *observance*, but the *infraction* of the holy law, which is the cause of national war and civil strife ; of course then the gospel cannot claim any superiority over our Pentateuch in this respect, as the latter is altogether calculated, even more so than the former, to eradicate the cause of war, as the resistance to evil through legal means is permitted by the Pentateuch, but forbidden by the gospels, if taken literally ; and if we once commence spiritualising any precept, so as to remove its harsh and unpalatable features, it requires but the ingenuity of an ordinary lawyer to make its operations entirely ineffectual.—And if the Professor of Christianity had carefully compared our law with the gospels, I am confident he would not have fallen into the error which I felt constrained to expose.

(b)—" Nothing can be found in them, which," &c. I am sorry that I cannot even permit this to pass unnoticed, for the gospels contain at least two passages which do not even allow us to harbour a thought that Christianity could bring peace, much less to view it as the chief requisite of a Christian.—Matthew x. 34 : " Think not that I am come to send peace on earth ; I came not to send peace, but a sword."— The Notzry next states, that " a man's foes shall be of his own household ;" which prophecy, strange to tell, is the only one in the New Testament which has been literally fulfilled. (See also Luke xii. 51.) And I must maintain, that these two passages, supposing even the Notzry to have been a prophet, prove clearly, that the gospels sanction a state of war, as they predict that such shall be the consequence of the prevalence of Christianity.

(c)—" Assistance even from Heaven to protect himself," &c. If it is true that the so called Christ was to die, it is impossible that any assistance from Heaven could have been granted him, for in that case God would have used means to defeat his own immutable will, which is evidently an absurdity.—Besides *Peter did* fight, for he cut off the ear of one of the high-priest's servants ; and it appears, that in spite of the Notzry's prohibition, his chief servant, upon whom he said he would build his church, did resort to violence, of course he did not understand the sermon on the mount to prohibit war, or else he would have acted contrary to law, and what is the same, have been a man of violence and a sinner.

(d)—" Over the contrary state of peace," &c. I must remind my friend that I explicitly stated that war is a curse, and a curse of such magnitude even, that every other expedient of redress should be exhausted, before *it* ought to be resorted to. On the other side, however, there are evils greater even than direful war, which must be resisted at every hazard. Passive obedience and submission to usurped authority would, as the world is now constituted, open the door to every outrage, and every act of aggression, villany can conceive ; whereas the consciousness that violence will be met by violence, deters despots frequently from injuring surrounding nations, just as the dread of punishment by the hand of justice compels the wicked man to refrain from his meditated burglary or murder. War, therefore, and violence can only *then* cease, when the state of the world is different from what it is now. That the knowledge of the gospels cannot have the effect of producing this altered state of society, it is impossible to deny, though I am ready to confess that certain men professing Christianity have lived peaceably, even to such a degree as not to resist actual aggression. But as the Hebrew religion is, in fact, whatever our opponents may say to the contrary notwithstanding, a religion of love and mercy, its universal acknowledgment will eradicate all motives of violence and aggression, since the world will be enlightened in the knowledge of the Eternal to such a degree, that peace will be preferred by all mankind, and it therefore will abolish the possibility even of war, and this we are taught by our prophets. (Isaiah, chap. ii. v. 4.) Till, however, this universal knowledge reigns, violence, as has been said, must and may lawfully be resorted to, to ward off evils of great magnitude, which admit of no other remedy. Amputation of a limb is an evil, and would never be performed when it is in a healthy state; but if the limb be fractured, lacerated, or otherwise wounded, so as to endanger the life of the patient, amputation becomes necessary, and it is resorted to, to ward off the greater evil— death. Just so it is in the present state of the world. War is abhorrent to the benign principles of the divine religion revealed unto our ancestors when they had been redeemed from slavery ; violence is prohibited ; injustice of every kind is interdicted ; and peace, internal and external, is held up to our view as the greatest blessing the Supreme Ruler can bestow on the children of his creation. But should we be molested, our country invaded, our liberties attacked, our children slaughtered, or our sanctuary polluted, then it becomes our *duty* to rise in our manhood, to step forward, and do battle for " our people and the cities of our God," and we deserve to be branded with the epithets of cowards, slothful, and irreligious men, if we would fold our arms over our bosom, and say : " We dare not defend our lives, our honour, and our religion." Indeed, I must repeat, war is a curse, but there are greater curses than it, and to protect us against them, war is permitted and even commanded.

(*e*)—" Had been atoned for by suffering or repentance ?" If my friend means to assert in this sentence, the conclusion of which I have quoted, that no war can be, emphatically speaking, a holy war; but that even defensive war is hateful in the sight of Heaven : I am obliged to dissent from him, for our Holy Bible and even every day's experience prove, that never was a righteous people defeated, when their cause was righteous. The Philistines were enraged, that the fugitive David had been elected king of Israel, and they came with powerful armies to dispossess him of the government which he had rightfully obtained : the Israelites met them in battle, and the Philistines fell by the edge of the sword.—The Carthagenian Hannibal presumed to follow the aggression of the Romans, and to carry war and desolation to the gates of their city : his quarrel was unjust, and Carthage was humbled, its government abolished, and the walls broken down by the Romans, whose annihilation had been meditated.—The Austrians wished to oppress Switzerland, and invaded it with a powerful army, consisting of the flower of German chivalry : but near Sempach they were met by the Swiss peasantry, who overthrew them and drove them back in shame, and proved thus that the righteous cause must be victorious.—And but lately, when the Britons attempted to compel their colonies to pay obedience to laws unjustly enacted : the colonists rose in arms, and, trusting in the God of battles, overcame the bravest armies which England ever sent from her shores, and the liberty and independence of these United States were achieved.—There are many other examples which history affords, but it is perfectly useless to prove the matter any further.—It will thus be seen, that *all* wars are not abhorrent to God ; and of course we must admit, that they are a part of the economy of God, and are a scourge which He wields to punish the aggressor and the ambitious conqueror, while they at the same time promote the enlargement of the oppressed, and secure the liberties of an upright people.—But if my friend means to say, that war shall one day cease, and that no more injury shall in those days be done from man to man, I am compelled to agree with him, for *this is* what the prophets predict, and this is the mark by which we are to distinguish the time of the true Messiah.—To the question of my friend : " If God was not able to save the Israelites without war ?" I must answer in the affirmative ; but I do not know what advantage can be gained from this my concession. Suppose God had saved them without war, we should then have found it so recorded ; but, if we read the book of Judges, we shall discover that God absolutely commanded Gideon and Barak to go to war; of course we must conclude, that although He could have saved them without war, yet He preferred to save them through *their own* agency ; for as our wise men teach us, God will always employ some natural means, though the result effected is frequently entirely disproportionate to the end accomplished. For instance Gideon's battle ; he had but three hundred men, and he was enabled with this handful to overcome a mighty and well appointed army.—Moses was commanded to stretch his staff over the Red Sea ; the waters were divided as an effect of

35

Moses's doing as he was ordered, and yet the effect bears no proportion to the apparent cause. And the like will be found throughout
the Bible; and it follows, therefore, that as war is in certain respects
" a part of the divine economy in the government of the world," as
it is now constituted, the New Testament cannot claim any superiority over the Mosaic law; since to say that we shall not repel an
invading foe is evidently contrary to revelation, and if the New Testament indeed contains the doctrine contended for by the Society of
Friends, it speaks contrary to the divine law, and cannot be true, because no two *disagreeing* precepts can proceed from the Source of
everlasting wisdom and all-seeing Providence.

(*f*)—"Can constitute a valid objection," &c. I cheerfully subscribe
to this proposition; but whilst my friend claims this indulgence for
his creed, I claim with even more justice the same for the religion
which it is my happiness to profess. And if it even can be proved
that the Israelites carried on unjust wars, I hope that no candid man
will charge our law as the cause of this abomination, seeing that its
spirit, and even its letter, are so diametrically opposed to all violence
and oppression, as has been amply demonstrated.

(*g*)—"Cannot be overturned by all the wit and ingenuity of man."
My friend seems here to have grown a little warm, and he seems to
have supposed, that I had endeavoured to "turn the laugh" against
his society in my last essay. But this was not my intention; I lay no
claim to wit, or a large share of ingenuity;—my arguments are all
drawn from Scripture, the only fair and legitimate source of argument
in religious matters. I will repeat the confession, that Mr. William
Penn may have been, for aught I know, the greatest legislator next to
Moses; but this does not invalidate my assertion, that neither he nor
any body else ever observed the gospel strictly; and if they, I mean
Penn and his followers, actually did so, they are clearly to blame; for
it is one thing to abstain from injuring others, and another thing to
submit silently to the injustice of good or wicked men, if we have
lawful means of redress within our power. Besides the example of
Penn does not prove that the spirit of the gospel is the spirit of peace,
since the self-styled *holy* inquisition, and the good people of New
England, could demonstrate with equal clearness, that they were
commanded to torture Jews, hang Quakers, and burn old and infirm
women, and this by the benign gospel of their Christ, with which the
Society of Friends prove that it is absolutely necessary not to resist
evil. Add to this, that the prophets do not speak of peace among one
sect only, but through all the earth: and it will be seen, that the New
Testament and the state of Christians, either individual or collective,

cannot be considered as a fulfilment of the Holy Writ contained in the Jewish canon. And where then, I ask, can be the superiority of the gospels over the Pentateuch?

(*h*)—"And no farther." In this paragraph my friend and myself are perfectly agreed, and as far as Christianity is *founded upon the books proceeding from the revealed power of God* it is useful, for it is the duties enjoined in these books, which purify the heart, and if obeyed will make our condition in life useful to all the world, (for every man is able to do something for the good of society,) and render us fit to be children of immortality; but as soon as it exceeds this limit even by one iota, it is no longer entitled to respect much less obedience; for no *truth* can exist beyond the words of revelation, which revelation is contained solely in the Old Testament, as can be clearly proven.

(*i*)—" This spirit of truth was to teach," &c. My friend says, that I have taken a too limited view of the gospel; I shall debate this position, although I might shield myself behind the general acceptation of the word: my object only is to correct a very important error of my friend in his position, which he has founded upon passages from the New Testament. If I would, I could demand of him, before I should even permit myself to debate its doctrines, to prove its historical accuracy; but I need not be so very dignified, and I am even content to do him battle upon his own terms. The spirit, or rather Holy Ghost, so says John, was "to teach *his* followers *all things*." This is said by John, but I say, that this has never happened; for if the spirit were diffused over the followers of the Notzry, the consequence would be that they would all think alike in matters of religion at least: instead of which even the apostles disagreed; for upon referring to Paul's Epistle to the Galatians it will be discovered in chap. ii. v. 11: " But when Peter was come to Antioch, I withstood him to the face, because he was to be blamed." Thus we see, that Peter and Paul differed in matters of faith; and could this be the effect of the inward revelation, the working of the inward spirit, which deceiveth not? And at the present day, one person is impelled by the inward spirit of grace to become a methodist, another a baptist, a third a Roman catholic, a fourth something else, in short, every sect of Christians thinks itself *exclusively* right, and as far as I was ever able to decide, they all can find some warrant for their opinions in the New Testament; and if we then suppose that the true gospel is not the written gospel, *id est*: the books of Matthew, Mark, Luke and John, but an inward infusion of the (Christian) Holy Ghost, it appears that the revelation of this spirit is not the same to every body, and I might with equal justice believe myself inspired, as Matthew and Mark have done. From all which it appears: that the inward revelation produced by the Christian gospel is the parent of discord, and cannot therefore be the revelation from the Most High, for He ordered his prophet to say : "And all thy children shall be taught by the Eternal, and much peace shall be to thy children," which means, that when the time of the Messiah shall come, all the Israelites shall be taught by inward inspiration, and this then will cause all dissension to cease because all shall know what is right. Now I do not believe, that any man can be hardy enough to assert that this is the case with the followers of the Christ of the Christians, for they *disagree* about the interpretation of almost every passage in the New Testament.

(*k*)—" But the word is nigh unto thee," &c. My friend adduces two passages from the Old Testament, and he mistakes the character of both. The 31st chapter of Jeremiah refers to the revelation contained in the Pentateuch, as can be easily proved ; and the passage from the 30th of Deuteronomy, when taken in connection with what precedes and follows, will also be found to refer to the Mosaic law ; and Moses meant to say, that the Israelites could not complain of not knowing the will and the word of God, for it had been but on that very day taught to them by the legislator who spoke these words, and it was therefore, so to say, within their mouth and heart. Besides, it must be remembered, that Moses wrote the law in a book, and commanded the Levites to teach it to the Israelites, so as to put it in their mouth ; that is to say, that the Israelites were to be taught until the law was so familiar to them that they might know it by heart, and converse about it with ease. We believe, that the law will one day be inscribed on the hearts of all mankind; but we contend that this has not yet come to pass. It matters not what may be advanced about the beauty of the gospels, and about the language of the apostles : the fact is otherwise, for it appears that at the time the inward revelation will be general, evil will of itself cease to exist, and universal knowledge and universal peace will go hand in hand over the face of the renovated earth ; and in the language of the 85th psalm : " Mercy and truth shall then meet together, and righteousness and peace shall kiss each other, and truth shall spring out of the earth, and righteousness shall look down from heaven." This is to be the effect of God's pouring out his spirit over all flesh, which will take place at the time of the true Messiah.

(*l*)—" Which, indeed, did raise up the tribes of Jacob," &c. I agree with my friend in maintaining, that whoever acts righteously, whether Jew, Brahmin, or Nazarene, is a child of eternal salvation, for this idea is founded upon the universal *justice* of God, although the gospels, chiefly Mark in the conclusion of his last chapter, assert that the faith in Christianity is necessary to ensure salvation, although a man had observed every precept of the law; and this is also the opinion of Paul. But having agreed thus far with my friend, I must dissent from him in the use he makes of the several passages of Scripture adduced by him : for he again spiritualises, which ought not to be done, according to our mode of interpretation.—It is true, that we need not look for any Messiah to teach us what to believe and do to become righteous, for that has been taught us in the Mosaic law ; but nevertheless a Messiah is predicted, a Messiah is expected, and this Messiah will come to fulfil the prophecies, and to restore the Israelites to their land, and peace and harmony throughout the world.

(*m*)—" That thou mayst do it." This is the passage cited from Deut. chap. xxx. ; but it relates, as has been shown, to the Mosaic law—the law written down by the command of the God of nature—a law existing uncorrupted and unequalled for three thousand years ; it is this of which Moses and the prophets speak, and to this we are always commanded to direct our attention. It is indeed surprising, how Christians are obliged to twist every passage in Scripture so as to avoid the force of our arguments ; for it is impossible to reconcile the gospel, written and unwritten, either to the letter or the obvious spirit of the Bible, and the consequence is, that every now and then we see a new sect coming into being, who interpret their new law differently from any sect which went before them. This evidently proves no superiority of the gospels over the Bible—this surely does not establish that the kingdom of peace is prevalent on earth. On the other hand, let the world look at us, who have been scattered in every country of God's earth, and driven to slaughter in almost every age, whose books have been burnt, whenever the adversary could lay hold of them—let, I say, the world look at us, who are yet united and one people, and then let them consider if the finger of the Almighty God has not done this ; I must, therefore, now conclude this volume with the words of the blessed lawgiver, the last words he spoke to the people of Israel, whom he had loved so well and served so faithfully :

" Happy art thou, O Israel : who is like unto thee, O people assisted by the Lord, who is the shield of thy help, and who is the sword of thy excellency ! and thy enemies shall cower down before thee, but thou shalt tread upon their high places."

May everlasting life of blessedness be the portion of all mankind, and may the Messiah soon be sent to redeem the captives of Israel. Amen !

NOTICE TO SUBSCRIBERS.

As fully three years have elapsed since this work was announced, the subscribers are notified, that, if they do not wish to take the work, they will be entirely exonerated; and those who are yet kind enough to continue their subscription, are respectfully informed, that the non-appearance of the book was owing to the want of encouragement held out, and although several subscriptions have been received lately, particularly the very liberal one of Mr. Abraham Hart, of the house of Carey & Hart of this city, the subscriptions will not meet the expense of the publication. The work would certainly not have been put to press with so little encouragement, if it had not been announced; and I did not wish it thought that I was afraid of meeting a small pecuniary loss, where the object is a defence of our religion.—To this want of encouragement it is also owing that the number of copies printed is fully one fourth less than the edition printed of the Instruction in the Mosaic Religion.   I. L.

CORRECTION.—In page 257, line 14, for *latter* read *letter*—in part of the edition.

LaVergne, TN USA
01 September 2009
156604LV00004B/60/P